Super Easy

MEDITERRANEAN DIET COOKBOOK
for Beginners

2000 Days of Budget-Friendly, Tasty & Nutritious Recipes Book for a Better and Healthier Lifestyle | Stress-Free 30-Day Meal Plan

Beatrice Dias Santos

TABLE OF CONTENTS

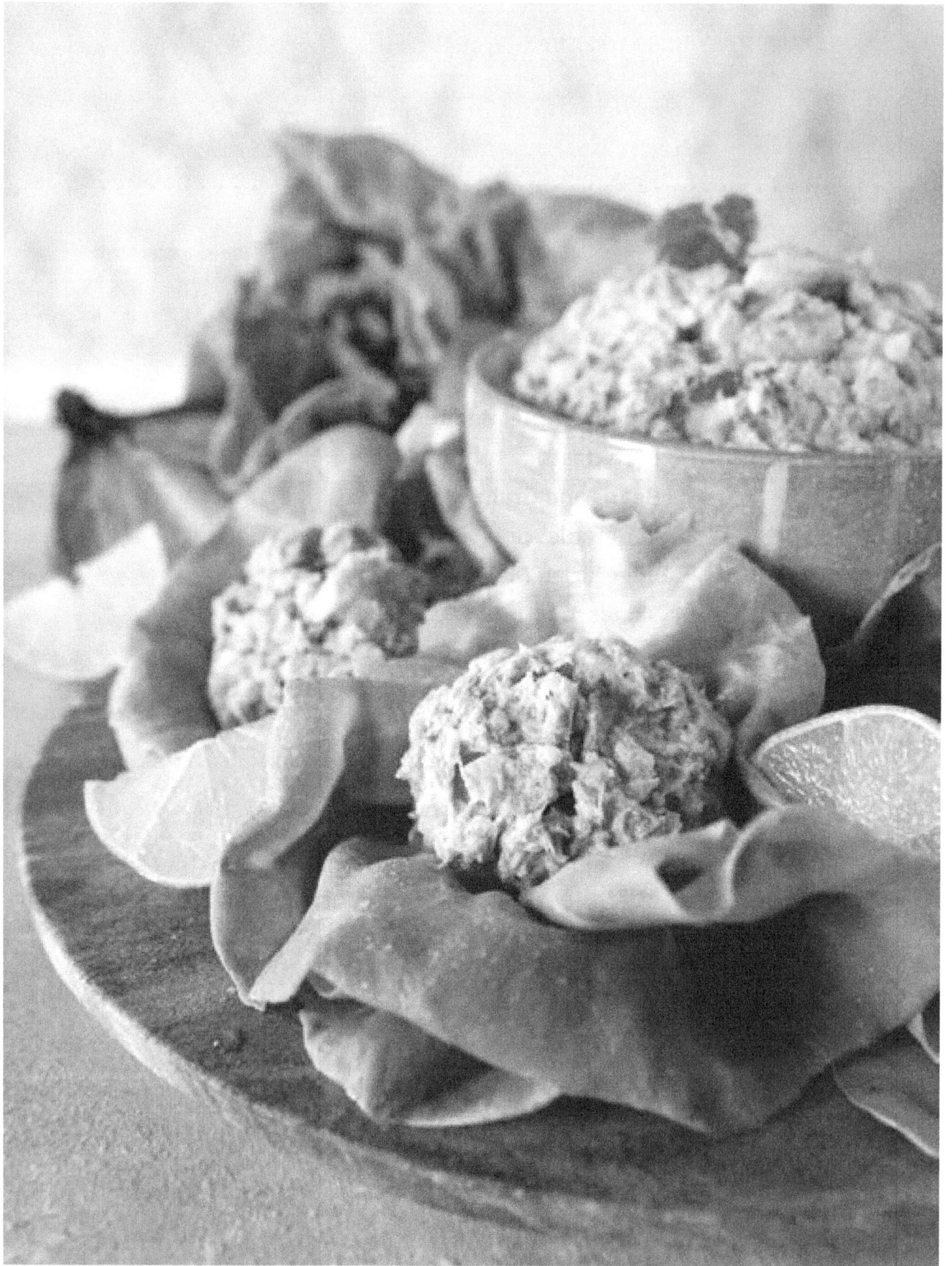

INTRODUCTION

In this cookbook, we delve into the heart of Mediterranean traditions, exploring the culinary heritage that has been passed down through generations. Each recipe is a reflection of the region's rich cultural mosaic, blending influences from various countries that border the Mediterranean Sea. From the sun-drenched coasts of Southern Italy to the bustling markets of Morocco, this book invites you to experience the diversity and vibrancy of Mediterranean cuisine.

The Mediterranean Pantry: Ingredients that Define a Region

A journey through Mediterranean cooking begins with understanding the essential ingredients that define this rich culinary tradition. The Mediterranean pantry is stocked with a variety of fresh, seasonal produce, whole grains, legumes, and a treasure trove of aromatic herbs and spices. Olive oil, often referred to as liquid gold, plays a pivotal role in many dishes, providing a healthy source of fat and a distinctive flavor.

Fresh vegetables such as tomatoes, eggplants, zucchinis, and bell peppers are staples in Mediterranean kitchens, often featured in dishes like ratatouille, caponata, and stuffed peppers. Fruits like figs, pomegranates, and citrus add a burst of natural sweetness and complexity to both savory and sweet recipes. Whole grains, including bulgur, farro, and couscous, form the foundation of many meals, providing essential fiber and nutrients.

Herbs such as basil, oregano, rosemary, and thyme, along with spices like cumin, coriander, and saffron, are used liberally to enhance the flavors of dishes. These ingredients not only contribute to the taste but also offer numerous health benefits, embodying the philosophy of food as medicine.

The Art of Mediterranean Cooking

Mediterranean cooking is characterized by its simplicity and emphasis on high-quality, fresh ingredients. The cooking techniques are straightforward, designed to bring out the natural flavors of the food. Grilling, roasting, and braising are common methods that enhance the taste and texture of the ingredients without overpowering them.

Grilling is a favorite technique in the Mediterranean, used for vegetables, fish, and meats. The smoky flavor imparted by the grill complements the freshness of the produce and the richness of the proteins. Roasting, another popular method, intensifies the flavors of vegetables and meats, creating dishes that are both hearty and delicious. Braising, often done with legumes and tougher cuts of meat, results in tender, flavorful meals that are comforting and satisfying.

One of the key aspects of Mediterranean cooking is the use of simple, yet flavorful, combinations. A typical dish might combine a handful of ingredients, each contributing its unique taste and texture to the final creation. For example, a traditional Greek salad features ripe tomatoes, crisp cucumbers, briny olives, and creamy feta cheese, all brought together with a drizzle of olive oil and a sprinkle of oregano. This simplicity allows the quality of the ingredients to shine through, creating dishes that are both nourishing and delightful.

Embracing Mediterranean Culture

The Mediterranean diet is deeply intertwined with the region's culture and way of life. Meals are more than just a time to eat; they are a time to connect with family and friends, to relax and enjoy the moment. This cultural aspect of the Mediterranean diet is as important as the food itself, contributing to a holistic approach to health and well-being.

Sharing meals is a cherished tradition in Mediterranean cultures. Whether it's a leisurely Sunday lunch with extended family or a casual dinner with friends, these gatherings foster a sense of community and belonging. This social aspect of dining is believed to contribute to the overall health and happiness of the Mediterranean people, reinforcing the connection between food and well-being.

In addition to social dining, the Mediterranean lifestyle encourages regular physical activity and a mindful approach to eating. Walking, gardening, and outdoor activities are integral parts of daily life, promoting physical fitness and mental well-being. Mindful eating practices, such as savoring each bite and paying attention to hunger and fullness cues, help to cultivate a healthy relationship with food.

Your Mediterranean Adventure Begins

As you explore this cookbook, you will not only learn to prepare delicious and nutritious meals but also gain a deeper appreciation for the Mediterranean way of life. Each recipe is an invitation to embrace the principles of the Mediterranean diet, incorporating fresh, wholesome ingredients into your meals and adopting a more mindful, balanced approach to eating.

By bringing the flavors and traditions of the Mediterranean into your kitchen, you will embark on a culinary adventure that celebrates health, happiness, and the joy of good food. Welcome to the Mediterranean diet cookbook – a gateway to a healthier, more flavorful way of living. Buon appetito!

Chapter **1**

Unveiling the Mediterranean Diet

Chapter 1: Unveiling the Mediterranean Diet

The Mediterranean diet, celebrated worldwide for its health benefits and delicious flavors, is more than a dietary regimen; it's a holistic lifestyle that has been nurtured by generations of people living in countries around the Mediterranean Sea. This chapter will introduce you to the fundamentals of the Mediterranean diet, its key principles, and the Mediterranean Diet Pyramid, a visual guide that helps us incorporate this nourishing lifestyle into our daily lives.

Understanding the Mediterranean Diet

The Mediterranean diet is rooted in the traditional eating habits of countries such as Greece, Italy, Spain, and Turkey. These populations have been observed for their remarkable health and longevity, which scientists and nutritionists attribute largely to their diet. Unlike many modern diets that focus on restriction, the Mediterranean diet emphasizes abundance—particularly the abundance of fresh, whole foods.

Key Principles of the Mediterranean Diet:

1. Plant-Based Focus: The diet is rich in vegetables, fruits, whole grains, legumes, nuts, and seeds. These foods are packed with essential nutrients like vitamins, minerals, fiber, and antioxidants. A typical Mediterranean meal might include a variety of colorful vegetables, hearty grains, and protein-rich legumes, all prepared in simple but flavorful ways.

2. Healthy Fats: Olive oil, especially extra virgin olive oil, is the cornerstone of the Mediterranean diet. It is used generously in cooking, dressings, and even as a dip for bread. This oil is high in monounsaturated fats, which are beneficial for heart health. Other sources of healthy fats include nuts, seeds, and avocados.

3. Moderate Protein Intake: The diet includes moderate amounts of fish and seafood, which are excellent sources of lean protein and omega-3 fatty acids. Poultry and dairy products like cheese and yogurt are also part of the diet but are consumed in smaller quantities. Red meat is eaten sparingly, and processed meats are limited.

4. Flavorful Herbs and Spices: Instead of relying on salt, Mediterranean cuisine uses a variety of herbs and spices to flavor dishes. Commonly used herbs include basil, oregano, rosemary, and thyme, while garlic, onion, and lemon are also key flavor components. This not only enhances the taste but also adds health benefits.

5. Limited Sweets and Processed Foods: Desserts and processed foods are enjoyed infrequently, reserved for special occasions. When sweets are consumed, they are often made from natural ingredients like honey, nuts, and dried fruits.

6. Moderate Alcohol Consumption: In many Mediterranean cultures, moderate consumption of wine, particularly red wine, is common and typically enjoyed with meals. This is believed to contribute to the overall benefits of the diet, though it should be approached with moderation and can be omitted altogether if preferred.

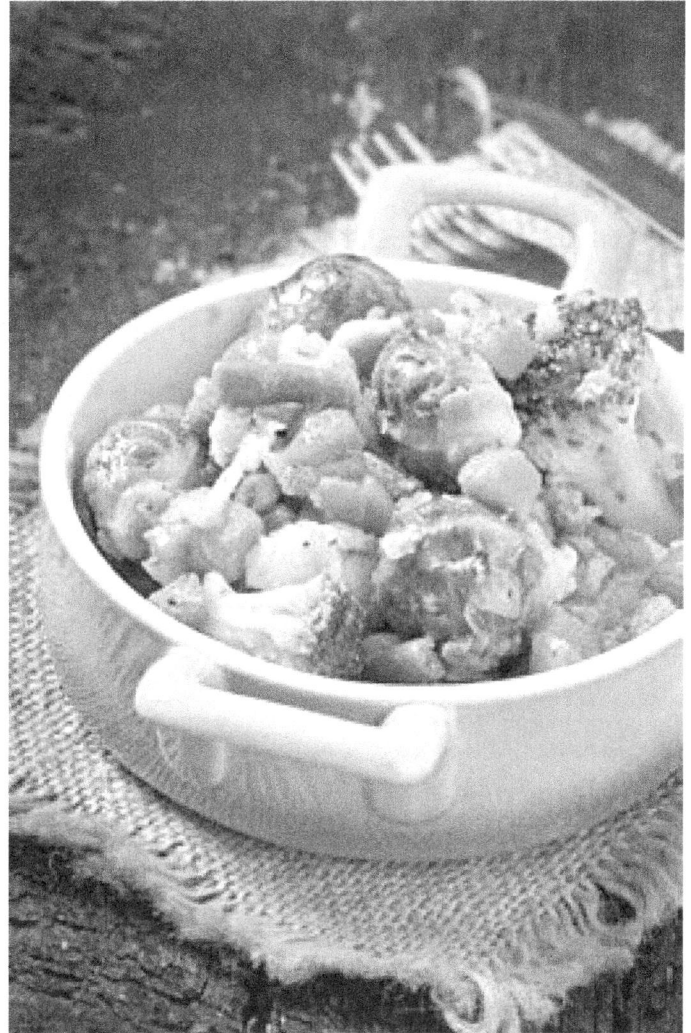

The Mediterranean Diet Pyramid

The Mediterranean Diet Pyramid is a visual representation that illustrates the recommended frequency and proportions of different food groups in the diet. Developed by nutrition experts, this pyramid serves as a practical guide for those looking to adopt the Mediterranean way of eating.

※ **Base of the Pyramid:** Daily Physical Activity and Social Connections

- At the base of the pyramid, you'll find the foundation of the Mediterranean lifestyle: regular physical activity and social engagement. Daily exercise, such as walking, gardening, or other forms of physical activity, is encouraged. Equally important is the social aspect of meals, which emphasizes enjoying food with family and friends, fostering a sense of community and belonging.

※ **First Tier:** Vegetables, Fruits, Whole Grains, and Healthy Fats

- The first tier consists of foods that should be eaten at every meal. These include a wide variety of vegetables and fruits, which are rich in essential vitamins, minerals, and antioxidants. Whole grains like barley, oats, and brown rice provide fiber and sustained energy. Healthy fats, primarily from olive oil, nuts, and seeds, are also integral to this tier, promoting heart health and satiety.

※ **Second Tier: Fish and Seafood**

- Fish and seafood occupy the next tier and are recommended for consumption at least twice a week. These foods are rich in omega-3 fatty acids, which are essential for heart and brain health. Common choices include salmon, sardines, mackerel, and shellfish.

※ **Third Tier: Poultry, Eggs, Cheese, and Yogurt**

- The third tier includes moderate portions of poultry, eggs, cheese, and yogurt. These foods provide valuable protein and calcium but should be consumed in moderation compared to plant-based foods and fish. Poultry and eggs offer lean protein, while cheese and yogurt provide probiotics and calcium.

※ **Fourth Tier: Meats and Sweets**

- At the top of the pyramid are meats and sweets, which should be consumed sparingly. Red meat is limited to a few times a month, and sweets are enjoyed occasionally. When indulging in sweets, Mediterranean desserts often include natural sweeteners like honey and fruits, and are made with whole ingredients.

※ **Wine:**

- Wine, particularly red wine, is enjoyed in moderation, usually with meals. The suggested amount is up to one glass per day for women and up to two glasses per day for men. However, alcohol consumption is optional and should be approached responsibly.

The Mediterranean Diet Pyramid provides a balanced approach to nutrition, emphasizing variety, moderation, and the enjoyment of meals in a social context. By following the principles outlined in the pyramid, individuals can enjoy a rich and varied diet that supports overall health and well-being.

The Health Benefits of the Mediterranean Diet

The Mediterranean diet is one of the most extensively researched dietary patterns, with numerous studies highlighting its wide-ranging health benefits. Here are some of the key advantages associated with following this diet:

1. Cardiovascular Health: The high content of healthy fats, fiber, and antioxidants helps reduce the risk of heart disease. Studies have shown that the Mediterranean diet can lower levels of bad cholesterol (LDL) and increase levels of good cholesterol (HDL), thereby improving overall heart health.

2. Weight Management: The diet's emphasis on whole, unprocessed foods and healthy fats promotes satiety and helps maintain a healthy weight. The balanced intake of macronutrients ensures that energy levels remain stable, reducing the likelihood of overeating.

3. Diabetes Prevention and Management: The Mediterranean diet aids in regulating blood sugar levels, making it effective for both preventing and managing type 2 diabetes. The high fiber content from fruits, vegetables, and whole grains helps slow the absorption of sugar into the bloodstream.

4. Longevity: Adherence to the Mediterranean diet has been linked to a lower risk of mortality and increased life expectancy. The diet's nutrient-rich profile supports overall health, reducing the risk of chronic diseases.

5. Mental Health: The Mediterranean diet's rich content of omega-3 fatty acids, vitamins, and minerals supports brain health. Research suggests that the diet may help reduce the risk of cognitive decline and conditions such as depression and anxiety.

6. Reduced Inflammation: The diet's high levels of antioxidants and healthy fats help reduce inflammation in the body. Chronic inflammation is linked to various diseases, including heart disease, cancer, and arthritis.

Embracing the Mediterranean Lifestyle

Adopting the Mediterranean diet is not just about changing what you eat; it's about embracing a lifestyle that values physical activity, social connections, and mindful eating. Here's how you can incorporate these elements into your daily life:

※ **Regular Physical Activity:** Incorporate exercise into your daily routine. This could be a morning walk, a swim, cycling, or even tending to a garden. The goal is to stay active and make physical movement a regular part of your day.

※ **Social Engagement:** Make meals a time to connect with family and friends. Sharing food, conversation, and laughter around the table enhances the dining experience and contributes to emotional well-being.

※ **Mindful Eating:** Pay attention to what you eat and savor each bite. Eating slowly and without distractions can improve digestion and help you enjoy your food more. This practice also helps you recognize hunger and fullness cues, preventing overeating.

※ **Culinary Exploration:** Experiment with Mediterranean recipes and discover new flavors and ingredients. Cooking at home allows you to control the quality of your ingredients and enjoy the process of preparing meals.

Your Mediterranean Adventure Begins

As you embark on this journey with the Mediterranean diet, this chapter provides a comprehensive overview of its principles, the Mediterranean Diet Pyramid, and the numerous health benefits associated with this way of eating. Embrace the vibrant flavors, diverse ingredients, and healthful practices of the Mediterranean diet, and look forward to a life of enhanced well-being and culinary delight.

In the following chapters, you will find a variety of recipes that will guide you in preparing delicious and nutritious meals inspired by Mediterranean cuisine. From breakfast to dinner, and everything in between, these recipes will help you integrate the Mediterranean diet into your daily life with ease and joy. Welcome to the Mediterranean diet cookbook – your gateway to a healthier, more flavorful way of living. Buon appetito!

30-Day Meal Plan

DAYS	BREAKFAST	LUNCH	DINNER	SNACK/DESSERT
1	Cardamom-Infused Apple Steel-Cut Oats 11	Curried Apple and Leek Couscous 22	Pomegranate-Glazed Chicken Breasts with Fresh Seeds 50	Vegetable Pot Stickers 74
2	Quinoa and Yogurt Breakfast Bowls 17	Garlicky Split Chickpea Curry 19	Spicy Harissa Yogurt-Roasted Chicken Thighs 53	Crispy Greek Hummus Tacos 75
3	Peach Sunrise Smoothie 11	Mediterranean Pea and Potato Casserole 25	Deconstructed Greek Chicken Kebabs 54	Flatbread with Ricotta and Orange-Raisin Relish 76
4	Fruity Yogurt Bliss Smoothie 13	Za'atar Chickpea and Spinach Bulgur Salad 23	Skillet Parsley Chicken with Golden Potatoes 52	Sumac-Spiced Maple Nut Mix 72
5	Nutty Ricotta Fruit Toast 14	Lentil and Zucchini Boats 21	Balsamic Chicken Thighs with Tomato and Basil 52	Smoky Grilled Baba Ghanoush 77
6	Jalapeño Popper Egg Cups 13	Mediterranean Giant Beans with Tomatoes and Herbs 19	Coconut Curry Chicken 54	Mediterranean Pesto & Olive Fat Bombs 72
7	Red Pepper and Feta Egg Bites 13	Cumin-Scented Lentil and Basmati Pilaf 19	Slow-Cooked Pesto Chicken with Red Potatoes 50	Creamy Shrimp-Stuffed Cucumber Pirogues 73
8	Herbed Veggie Steel-Cut Oats 16	Mediterranean Lentil Casserole 19	Garlic Dill Wings 50	Nutty Fig Energy Bites 76
9	Garlic Scrambled Eggs with Basil 14	Domatorizo (Greek Tomato Rice) 23	Easy Turkey Tenderloin 50	Citrus-Infused Melon Salad 72
10	Spicy Harissa Shakshuka with Peppers and Tomatoes 17	Lentils in Tomato Sauce 20	Caribbean Jerk Chicken Skewers 52	Zesty Black-Eyed Pea Salsa 75
11	Peachy Power Smoothie Bowl 14	Creamy Puréed Red Lentil Soup 21	Baked Chicken Caprese 53	Marinated Feta and Artichokes 75
12	Nutty Coconut Cinnamon Porridge 12	Ginger-Spiced Whole Brown Lentil Dhal 23	Italian Marinated Cube Steak Roll-Ups with Peppers and Mushrooms 56	Crispy Tuna Almond Croquettes 75
13	Mediterranean Avocado Egg Pita 14	Hearty Two-Bean Bulgur Chili 21	Marinated Chicken 52	Quick Garlic Mushrooms 74
14	Spanish Potato and Onion Omelet	Zesty Black Bean and Corn Salad	Slow-Cooked Fenugreek Spiced Chicken	Nutty Apple Salad
15	Savory Cottage Cheese Breakfast Bowl 12	Creamy Garbanzo and Pita Layered Delight 24	Ground Beef Taco Rolls 56	Sweet-and-Spicy Nuts 73
16	Creamy Orange Pecan Polenta Bowl 17	Rice Pilaf 30	Mozzarella Chicken Nuggets 51	Mediterranean Mixed-Vegetable Caponata 74

DAYS	BREAKFAST	LUNCH	DINNER	SNACK/DESSERT
17	Fig-Walnut Breakfast Quinoa Bowl 15	Cilantro Lime Rice 23	Stuffed Pepper Stew 36	Shrimp and Chickpea Fritters 72
18	Peach Pecan Oatmeal Delight 15	Farro and Mushroom Risotto 24	Root Vegetable Soup with Garlic Aioli Drizzle 36	White Bean Harissa Dip 74
19	Homemade Pumpkin Parfait 15	Mediterranean Lentil and Rice Salad 22	Crispy Eggplant Rounds 37	Turmeric Crunch Chickpeas 77
20	Blueberry-Lemon Tea Cakes 15	Savory Herbed Wild Rice Pilaf 24	Crispy Za'atar-Spiced Chicken Tenders 53	Spiced Baked Pears with Mascarpone 88
21	Apple and Tahini Toast 13	Turkish Shepherd's Salad with Feta 43	Zesty Serrano Pork Kebabs 59	Pomegranate-Wine Poached Pears with Pomegranate Seeds 88
22	Buffalo Egg Cups 11	Garlic-Rosemary Infused Olive Oil 94	Chicken and Chickpea Skillet with Berbere Spice 54	Slow-Cooked Fruit Medley 88
23	Citrus-Walnut Baklava Porridge 12	Creamy Yellow Lentil Soup 22	Crustless Spanakopita 40	Maple Cornmeal Steamed Bread 89
24	Herbed Vegetable Mediterranean Omelet 16	Moroccan Tomato and Roasted Chile Salad 46	Cheesy Zucchini Spinach Lasagna 36	Olive Oil Greek Yogurt Brownies 91
25	Turmeric Veggie Egg Bake 16	Rice with Pork Chops 20	Slow-Cooked Chicken Caprese Bake 51	Minty Watermelon Salad 90
26	Cauliflower Avocado Toast 16	Slow-Cooked Chickpea Falafel Patties 21	Pesto Spinach Flatbread 37	Air-Fried S'mores Delight 90
27	Lemon Olive Oil Breakfast Cakes with Berry Syrup 13	Quinoa with Kale, Carrots, and Walnuts 25	Tortellini in Red Pepper Sauce 39	Pumpkin-Ricotta Cheesecake 91
28	Sunny-Side Up Baked Eggs with Swiss Chard, Feta, and Basil 15	Savory Tomato and Bulgur Pilaf 26	Broccoli Crust Pizza 38	Grilled Halloumi with Watermelon, Cherry Tomatoes, Olives, and Herb Oil 76
29	Polenta with Sautéed Chard and Fried Eggs 12	Pilaf with Eggplant and Raisins 22	Italian Braised Pork 56	Tirokafteri (Spicy Feta and Yogurt Dip) 76
30	Smoked Salmon Egg Scramble with Dill and Chives 14	Quinoa Salad in Endive Boats 20	Hearty Moroccan Vegetable Tagine 37	Lebanese Muhammara 73

Chapter 2
Breakfasts

Chapter 2 Breakfasts

Cardamom-Infused Apple Steel-Cut Oats

Prep time: 10 minutes | Cook time: 7 minutes | Serves 4

- 1 tablespoon light olive oil
- 1 large Granny Smith, Honeycrisp, or Pink Lady apple, peeled, cored, and diced
- ½ teaspoon ground cardamom
- 1 cup steel-cut oats
- 3 cups water
- ¼ cup maple syrup
- ½ teaspoon salt

1. Press the Sauté button on the Instant Pot® and heat oil. Add apple and cardamom and cook until apple is just softened, about 2 minutes. Press the Cancel button. 2. Add oats, water, maple syrup, and salt to pot, and stir well. Close lid, set steam release to Sealing, press the Manual button, and set time to 5 minutes. 3. When the timer beeps, let pressure release naturally for 10 minutes, then quick-release the remaining pressure until the float valve drops. Press the Cancel button, open lid, and stir well. Serve hot.

Per Serving:
calories: 249 | fat: 6g | protein: 6g | carbs: 48g | fiber: 5g | sodium: 298mg

Spanish Potato and Onion Omelet

Prep time: 10 minutes | Cook time: 40 minutes | Serves 4

- 1½ pounds (680 g) Yukon gold potatoes, scrubbed and thinly sliced
- 3 tablespoons olive oil, divided
- 1 teaspoon kosher salt, divided
- 1 sweet white onion, thinly sliced
- 3 cloves garlic, minced
- 8 eggs
- ½ teaspoon ground black pepper

1. Preheat the oven to 350°F(180ºC). Line 2 baking sheets with parchment paper. 2. In a large bowl, toss the potatoes with 1 tablespoon of the oil and ½ teaspoon of the salt until well coated. Spread over the 2 baking sheets in a single layer. Roast the potatoes, rotating the baking sheets halfway through cooking, until tender but not browned, about 15 minutes. Using a spatula, remove the potatoes from the baking sheets and let cool until warm. 3. Meanwhile, in a medium skillet over medium-low heat, cook the onion in 1 tablespoon of the oil, stirring, until soft and golden, about 10 minutes. Add the garlic and cook until fragrant, about 2 minutes. Transfer the onion and garlic to a plate and let cool until warm. 4. In a large bowl, beat the eggs, pepper, and the remaining ½ teaspoon salt vigorously until the yolks and whites are completely combined and slightly frothy. Stir in the potatoes and onion and garlic and combine well, being careful not to break too many potatoes. 5. In the same skillet over medium-high heat,

warm the remaining 1 tablespoon oil until shimmering, swirling to cover the whole surface. Pour in the egg mixture and spread the contents evenly. Cook for 1 minute and reduce the heat to medium-low. Cook until the edges of the egg are set and the center is slightly wet, about 8 minutes. Using a spatula, nudge the omelet to make sure it moves freely in the skillet. 6. Place a rimless plate, the size of the skillet, over the omelet. Place one hand over the plate and, in a swift motion, flip the omelet onto the plate. Slide the omelet back into the skillet, cooked side up. Cook until completely set, a toothpick inserted into the middle comes out clean, about 6 minutes. 7. Transfer to a serving plate and let cool for 5 minutes. Serve warm or room temperature.

Per Serving:
calories: 376 | fat: 19g | protein: 15g | carbs: 37g | fiber: 5g | sodium: 724mg

Buffalo Egg Cups

Prep time: 10 minutes | Cook time: 15 minutes | Serves 2

- 4 large eggs
- 2 ounces (57 g) full-fat cream cheese
- 2 tablespoons buffalo sauce
- ½ cup shredded sharp Cheddar cheese

1. Begin by cracking the eggs into two ramekins, ensuring they are evenly distributed. 2. In a small bowl that is safe for microwave use, combine the cream cheese, buffalo sauce, and Cheddar cheese. Microwave this mixture for 20 seconds, then stir until smooth. Spoon a generous amount of the mixture into each ramekin on top of the eggs. 3. Carefully place the ramekins into the air fryer basket. 4. Set the air fryer temperature to 320ºF (160ºC) and cook for 15 minutes. 5. Once cooked, serve the ramekins warm for the best taste.

Per Serving:
calories: 354 | fat: 29g | protein: 21g | carbs: 3g | fiber: 0g | sodium: 343mg

Peach Sunrise Smoothie

Prep time: 10 minutes | Cook time: 0 minutes | Serves 1

- 1 large unpeeled peach, pitted and sliced (about ½ cup)
- 6 ounces (170 g) vanilla or
- peach low-fat Greek yogurt
- 2 tablespoons low-fat milk
- 6 to 8 ice cubes

1. Gather all the ingredients and place them in a blender. Blend the mixture until it reaches a thick and creamy consistency. 2. Serve immediately for the best flavor and texture.

Per Serving:
calories: 228 | fat: 3g | protein: 11g | carbs: 42g | fiber: 3g | sodium: 127mg

Nutty Coconut Cinnamon Porridge

Prep time: 10 minutes | Cook time: 10 minutes | Serves 2

- ¼ cup coconut milk
- ¾ cup unsweetened almond milk or water
- ¼ cup almond butter or hazelnut butter
- 1 tablespoon virgin coconut oil
- 2 tablespoons chia seeds
- 1 tablespoon flax meal
- 1 teaspoon cinnamon
- ¼ cup macadamia nuts
- ¼ cup hazelnuts
- 4 Brazil nuts
- Optional: low-carb sweetener, to taste
- ¼ cup unsweetened large coconut flakes
- 1 tablespoon cacao nibs

1. In a small saucepan, mix the coconut milk and almond milk and heat over medium heat. Once hot (not boiling), take off the heat. Add the almond butter and coconut oil. Stir until well combined. If needed, use an immersion blender and process until smooth. 2. Add the chia seeds, flax meal, and cinnamon, and leave to rest for 5 to 10 minutes. Roughly chop the macadamias, hazelnuts, and Brazil nuts and stir in. Add sweetener, if using, and stir. Transfer to serving bowls. In a small skillet, dry-roast the coconut flakes over medium-high heat for 1 to 2 minutes, until lightly toasted and fragrant. Top the porridge with the toasted coconut flakes and cacao nibs (or you can use chopped 100% chocolate). Serve immediately or store in the fridge for up to 3 days.

Per Serving:
calories: 646 | fat: 61g | protein: 13g | carbs: 23g | fiber: 10g | sodium: 40mg

Polenta with Sauté ed Chard and Fried Eggs

Prep time: 5 minutes | Cook time: 20 minutes | Serves 4

For the Polenta:
- 2½ cups water
- ½ teaspoon kosher salt
- ¾ cups whole-grain cornmeal

For the Chard:
- 1 tablespoon extra-virgin olive oil
- 1 bunch (about 6 ounces / 170 g) Swiss chard, leaves and stems chopped and separated

For the Eggs:
- 1 tablespoon extra-virgin olive oil

- ¼ teaspoon freshly ground black pepper
- 2 tablespoons grated Parmesan cheese

- 2 garlic cloves, sliced
- ¼ teaspoon kosher salt
- ⅛ teaspoon freshly ground black pepper
- Lemon juice (optional)

- 4 large eggs

Prepare the Polenta: 1. In a medium saucepan, bring water and salt to a rolling boil over high heat. Gradually whisk in the cornmeal, ensuring to mix continuously. 2. Lower the heat to a simmer, cover the pot, and let it cook for 10 to 15 minutes, stirring frequently to prevent lumps from forming. Once thickened, mix in the pepper and Parmesan cheese, then spoon the mixture into four bowls. Sauté the Chard: 3. In a large skillet, heat oil over medium heat. Add the chard stems, along with garlic, salt, and pepper; sauté for about 2 minutes. 4. Incorporate the chard leaves and continue cooking until they are wilted, roughly 3 to 5 minutes. 5. If desired, add a splash of lemon juice, toss everything together, and evenly distribute it over the polenta. Cook the Eggs: 6. Using the same large skillet, heat oil over medium-high heat. Gently crack each egg into the skillet, ensuring there's ample space between them to avoid crowding. Cook until the whites are firm and the edges are golden, about 2 to 3 minutes. 7. Serve the eggs sunny-side up, or carefully flip them for over-easy, cooking for an additional minute. Top each bowl of polenta and chard with one egg.

Per Serving:
calories: 310 | fat: 18g | protein: 17g | carbs: 21g | fiber: 1g | sodium: 500mg

Citrus-Walnut Baklava Porridge

Prep time: 5 minutes | Cook time: 5 minutes | Serves 2

- 2 cups riced cauliflower
- ¾ cup unsweetened almond, flax, or hemp milk
- 4 tablespoons extra-virgin olive oil, divided
- 2 teaspoons grated fresh orange peel (from ½ orange)
- ½ teaspoon ground cinnamon
- ½ teaspoon almond extract or vanilla extract
- ⅛ teaspoon salt
- 4 tablespoons chopped walnuts, divided
- 1 to 2 teaspoons liquid stevia, monk fruit, or other sweetener of choice (optional)

1. In medium saucepan, combine the riced cauliflower, almond milk, 2 tablespoons olive oil, grated orange peel, cinnamon, almond extract, and salt. Stir to combine and bring just to a boil over medium-high heat, stirring constantly. 2. Remove from heat and stir in 2 tablespoons chopped walnuts and sweetener (if using). Stir to combine. 3. Divide into bowls, topping each with 1 tablespoon of chopped walnuts and 1 tablespoon of the remaining olive oil.

Per Serving:
calories: 414 | fat: 38g | protein: 6g | carbs: 16g | fiber: 4g | sodium: 252mg

Savory Cottage Cheese Breakfast Bowl

Prep time: 10 minutes | Cook time: 0 minutes | Serves 4

- 2 cups low-fat cottage cheese
- 2 tablespoons chopped mixed fresh herbs, such as basil, dill, flat-leaf parsley, and oregano
- ½ teaspoon ground black pepper
- 1 large tomato, chopped
- 1 small cucumber, peeled and chopped
- ¼ cup pitted kalamata olives, halved
- 1 tablespoon extra-virgin olive oil

1. Begin by mixing the cottage cheese, herbs, and pepper together in a medium-sized bowl until well blended. 2. Next, add the diced tomato, cucumber, and olives to the bowl and gently fold everything together to combine. 3. Drizzle olive oil over the mixture just before serving for added flavor.

Per Serving:
calories: 181 | fat: 10g | protein: 15g | carbs: 8g | fiber: 1g | sodium: 788mg

Jalapeño Popper Egg Cups

Prep time: 10 minutes | Cook time: 10 minutes | Serves 2

- 4 large eggs
- ¼ cup chopped pickled jalapeños
- 2 ounces (57 g) full-fat

- cream cheese
- ½ cup shredded sharp Cheddar cheese

1. Begin by cracking the eggs into a medium-sized mixing bowl and whisking them thoroughly. Next, distribute the beaten eggs evenly into four silicone muffin cups. 2. In a large bowl that is safe for microwave use, combine the jalapeños, cream cheese, and Cheddar cheese. Heat this mixture in the microwave for 30 seconds, then stir well. Take about a quarter of this mixture and carefully spoon it into the center of each egg cup. Continue this process until all the mixture is used up. 3. Place the filled egg cups into the air fryer basket, ensuring they are stable. 4. Set the air fryer temperature to 320ºF (160ºC) and cook the cups for a duration of 10 minutes. 5. Once finished, remove the egg cups from the air fryer and enjoy them while they are still warm.

Per Serving:
calories: 375 | fat: 30g | protein: 23g | carbs: 3g | fiber: 0g | sodium: 445mg

Fruity Yogurt Bliss Smoothie

Prep time: 5 minutes | Cook time: 0 minutes | Serves 1

- ½ cup vanilla low-fat Greek yogurt
- ¼ cup low-fat milk
- ½ cup fresh or frozen

- blueberries or strawberries (or a combination)
- 6 to 8 ice cubes

1. Place the Greek yogurt, milk, and berries in a blender and blend until the berries are liquefied. Add the ice cubes and blend on high until thick and smooth. Serve immediately.

Per Serving:
calories: 158 | fat: 3g | protein: 9g | carbs: 25g | fiber: 1g | sodium: 110mg

Red Pepper and Feta Egg Bites

Prep time: 5 minutes | Cook time: 8 minutes | Serves 6

- 1 tablespoon olive oil
- ½ cup crumbled feta cheese
- ¼ cup chopped roasted red peppers

- 6 large eggs, beaten
- ¼ teaspoon ground black pepper
- 1 cup water

1. Begin by lightly greasing silicone muffin or poaching cups with oil. Evenly distribute the feta cheese and roasted red peppers into the prepared cups. In a separate bowl with a spout, whisk the eggs together with black pepper until well combined. 2. Position the rack inside the Instant Pot® and pour in the water. Place the prepared cups on the rack. Carefully pour the egg mixture into each cup. Secure the lid, ensure the steam release valve is set to Sealing, then press the Manual button and adjust the time to 8 minutes. 3. Once the timer signals, perform a quick release of the pressure until the float valve drops, then carefully open the lid. Gently remove the silicone cups and slide the eggs onto plates. Enjoy them while warm.

Per Serving:
calories: 145 | fat: 11g | protein: 10g | carbs: 3g | fiber: 1g | sodium: 294mg

Lemon Olive Oil Breakfast Cakes with Berry Syrup

Prep time: 5 minutes | Cook time: 10 minutes | Serves 4

For the Pancakes:
- 1 cup almond flour
- 1 teaspoon baking powder
- ¼ teaspoon salt
- 6 tablespoon extra-virgin olive oil, divided

- 2 large eggs
- Zest and juice of 1 lemon
- ½ teaspoon almond or vanilla extract

For the Berry Sauce:
- 1 cup frozen mixed berries
- 1 tablespoon water or lemon

- juice, plus more if needed
- ½ teaspoon vanilla extract

Make the Pancakes: 1. Begin by mixing almond flour, baking powder, and salt in a large bowl, whisking to ensure there are no clumps. 2. Add in the 4 tablespoons of olive oil, eggs, lemon zest and juice, and almond extract, whisking everything together until well combined. 3. In a skillet, heat 1 tablespoon of olive oil, then pour about 2 tablespoons of the batter for each of the 4 pancakes. Cook for 4 to 5 minutes until bubbles start to form, then flip them over. Cook for another 2 to 3 minutes on the other side. Repeat the process with the remaining 1 tablespoon of olive oil and the rest of the batter.

Prepare the Berry Sauce: 1. In a small saucepan, combine the frozen berries, water, and vanilla extract, heating over medium-high heat for 3 to 4 minutes until it becomes bubbly, adding extra water if it's too thick. Use a spoon or fork to mash the berries, then whisk the mixture until it is smooth.

Per Serving:
calories: 381 | fat: 35g | protein: 8g | carbs: 12g | fiber: 4g | sodium: 183mg

Apple and Tahini Toast

Prep time: 10 minutes | Cook time: 0 minutes | Serves 1

- 2 tablespoons tahini
- 2 slices whole-wheat bread, toasted
- 1 small apple of your

- choice, cored and thinly sliced
- 1 teaspoon honey

1. Start by generously spreading tahini over the toasted bread until it's well-coated. 2. Arrange the apple slices on top of the tahini-covered bread and drizzle with honey for added sweetness. Serve right away for the best taste.

Per Serving:
calories: 439 | fat: 19g | protein: 13g | carbs: 60g | fiber: 10g | sodium: 327mg

Smoked Salmon Egg Scramble with Dill and Chives

Prep time: 5 minutes | Cook time: 5 minutes | Serves 2

- 4 large eggs
- 1 tablespoon milk
- 1 tablespoon fresh chives, minced
- 1 tablespoon fresh dill, minced
- ¼ teaspoon kosher salt
- ⅛ teaspoon freshly ground black pepper
- 2 teaspoons extra-virgin olive oil
- 2 ounces (57 g) smoked salmon, thinly sliced

1. In a large bowl, thoroughly whisk together the eggs, milk, chives, dill, salt, and pepper until well combined. 2. In a medium skillet or sauté pan, heat the olive oil over medium heat. Pour in the egg mixture and cook for approximately 3 minutes, stirring occasionally to ensure even cooking. 3. Gently fold in the salmon and continue cooking until the eggs are set but still moist, which should take about 1 minute.

Per Serving:
calories: 325 | fat: 26g | protein: 23g | carbs: 1g | fiber: 0g | sodium: 455mg

Peachy Power Smoothie Bowl

Prep time: 15 minutes | Cook time: 0 minutes | Serves 2

- 2 cups packed partially thawed frozen peaches
- ½ cup plain or vanilla Greek yogurt
- ½ ripe avocado
- 2 tablespoons flax meal
- 1 teaspoon vanilla extract
- 1 teaspoon orange extract
- 1 tablespoon honey (optional)

1. Combine all of the ingredients in a blender and blend until smooth. 2. Pour the mixture into two bowls, and, if desired, sprinkle with additional toppings.

Per Serving:
calories: 213 | fat: 13g | protein: 6g | carbs: 23g | fiber: 7g | sodium: 41mg

Garlic Scrambled Eggs with Basil

Prep time: 5 minutes | Cook time: 5 minutes | Serves 2

- 4 large eggs
- 2 tablespoons finely chopped fresh basil
- 2 tablespoons grated Gruyère cheese
- 1 tablespoon cream
- 1 tablespoon olive oil
- 2 cloves garlic, minced
- Sea salt and freshly ground pepper, to taste

1. In a spacious bowl, whisk together the eggs, basil, cheese, and cream until they are just combined. 2. In a large, heavy nonstick skillet, heat the oil over medium-low heat. Add the garlic and sauté until it turns golden, which should take about 1 minute. 3. Pour the egg mixture into the skillet, directly over the garlic. Continuously stir the eggs as they cook, until they become fluffy and soft. 4. Season the mixture with sea salt and freshly ground pepper

according to your taste. Split the fluffy eggs between two plates and serve right away.

Per Serving:
calories: 267 | fat: 21g | protein: 16g | carbs: 3g | fiber: 0g | sodium: 394mg

Nutty Ricotta Fruit Toast

Prep time: 5 minutes | Cook time: 0 minutes | Serves 2

- ¼ cup full-fat ricotta cheese
- 1½ teaspoons honey, divided
- 3 drops almond extract
- 2 slices whole-grain bread, toasted
- ½ medium banana, peeled
- and cut into ¼-inch slices
- ½ medium pear (any variety), thinly sliced
- 2 teaspoons chopped walnuts
- 2 pinches of ground cinnamon

1. In a small bowl, combine the ricotta, ¼ teaspoon honey, and the almond extract. Stir well. 2. Spread 1½ tablespoons of the ricotta mixture over each slice of toast. 3. Divide the pear slices and banana slices equally on top of each slice of toast. 4. Drizzle equal amounts of the remaining honey over each slice, and sprinkle 1 teaspoon of the walnuts over each slice. Top each serving with a pinch of cinnamon.

Per Serving:
calories: 207 | fat: 7g | protein: 8g | carbs: 30g | fiber: 4g | sodium: 162mg

Mediterranean Avocado Egg Pita

Prep time: 5 minutes | Cook time: 7 minutes | Serves 2

- 2 eggs
- 1 small avocado, peeled, halved, and pitted
- ¼ teaspoon fresh lemon juice
- Pinch of salt
- ¼ teaspoon freshly ground black pepper
- 1 (8-inch) whole-wheat
- pocket pita bread, halved
- 12 (¼-inch) thick cucumber slices
- 6 oil-packed sun-dried tomatoes, rinsed, patted dry, and cut in half
- 2 tablespoons crumbled feta
- ½ teaspoon extra virgin olive oil

1. Fill a small saucepan with water and place it over medium heat. When the water is boiling, use a slotted spoon to carefully lower the eggs into the water. Gently boil for 7 minutes, then remove the pan from the heat and transfer the eggs to a bowl of cold water. Set aside. 2. In a small bowl, mash the avocado with a fork and then add the lemon juice and salt. Mash to combine. 3. Peel and slice the eggs, then sprinkle the black pepper over the egg slices. 4. Spread half of the avocado mixture over one side of the pita half. Top the pita half with 1 sliced egg, 6 cucumber slices, and 6 sun-dried tomato pieces. 5. Sprinkle 1 tablespoon crumbled feta over the top and drizzle ¼ teaspoon olive oil over the feta. Repeat with the other pita half. Serve promptly.

Per Serving:
calories: 427 | fat: 28g | protein: 14g | carbs: 36g | fiber: 12g | sodium: 398mg

Blueberry-Lemon Tea Cakes

Prep time: 10 minutes | Cook time: 25 minutes | Serves 12

4 eggs

- ½ cup granulated sugar
- Grated peel of 1 lemon
- 1½ cups all-purpose flour
- ¾ cup fine cornmeal
- 2 teaspoons baking powder
- 1 teaspoon kosher salt
- 1 cup extra-virgin olive oil
- 1½ cups fresh or frozen blueberries

1. Begin by preheating the oven to 350°F (180°C). Grease a 12-cup muffin pan or line it with paper liners. 2. Using an electric mixer on medium speed, beat the eggs and sugar together until the mixture becomes pale and fluffy. Stir in the lemon zest. 3. In a separate medium bowl, combine the flour, cornmeal, baking powder, and salt. With the mixer set to low speed, gradually add the flour mixture and oil to the egg mixture in alternating additions. Gently fold in the blueberries. 4. Spoon the batter into the prepared muffin pan. Bake until the tops are golden brown and a toothpick inserted into the center comes out clean, which should take about 20 to 25 minutes.

Per Serving:
calories: 317 | fat: 20g | protein: 4g | carbs: 31g | fiber: 2g | sodium: 217mg

Peach Pecan Oatmeal Delight

Prep time: 10 minutes | Cook time: 4 minutes | Serves 4

- 4 cups water
- 2 cups rolled oats
- 1 tablespoon light olive oil
- 1 large peach, peeled, pitted,
- and diced
- ¼ teaspoon salt
- ½ cup toasted pecans
- 2 tablespoons maple syrup

1. Place water, oats, oil, peach, and salt in the Instant Pot®. Stir well. Close lid, set steam release to Sealing, press the Manual button, and set time to 4 minutes. 2. When the timer beeps, quick-release the pressure until the float valve drops. Press the Cancel button, open lid, and stir well. Serve oatmeal topped with pecans and maple syrup.

Per Serving:
calories: 399 | fat: 27g | protein: 8g | carbs: 35g | fiber: 7g | sodium: 148mg

Homemade Pumpkin Parfait

Prep time: 5 minutes | Cook time: 0 minutes | Serves 4

- 1 (15-ounce / 425-g) can pure pumpkin purée
- 4 teaspoons honey, additional to taste
- 1 teaspoon pumpkin pie spice
- ¼ teaspoon ground cinnamon
- 2 cups plain, unsweetened, full-fat Greek yogurt
- 1 cup honey granola

1. In a large mixing bowl, combine the pumpkin purée, honey, pumpkin pie spice, and cinnamon. Cover the bowl and refrigerate for a minimum of 2 hours. 2. To assemble the parfaits, layer each cup with ¼ cup of the pumpkin mixture, followed by ¼ cup of yogurt and then ¼ cup of granola. Repeat the layers of Greek yogurt and pumpkin mixture, finishing with a sprinkle of honey granola on top.

Per Serving:
calories: 264 | fat: 9g | protein: 15g | carbs: 35g | fiber: 6g | sodium: 90mg

Fig-Walnut Breakfast Quinoa Bowl

Prep time: 10 minutes | Cook time: 12 minutes | Serves 4

- 1½ cups quinoa, rinsed and drained
- 2½ cups water
- 1 cup almond milk
- 2 tablespoons honey
- 1 teaspoon vanilla extract
- ½ teaspoon ground
- cinnamon
- ¼ teaspoon salt
- ½ cup low-fat plain Greek yogurt
- 8 fresh figs, quartered
- 1 cup chopped toasted walnuts

1. Place quinoa, water, almond milk, honey, vanilla, cinnamon, and salt in the Instant Pot®. Stir to combine. Close lid, set steam release to Sealing, press the Rice button, and set time to 12 minutes. When the timer beeps, let pressure release naturally, about 20 minutes. 2. Press the Cancel button, open lid, and fluff quinoa with a fork. Serve warm with yogurt, figs, and walnuts.

Per Serving:
calories: 413 | fat: 25g | protein: 10g | carbs: 52g | fiber: 7g | sodium: 275mg

Sunny-Side Up Baked Eggs with Swiss Chard, Feta, and Basil

Prep time: 15 minutes | Cook time: 10 to 15 minutes | Serves 4

- 1 tablespoon extra-virgin olive oil, divided
- ½ red onion, diced
- ½ teaspoon kosher salt
- ¼ teaspoon nutmeg
- ⅛ teaspoon freshly ground
- black pepper
- 4 cups Swiss chard, chopped
- ¼ cup crumbled feta cheese
- 4 large eggs
- ¼ cup fresh basil, chopped or cut into ribbons

1. Begin by preheating the oven to 375°F (190°C). Arrange 4 ramekins on a half sheet pan or in a baking dish and lightly coat them with olive oil. 2. In a large skillet or sauté pan, heat the remaining olive oil over medium heat. Add the onion, salt, nutmeg, and pepper, sautéing until the onion becomes translucent, which should take about 3 minutes. Next, add the chard and continue cooking, stirring frequently, until it wilts, approximately 2 minutes. 3. Distribute the mixture evenly among the 4 ramekins. Top each with 1 tablespoon of feta cheese and crack an egg on top of the mixture in each ramekin. Bake for 10 to 12 minutes, or until the egg whites are fully set. 4. After baking, allow the ramekins to cool for 1 to 2 minutes. Carefully use a fork or spatula to transfer the eggs from the ramekins to a plate. Finish by garnishing with fresh basil.

Per Serving:
calories: 140 | fat: 10g | protein: 9g | carbs: 4g | fiber: 4g | sodium: 370mg

Cauliflower Avocado Toast

Prep time: 15 minutes | Cook time: 8 minutes | Serves 2

- 1 (12 ounces / 340 g) steamer bag cauliflower
- 1 large egg
- ½ cup shredded Mozzarella cheese
- 1 ripe medium avocado
- ½ teaspoon garlic powder
- ¼ teaspoon ground black pepper

1. Prepare the cauliflower by cooking it according to the package directions. Once cooked, transfer it from the bag and place it in cheesecloth or a clean towel to squeeze out any excess moisture. 2. In a large mixing bowl, combine the cauliflower with the egg and Mozzarella cheese. Cut a piece of parchment paper to fit your air fryer basket. Divide the cauliflower mixture into two portions and form two mounds on the parchment paper. Flatten the mounds into a rectangle about ¼ inch thick, then place the parchment into the air fryer basket. 3. Set the air fryer to 400°F (204°C) and adjust the timer for 8 minutes. 4. Flip the cauliflower halfway through the cooking time to ensure even cooking. 5. When the timer sounds, carefully remove the parchment from the air fryer and let the cauliflower cool for 5 minutes. 6. Halve the avocado and take out the pit. Scoop the flesh into a medium bowl and mash it together with garlic powder and pepper. Spread this mixture over the cauliflower. Serve immediately.

Per Serving:
calories: 321 | fat: 22g | protein: 16g | carbs: 19g | fiber: 10g | sodium: 99mg

Turmeric Veggie Egg Bake

Prep time: 15 minutes | Cook time: 20 minutes | Serves 2

- 2 tablespoons extra-virgin avocado oil or ghee
- 2 medium spring onions, white and green parts separated, sliced
- 1 clove garlic, minced
- 3½ ounces (99 g) Swiss chard or collard greens, stalks and leaves separated, chopped
- 1 medium zucchini, sliced into coins
- 2 tablespoons water
- 1 teaspoon Dijon or yellow mustard
- ½ teaspoon ground turmeric
- ¼ teaspoon black pepper
- Salt, to taste
- 4 large eggs
- ¾ cup grated Manchego or Pecorino Romano cheese
- 2 tablespoons (30 ml) extra-virgin olive oil

1. Preheat the oven to 360°F (182°C) fan assisted or 400°F (205°C) conventional. 2. Grease a large, ovenproof skillet (with a lid) with the avocado oil. Cook the white parts of the spring onions and the garlic for about 1 minute, until just fragrant. Add the chard stalks, zucchini, and water. Stir, then cover with a lid. Cook over medium-low heat for about 10 minutes or until the zucchini is tender. Add the mustard, turmeric, pepper, and salt. Add the chard leaves and cook until just wilted. 3. Use a spatula to make 4 wells in the mixture. Crack an egg into each well and cook until the egg whites start to set while the yolks are still runny. Top with the cheese, transfer to the oven, and bake for 5 to 7 minutes. Remove from the oven and sprinkle with the reserved spring onions. Drizzle with the olive oil and serve warm.

Per Serving:
calories: 600 | fat: 49g | protein: 31g | carbs: 10g | fiber: 4g | sodium: 213mg

Herbed Vegetable Mediterranean Omelet

Prep time: 10 minutes | Cook time: 12 minutes | Serves 2

- 2 teaspoons extra-virgin olive oil, divided
- 1 garlic clove, minced
- ½ red bell pepper, thinly sliced
- ½ yellow bell pepper, thinly sliced
- ¼ cup thinly sliced red onion
- 2 tablespoons chopped fresh basil
- 2 tablespoons chopped fresh parsley, plus extra for garnish
- ½ teaspoon salt
- ½ teaspoon freshly ground black pepper
- 4 large eggs, beaten

1. In a large, heavy skillet, heat 1 teaspoon of the olive oil over medium heat. Add the garlic, peppers, and onion to the pan and sauté, stirring frequently, for 5 minutes. 2. Add the basil, parsley, salt, and pepper, increase the heat to medium-high, and sauté for 2 minutes. Slide the vegetable mixture onto a plate and return the pan to the heat. 3. Heat the remaining 1 teaspoon olive oil in the same pan and pour in the beaten eggs, tilting the pan to coat evenly. Cook the eggs just until the edges are bubbly and all but the center is dry, 3 to 5 minutes. 4. Either flip the omelet or use a spatula to turn it over. 5. Spoon the vegetable mixture onto one-half of the omelet and use a spatula to fold the empty side over the top. Slide the omelet onto a platter or cutting board. 6. To serve, cut the omelet in half and garnish with fresh parsley.

Per Serving:
calories: 218 | fat: 14g | protein: 14g | carbs: 9g | fiber: 1g | sodium: 728mg

Herbed Veggie Steel-Cut Oats

Prep time: 10 minutes | Cook time: 15 minutes | Serves 2

- ½ cup steel-cut oats
- 1 cup water
- 1 large tomato, chopped
- 1 medium cucumber, chopped
- 1 tablespoon olive oil
- Freshly grated, low-fat Parmesan cheese
- Flat-leaf parsley or mint, chopped, for garnish
- Sea salt and freshly ground pepper, to taste

1. Put the oats and 1 cup of water in a medium saucepan and bring to a boil on high heat. 2. Stir continuously until water is absorbed, about 15 minutes. 3. To serve, divide the oatmeal between 2 bowls and top with the tomatoes and cucumber. 4. Drizzle with olive oil, then top with the Parmesan cheese and parsley or mint. 5. Season to taste. 6. Serve immediately.

Per Serving:
calories: 240 | fat: 10g | protein: 8g | carbs: 32g | fiber: 6g | sodium: 10mg

Creamy Orange Pecan Polenta Bowl

Prep time: 5 minutes |Cook time: 10 minutes| Serves: 6

- 2 (18-ounce / 510-g) tubes plain polenta
- 2¼ to 2½ cups 2% milk, divided
- 2 oranges, peeled and chopped
- ½ cup chopped pecans
- ¼ cup 2% plain Greek yogurt
- 8 teaspoons honey

1. Slice the polenta into rounds and place in a microwave-safe bowl. Heat in the microwave on high for 45 seconds. 2. Transfer the polenta to a large pot, and mash it with a potato masher or fork until coarsely mashed. Place the pot on the stove over medium heat. 3. In a medium, microwave-safe bowl, heat the milk in the microwave on high for 1 minute. Pour 2 cups of the warmed milk into the pot with the polenta, and stir with a whisk. Continue to stir and mash with the whisk, adding the remaining milk a few tablespoons at a time, until the polenta is fairly smooth and heated through, about 5 minutes. Remove from the stove. 4. Divide the polenta among four serving bowls. Top each bowl with one-quarter of the oranges, 2 tablespoons of pecans, 1 tablespoon of yogurt, and 2 teaspoons of honey before serving.

Per Serving:

calories: 319 | fat: 9g | protein: 8g | carbs: 54g | fiber: 4g | sodium: 428mg

Quinoa and Yogurt Breakfast Bowls

Prep time: 10 minutes | Cook time: 12 minutes | Serves 8

- 2 cups quinoa, rinsed and drained
- 4 cups water
- 1 teaspoon vanilla extract
- ¼ teaspoon salt
- 2 cups low-fat plain Greek yogurt
- 2 cups blueberries
- 1 cup toasted almonds
- ½ cup pure maple syrup

1. In the Instant Pot®, combine quinoa, water, vanilla, and salt. Secure the lid and ensure the steam release is set to Sealing. Press the Rice button and adjust the time to 12 minutes. 2. Once the timer signals, allow the pressure to release naturally for approximately 20 minutes. Carefully open the lid and fluff the quinoa using a fork. 3. Mix in yogurt. Serve while warm, garnished with berries, almonds, and a drizzle of maple syrup.

Per Serving:

calories: 376 | fat: 13g | protein: 16g | carbs: 52g | fiber: 6g | sodium: 105mg

Spicy Harissa Shakshuka with Peppers and Tomatoes

Prep time: 10 minutes | Cook time: 20 minutes | Serves 4

- 1½ tablespoons extra-virgin olive oil
- 2 tablespoons harissa
- 1 tablespoon tomato paste
- ½ onion, diced
- 1 bell pepper, seeded and diced
- 3 garlic cloves, minced
- 1 (28-ounce / 794-g) can no-salt-added diced tomatoes
- ½ teaspoon kosher salt
- 4 large eggs
- 2 to 3 tablespoons fresh basil, chopped or cut into ribbons

1. Preheat the oven to 375ºF (190ºC). 2. Heat the olive oil in a 12-inch cast-iron pan or ovenproof skillet over medium heat. Add the harissa, tomato paste, onion, and bell pepper; sauté for 3 to 4 minutes. Add the garlic and cook until fragrant, about 30 seconds. Add the diced tomatoes and salt and simmer for about 10 minutes. 3. Make 4 wells in the sauce and gently break 1 egg into each. Transfer to the oven and bake until the whites are cooked and the yolks are set, 10 to 12 minutes. 4. Allow to cool for 3 to 5 minutes, garnish with the basil, and carefully spoon onto plates.

Per Serving:

calories: 190 | fat: 10g | protein: 9g | carbs: 15g | fiber: 4g | sodium: 255mg

Chapter 3

Beans and Grains

Chapter 3 Beans and Grains

Mediterranean Giant Beans with Tomatoes and Herbs

Prep time: 10 minutes | Cook time: 54 minutes | Serves 8

- 2 tablespoons light olive oil
- 1 medium white onion, peeled and chopped
- 2 cloves garlic, peeled and minced
- 1 pound (454 g) dried giant beans, soaked overnight and drained
- 2 thyme sprigs
- 1 bay leaf
- 5 cups water
- 1 (15-ounce / 425-g) can

- diced tomatoes, drained
- 1 (8-ounce / 227-g) can tomato sauce
- ¼ cup chopped fresh flat-leaf parsley
- 2 tablespoons chopped fresh oregano
- 1 tablespoon chopped fresh dill
- ½ cup crumbled feta cheese
- 1 small lemon, cut into 8 wedges

1. Press the Sauté button on the Instant Pot® and heat oil. Add onion and cook until tender, about 3 minutes. Add garlic and cook until fragrant, about 30 seconds. Press the Cancel button. 2. Add beans, thyme, bay leaf, and water to the Instant Pot®. Close lid, set steam release to Sealing, press the Manual button, and set time to 50 minutes. When the timer beeps, quick-release the pressure until the float valve drops. Open lid and check that beans are soft. If they are not tender, close lid and cook under pressure for 10 minutes more. 3. Add diced tomatoes and tomato sauce. Close lid and let stand on the Keep Warm setting for 10 minutes to heat through. Remove and discard bay leaf. Stir in herbs and ladle into soup bowls. Garnish with feta and lemon slices, and serve hot.

Per Serving:
calories: 241 | fat: 6g | protein: 14g | carbs: 33g | fiber: 10g | sodium: 458mg

Garlicky Split Chickpea Curry

Prep time: 10 minutes | Cook time: 4 to 6 hours | Serves 6

- 1½ cups split gram
- 1 onion, finely chopped
- 2 tomatoes, chopped
- 1 tablespoon freshly grated ginger
- 1 teaspoon cumin seeds, ground or crushed with a mortar and pestle
- 2 teaspoons turmeric
- 2 garlic cloves, crushed

- 1 hot green Thai or other fresh chile, thinly sliced
- 3 cups hot water
- 1 teaspoon salt
- 2 tablespoons rapeseed oil
- 1 teaspoon cumin seeds, crushed
- 1 garlic clove, sliced
- 1 fresh green chile, sliced

1. Set the slow cooker to high heat. Combine the split gram, onion, tomatoes, ginger, crushed cumin seeds, turmeric, crushed garlic, hot chile, water, and salt in the pot, and stir well. 2. Cover the

slow cooker and cook on high for 4 hours, or on low for 6 hours, until the split gram is tender. 3. Just before serving, heat oil in a saucepan. Once the oil is hot, add the cumin seeds and sliced garlic. Sauté until the garlic turns golden brown, then pour this mixture over the dhal. 4. To serve, garnish with sliced green chile.

Per Serving:
calories: 119 | fat: 5g | protein: 4g | carbs: 15g | fiber: 3g | sodium: 503mg

Cumin-Scented Lentil and Basmati Pilaf

Prep time: 5 minutes | Cook time: 50 minutes | Serves 6

- ¼ cup extra-virgin olive oil
- 1 large onion, chopped
- 6 cups water
- 1 teaspoon ground cumin

- 1 teaspoon salt
- 2 cups brown lentils, picked over and rinsed
- 1 cup basmati rice

1. In a medium pot over medium heat, cook the olive oil and onions for 7 to 10 minutes until the edges are browned. 2. Turn the heat to high, add the water, cumin, and salt, and bring this mixture to a boil, boiling for about 3 minutes. 3. Add the lentils and turn the heat to medium-low. Cover the pot and cook for 20 minutes, stirring occasionally. 4. Stir in the rice and cover; cook for an additional 20 minutes. 5. Fluff the rice with a fork and serve warm.

Per Serving:
calories: 397 | fat: 11g | protein: 18g | carbs: 60g | fiber: 18g | sodium: 396mg

Mediterranean Lentil Casserole

Prep time: 15 minutes | Cook time: 8 to 10 hours | Serves 6

- 1 pound (454 g) lentils, rinsed well under cold water and picked over to remove debris
- 4 cups low-sodium vegetable broth
- 3 carrots, diced
- 3 cups chopped kale

- 1 small onion, diced
- 2 garlic cloves, minced
- 1 teaspoon sea salt
- 1 teaspoon dried basil
- 1 teaspoon dried oregano
- ½ teaspoon dried parsley
- 1 lemon, thinly sliced

1. In a slow cooker, add the lentils, vegetable broth, carrots, kale, onion, garlic, salt, basil, oregano, and parsley. Stir everything together until well combined. 2. Cover the slow cooker and set it to cook on Low heat for 8 to 10 hours, or until the lentils are tender. 3. Serve the dish garnished with lemon slices.

Per Serving:
calories: 302 | fat: 2g | protein: 22g | carbs: 54g | fiber: 26g | sodium: 527mg

Quinoa Salad in Endive Boats

Prep time: 10 minutes | Cook time: 3 minutes | Serves 4

- 1 tablespoon walnut oil
- 1 cup quinoa, rinsed and drained
- 2½ cups water
- 2 cups chopped jarred artichoke hearts
- 2 cups diced tomatoes
- ½ small red onion, peeled
- and thinly sliced
- 2 tablespoons olive oil
- 1 tablespoon balsamic vinegar
- 4 large Belgian endive leaves
- 1 cup toasted pecans

1. Begin by pressing the Sauté button on the Instant Pot® and heating walnut oil. Add the quinoa and toss it for about 1 minute until it becomes slightly browned. Then, add water and stir the mixture. Press the Cancel button to stop sautéing. 2. Secure the lid, set the steam release to Sealing, press the Manual button, and set the timer for 2 minutes. Once the timer beeps, allow the pressure to release naturally for 10 minutes. Afterward, perform a quick release for any remaining pressure until the float valve drops, then open the lid. Drain any excess liquid and transfer the quinoa to a serving bowl. 3. To the quinoa, add the artichoke hearts, tomatoes, onion, olive oil, and vinegar, stirring everything together until well combined. Cover the bowl and refrigerate the mixture for at least 1 hour or up to overnight for the flavors to meld. 4. Arrange the endive leaves on four plates. Spoon ¼ cup of the quinoa mixture onto each endive leaf, then sprinkle toasted pecans over the top of each endive boat before serving.

Per Serving:

calories: 536 | fat: 35g | protein: 13g | carbs: 46g | fiber: 13g | sodium: 657mg

Zesty Black Bean and Corn Salad

Prep time: 20 minutes | Cook time: 30 minutes | Serves 6

- ½ pound (227 g) dried black beans, soaked overnight and drained
- 1 medium white onion, peeled and sliced in half
- 2 cloves garlic, peeled and lightly crushed
- 8 cups water
- 1 cup corn kernels
- 1 large tomato, seeded and chopped
- ½ medium red onion, peeled and chopped
- ¼ cup minced fresh cilantro
- ½ teaspoon ground cumin
- ¼ teaspoon smoked paprika
- ¼ teaspoon ground black pepper
- ¼ teaspoon salt
- 3 tablespoons extra-virgin olive oil
- 3 tablespoons lime juice

1. Add beans, white onion, garlic, and water to the Instant Pot®. Close lid, set steam release to Sealing, press the Bean button, and cook for the default time of 30 minutes. When the timer beeps, let pressure release naturally, about 20 minutes. 2. Open lid and remove and discard onion and garlic. Drain beans well and transfer to a medium bowl. Cool to room temperature, about 30 minutes. 3. In a separate small bowl, combine corn, tomato, red onion, cilantro, cumin, paprika, pepper, and salt. Toss to combine. Add to black beans and gently fold to mix. Whisk together olive oil and lime juice in a small bowl and pour over black bean mixture. Gently

toss to coat. Serve at room temperature or refrigerate for at least 2 hours.

Per Serving:

calories: 216 | fat: 7g | protein: 8g | carbs: 28g | fiber: 6g | sodium: 192mg

Lentils in Tomato Sauce

Prep time: 10 minutes | Cook time: 11 minutes | Serves 6

- 2 cups red, green, or brown dried lentils, rinsed and drained
- ½ teaspoon salt
- 4 cups water
- 1 (24-ounce / 680-g) jar marinara sauce
- 1 tablespoon extra-virgin olive oil
- 1 tablespoon chopped fresh oregano
- 1 teaspoon ground fennel
- ¼ teaspoon ground black pepper
- ½ cup grated Parmesan cheese
- ½ cup minced fresh flat-leaf parsley

1. In the Instant Pot®, combine the lentils, salt, and water. Secure the lid, set the steam release to Sealing, press the Manual button, and set the timer for 6 minutes. When the timer beeps, perform a quick release until the float valve drops. Press the Cancel button and then open the lid, draining any excess liquid. 2. Stir in the sauce, oil, oregano, fennel, and pepper into the pot, mixing thoroughly. Close the lid again, set the steam release to Sealing, press the Manual button, and adjust the timer to 5 minutes. Once the timer beeps, allow the pressure to release naturally for 10 minutes, then quick-release any remaining pressure until the float valve drops. Open the lid and finish by topping with cheese and parsley.

Per Serving:

calories: 342 | fat: 8g | protein: 21g | carbs: 48g | fiber: 9g | sodium: 640mg

Rice with Pork Chops

Prep time: 10 minutes | Cook time: 3 to 5 hours | Serves 4

- 1 cup raw long-grain brown rice, rinsed
- 2½ cups low-sodium chicken broth
- 1 cup sliced tomato
- 8 ounces (227 g) fresh spinach, chopped
- 1 small onion, chopped
- 2 garlic cloves, minced
- 2 teaspoons dried oregano
- 2 teaspoons dried basil
- 1 teaspoon sea salt
- ½ teaspoon freshly ground black pepper
- 4 thick-cut pork chops
- ¼ cup grated Parmesan cheese

1. In a slow cooker, mix together the rice, chicken broth, tomato, spinach, onion, garlic, oregano, basil, salt, and pepper until well combined. 2. Lay the pork chops on top of the rice mixture. 3. Cover the slow cooker and set it to cook on Low heat for 3 to 5 hours. 4. Before serving, sprinkle the dish with Parmesan cheese.

Per Serving:

calories: 482 | fat: 11g | protein: 51g | carbs: 44g | fiber: 4g | sodium: 785mg

Lentil and Zucchini Boats

Prep time: 15 minutes | Cook time: 50 minutes | Serves 4

- 1 cup dried green lentils, rinsed and drained
- ¼ teaspoon salt
- 2 cups water
- 1 tablespoon olive oil
- ½ medium red onion, peeled and diced
- 1 clove garlic, peeled and minced
- 1 cup marinara sauce
- ¼ teaspoon crushed red pepper flakes
- 4 medium zucchini, trimmed and cut lengthwise
- ½ cup shredded part-skim mozzarella cheese
- ¼ cup chopped fresh flat-leaf parsley

1. In the Instant Pot®, combine the lentils, salt, and water. Secure the lid, set the steam release to Sealing, press the Manual button, and adjust the timer to 12 minutes. Once the timer beeps, perform a quick release until the float valve drops. Press the Cancel button, then carefully open the lid and drain any excess liquid. Transfer the lentils to a medium bowl and set aside. 2. Press the Sauté button and heat oil in the pot. Add the onion and cook until it becomes tender, about 3 minutes. Stir in the garlic and cook until fragrant, approximately 30 seconds. Add the marinara sauce and crushed red pepper flakes, stirring to combine. Press the Cancel button, then fold in the lentils. 3. Preheat your oven to 350°F (180ºC) and spray a 9" × 13" baking dish with nonstick cooking spray. 4. Using a teaspoon, scoop out the insides of each zucchini half. Arrange the hollowed zucchini in the prepared baking dish. Fill each zucchini with the lentil mixture and sprinkle cheese on top. Bake for 30 to 35 minutes, or until the zucchini are tender and the cheese is melted and golden brown. Garnish with parsley and serve hot.

Per Serving:
calories: 326 | fat: 10g | protein: 22g | carbs: 39g | fiber: 16g | sodium: 568mg

Hearty Two-Bean Bulgur Chili

Prep time: 10 minutes | Cook time: 30 minutes | Serves 4 to 5

- 2 tablespoons olive oil
- 1 onion, diced
- 2 celery stalks, diced
- 1 carrot, diced
- 1 jalapeño pepper, seeded and chopped
- 3 garlic cloves, minced
- 1 (28-ounce/ 794-g) can diced tomatoes
- 1 tablespoon tomato paste
- 1½ teaspoons chili powder
- 2 teaspoons dried oregano
- 2 teaspoons ground cumin
- 1 (15-ounce/ 425-g) can black beans, drained and rinsed
- 1 (15-ounce/ 425-g) can cannellini beans, drained and rinsed
- ¾ cup dried bulgur
- 4 cups chicken broth
- Sea salt
- Freshly ground black pepper

1. In a Dutch oven, heat the olive oil over medium-high heat. Add the onion, celery, carrot, jalapeño, and garlic and sauté until the vegetables are tender, about 4 minutes. 2. Reduce the heat to medium and add the diced tomatoes, tomato paste, chili powder, oregano, and cumin. Cook for 3 minutes, then add the black beans, cannellini beans, bulgur, and broth. 3. Increase the heat to high, cover, and bring to a boil. Reduce the heat to low and simmer until the chili is cooked to your desired thickness, about 30 minutes.

Season with salt and black pepper and serve.

Per Serving:
calories: 385 | fat: 9g | protein: 16g | carbs: 64g | fiber: 20g | sodium: 325mg

Creamy Puréed Red Lentil Soup

Prep time: 15 minutes | Cook time: 21 minutes | Serves 6

- 2 tablespoons olive oil
- 1 medium yellow onion, peeled and chopped
- 1 medium carrot, peeled and chopped
- 1 medium red bell pepper, seeded and chopped
- 1 clove garlic, peeled and minced
- 1 bay leaf
- ½ teaspoon ground black pepper
- ¼ teaspoon salt
- 1 (15-ounce / 425-g) can diced tomatoes, drained
- 2 cups dried red lentils, rinsed and drained
- 6 cups low-sodium chicken broth

1. Press the Sauté button on the Instant Pot® and heat oil. Add onion, carrot, and bell pepper. Cook until just tender, about 5 minutes. Add garlic, bay leaf, black pepper, and salt, and cook until fragrant, about 30 seconds. Press the Cancel button. 2. Add tomatoes, lentils, and broth, then close lid, set steam release to Sealing, press the Manual button, and set time to 15 minutes. When the timer beeps, let pressure release naturally, about 15 minutes. Open lid, remove and discard bay leaf, and purée with an immersion blender or in batches in a blender. Serve warm.

Per Serving:
calories: 289 | fat: 6g | protein: 18g | carbs: 39g | fiber: 8g | sodium: 438mg

Slow-Cooked Chickpea Falafel Patties

Prep time: 10 minutes | Cook time: 6 to 8 hours | Serves 4

- Nonstick cooking spray
- 2 cups canned reduced-sodium chickpeas, rinsed and drained
- 4 garlic cloves, peeled
- ¼ cup chickpea flour or all-purpose flour
- ¼ cup diced onion
- ¼ cup chopped fresh parsley
- ¼ cup chopped fresh cilantro
- 1 teaspoon sea salt
- 1 teaspoon ground cumin
- ½ teaspoon ground coriander
- ½ teaspoon freshly ground black pepper
- ⅛ teaspoon cayenne pepper

1. Generously coat a slow cooker insert with cooking spray. 2. In a blender or food processor, combine the chickpeas, garlic, flour, onion, parsley, cilantro, salt, cumin, coriander, black pepper, and cayenne pepper. Process until smooth. Form the mixture into 6 to 8 (2-inch) round patties and place them in a single layer in the prepared slow cooker. 3. Cover the cooker and cook for 6 to 8 hours on Low heat.

Per Serving:
calories: 174 | fat: 3g | protein: 9g | carbs: 30g | fiber: 8g | sodium: 594mg

Mediterranean Lentil and Rice Salad

Prep time: 5 minutes |Cook time: 25 minutes| Serves: 4

- 2¼ cups low-sodium or no-salt-added vegetable broth
- ½ cup uncooked brown or green lentils
- ½ cup uncooked instant brown rice
- ½ cup diced carrots (about 1 carrot)
- ½ cup diced celery (about 1 stalk)
- 1 (2¼-ounce / 64-g) can sliced olives, drained (about ½ cup)
- ¼ cup diced red onion
- (about ⅛ onion)
- ¼ cup chopped fresh curly-leaf parsley
- 1½ tablespoons extra-virgin olive oil
- 1 tablespoon freshly squeezed lemon juice (from about ½ small lemon)
- 1 garlic clove, minced (about ½ teaspoon)
- ¼ teaspoon kosher or sea salt
- ¼ teaspoon freshly ground black pepper

1. In a medium saucepan over high heat, bring the broth and lentils to a boil, cover, and lower the heat to medium-low. Cook for 8 minutes. 2. Raise the heat to medium, and stir in the rice. Cover the pot and cook the mixture for 15 minutes, or until the liquid is absorbed. Remove the pot from the heat and let it sit, covered, for 1 minute, then stir. 3. While the lentils and rice are cooking, mix together the carrots, celery, olives, onion, and parsley in a large serving bowl. 4. In a small bowl, whisk together the oil, lemon juice, garlic, salt, and pepper. Set aside. 5. When the lentils and rice are cooked, add them to the serving bowl. Pour the dressing on top, and mix everything together. Serve warm or cold, or store in a sealed container in the refrigerator for up to 7 days.

Per Serving:
calories: 183 | fat: 6g | protein: 5g | carbs: 30g | fiber: 3g | sodium: 552mg

Pilaf with Eggplant and Raisins

Prep time: 10 minutes | Cook time: 30 minutes | Serves 4

- 4 eggplant (preferably thinner, about 6 ounces/170g each) cut into ¼-inch (.5cm) thick slices (if the slices are too large, cut them in half)
- 1½ teaspoons fine sea salt, divided
- ½ cup extra virgin olive oil
- 1 medium onion (any variety), diced
- 4 garlic cloves, thinly sliced
- ¼ cup white wine
- 1 cup uncooked medium-grain rice
- 1 (15-ounce / 425-g) can crushed tomatoes
- 3 cups hot water
- 4 tablespoons black raisins
- 4 teaspoons finely chopped fresh parsley
- 4 teaspoons finely chopped fresh mint
- ¼ teaspoon freshly ground black pepper to serve

1. Place the eggplant in a colander and sprinkle it with ½ teaspoon of sea salt. Allow it to rest for 10 minutes, then rinse thoroughly and squeeze out any excess water. 2. In a medium pot over medium heat, add the olive oil. Once the oil begins to shimmer, incorporate the eggplant and sauté for 7 minutes, stirring continuously until it becomes soft. Then, add the onions and continue sautéing for an additional 2 minutes, stirring frequently. 3. Mix in the garlic and sauté for 1 more minute before adding the white wine to deglaze the pan. After about 1 minute, add the rice and stir until it is evenly coated with the oil. 4. Pour in the crushed tomatoes, hot water, and the remaining sea salt. Stir the mixture and bring it to a boil, then reduce the heat to low and let it simmer for 20 minutes. If the water level gets too low, add more hot water, ¼ cup at a time. 5. Add the raisins and stir well, then cover the pot and remove it from the heat. Let it sit for 15 minutes to cool. 6. To serve, sprinkle 1 teaspoon of mint and 1 teaspoon of parsley over each portion, and season with black pepper. Store any leftovers covered in the refrigerator for up to 3 days.

Per Serving:
calories: 612 | fat: 29g | protein: 11g | carbs: 84g | fiber: 21g | sodium: 859mg

Creamy Yellow Lentil Soup

Prep time: 15 minutes | Cook time: 20 minutes | Serves 6

- 2 tablespoons olive oil
- 1 medium yellow onion, peeled and chopped
- 1 medium carrot, peeled and chopped
- 2 cloves garlic, peeled and minced
- 1 teaspoon ground cumin
- ½ teaspoon ground black pepper
- ¼ teaspoon salt
- 2 cups dried yellow lentils, rinsed and drained
- 6 cups water

1. Start by pressing the Sauté button on the Instant Pot® and adding oil. Once the oil is hot, toss in the onion and carrot, cooking for about 3 minutes until they are just tender. Next, add the garlic, cumin, pepper, and salt, sautéing until the mixture becomes fragrant, which should take about 30 seconds. Press the Cancel button to stop sautéing. 2. Stir in the lentils and water, then secure the lid. Set the steam release to Sealing, press the Manual button, and adjust the timer to 15 minutes. Once the timer signals, allow the pressure to release naturally for about 15 minutes. 3. Afterward, open the lid and use an immersion blender to purée the mixture until smooth, or blend it in batches in a traditional blender. Serve the soup warm.

Per Serving:
calories: 248 | fat: 5g | protein: 15g | carbs: 35g | fiber: 8g | sodium: 118mg

Curried Apple and Leek Couscous

Prep time: 10 minutes | Cook time: 10 minutes | Serves 4

- 2 teaspoons olive oil
- 2 leeks, white parts only, sliced
- 1 Granny Smith apple, diced
- 2 cups cooked whole-wheat couscous
- 2 tablespoons curry powder
- ½ cup chopped pecans

1. Heat the olive oil in a large skillet on medium heat and add leeks. Cook until soft and tender, about 5 minutes. 2. Add diced apple and cook until soft. 3. Add couscous and curry powder, then stir to combine. Remove from heat, mix in nuts, and serve.

Per Serving:
calories: 255 | fat: 12g | protein: 5g | carbs: 34g | fiber: 6g | sodium: 15mg

Domatorizo (Greek Tomato Rice)

Prep time: 10 minutes | Cook time: 12 minutes | Serves 6

- 2 tablespoons extra-virgin olive oil
- 1 large onion, peeled and diced
- 1 cup Arborio rice
- 1 cup tomato juice
- 3 tablespoons dry white wine
- 2 cups water
- 1 tablespoon tomato paste
- ½ teaspoon salt
- ½ teaspoon ground black pepper
- ½ cup crumbled or cubed feta cheese
- ⅛ teaspoon dried Greek oregano
- 1 scallion, thinly sliced

1. Start by pressing the Sauté button on the Instant Pot® and adding oil. Sauté the onion until it becomes tender, approximately 3 minutes. Then, stir in the rice and continue cooking for an additional 2 minutes. 2. Pour in the tomato juice and wine, mixing them with the rice. Cook while stirring frequently until the liquid is mostly absorbed, about 1 minute. 3. In a small bowl, whisk together water and tomato paste, then add this mixture to the pot along with salt and pepper. Stir well to combine and then press the Cancel button. 4. Close the lid, set the steam release to Sealing, press the Manual button, and adjust the timer to 5 minutes. Once the timer beeps, allow the pressure to release naturally for 10 minutes, then perform a quick release for any remaining pressure until the float valve drops. 5. After opening the lid, stir the rice thoroughly. Serve the rice in bowls, topped with feta cheese, oregano, and scallion. Enjoy immediately.

Per Serving:
calories: 184 | fat: 9g | protein: 6g | carbs: 20g | fiber: 1g | sodium: 537mg

Za'atar Chickpea and Spinach Bulgur Salad

Prep time: 15 minutes | Cook time: 7 minutes | Serves 4 to 6

- 3 tablespoons extra-virgin olive oil, divided
- 1 onion, chopped fine
- ½ teaspoon table salt
- 3 garlic cloves, minced
- 2 tablespoons za'atar, divided
- 1 cup medium-grind bulgur, rinsed
- 1 (15-ounce/ 425-g) can chickpeas, rinsed
- 1½ cups water
- 5 ounces (142 g) baby spinach, chopped
- 1 tablespoon lemon juice, plus lemon wedges for serving

1. Using highest sauté function, heat 2 tablespoons oil in Instant Pot until shimmering. Add onion and salt and cook until onion is softened, about 5 minutes. Stir in garlic and 1 tablespoon za'atar and cook until fragrant, about 30 seconds. Stir in bulgur, chickpeas, and water. 2. Lock lid in place and close pressure release valve. Select high pressure cook function and cook for 1 minute. Turn off Instant Pot and quick-release pressure. Carefully remove lid, allowing steam to escape away from you. 3. Gently fluff bulgur with fork. Lay clean dish towel over pot, replace lid, and let sit for 5 minutes. Add spinach, lemon juice, remaining 1 tablespoon za'atar, and remaining 1 tablespoon oil and gently toss to combine.

Season with salt and pepper to taste. Serve with lemon wedges.

Per Serving:
calories: 200 | fat: 8g | protein: 6g | carbs: 28g | fiber: 6g | sodium: 320mg

Ginger-Spiced Whole Brown Lentil Dhal

Prep time: 10 minutes | Cook time: 6 to 8 hours | Serves 6

- 6⅓ cups hot water
- 2 cups whole brown lentils
- 1 tablespoon ghee
- 1 teaspoon freshly grated ginger
- 1 teaspoon sea salt
- 1 teaspoon turmeric
- 7 to 8 ounces (198 to 227 g) canned tomatoes
- 4 garlic cloves, finely chopped
- 1 or 2 fresh green chiles, finely chopped
- 1 onion, chopped
- 1 teaspoon garam masala
- Handful fresh coriander leaves, chopped

1. Wash and clean the lentils, then set them aside to drain. 2. Heat the slow cooker to high and add all of the ingredients except the garam masala and coriander leaves. 3. Cover and cook on high for 6 hours, or on low for 8 hours. 4. Add the garam masala and fresh coriander leaves before serving, and enjoy.

Per Serving:
calories: 263 | fat: 3g | protein: 16g | carbs: 44g | fiber: 8g | sodium: 401mg

Cilantro Lime Rice

Prep time: 10 minutes | Cook time: 32 minutes | Serves 8

- 2 tablespoons extra-virgin olive oil
- ½ medium yellow onion, peeled and chopped
- 2 cloves garlic, peeled and minced
- ½ cup chopped fresh cilantro, divided
- 2 cups brown rice
- 2¼ cups water
- 2 tablespoons lime juice
- 1 tablespoon grated lime zest
- ¼ teaspoon salt
- ½ teaspoon ground black pepper

1. Begin by pressing the Sauté button on the Instant Pot® and heating the oil. Add the onion and sauté until it becomes soft, which should take about 6 minutes. Then, add the garlic and ¼ cup of cilantro, cooking for an additional 30 seconds until fragrant. Next, add the rice and stir constantly for about 3 minutes, ensuring it is well coated and begins to toast. Press the Cancel button to stop sautéing. 2. Pour in the water and stir to combine. Secure the lid, set the steam release to Sealing, press the Manual button, and set the timer for 22 minutes. When the timer beeps, allow the pressure to release naturally for 10 minutes, then quick-release any remaining pressure. Open the lid and fluff the rice with a fork. 3. Gently fold in the remaining ¼ cup of cilantro, lime juice, lime zest, salt, and pepper. Serve warm.

Per Serving:
calories: 95 | fat: 4g | protein: 1g | carbs: 14g | fiber: 1g | sodium: 94mg

Creamy Garbanzo and Pita Layered Delight

Prep time: 10 minutes | Cook time: 10 minutes | Serves 4

- 4 cups Greek yogurt
- 3 cloves garlic, minced
- 1 teaspoon salt
- 2 (16-ounce/ 454-g) cans garbanzo beans, rinsed and
- drained
- 2 cups water
- 4 cups pita chips
- 5 tablespoons unsalted butter

1. In a large bowl, whisk together the yogurt, garlic, and salt. Set aside. 2. Put the garbanzo beans and water in a medium pot. Bring to a boil; let beans boil for about 5 minutes. 3. Pour the garbanzo beans and the liquid into a large casserole dish. 4. Top the beans with pita chips. Pour the yogurt sauce over the pita chip layer. 5. In a small saucepan, melt and brown the butter, about 3 minutes. Pour the brown butter over the yogurt sauce.

Per Serving:
calories: 772 | fat: 36g | protein: 39g | carbs: 73g | fiber: 13g | sodium: 1,003mg

French Lentils with Swiss Chard

Prep time: 15 minutes | Cook time: 17 minutes | Serves 6

- 2 tablespoons extra-virgin olive oil, plus extra for drizzling
- 12 ounces (340 g) Swiss chard, stems chopped fine, leaves sliced into ½-inch-wide strips
- 1 onion, chopped fine
- ½ teaspoon table salt
- 2 garlic cloves, minced
- 1 teaspoon minced fresh thyme or ¼ teaspoon dried
- 2½ cups water
- 1 cup French green lentils, picked over and rinsed
- 3 tablespoons whole-grain mustard
- ½ teaspoon grated lemon zest plus 1 teaspoon juice
- 3 tablespoons sliced almonds, toasted
- 2 tablespoons chopped fresh parsley

1. Set the Instant Pot to the highest sauté setting and heat the oil until it shimmers. Add the chard stems, onion, and salt, cooking until the vegetables are softened, which should take about 5 minutes. Then, stir in the garlic and thyme, cooking until fragrant, about 30 seconds. Pour in the water and add the lentils, mixing well. 2. Secure the lid on the Instant Pot and close the pressure release valve. Select the high-pressure cook function and set the cooking time for 11 minutes. Once done, turn off the Instant Pot and allow the pressure to release naturally for 15 minutes. Perform a quick release for any remaining pressure, then carefully remove the lid, ensuring to direct the steam away from you. 3. Gently stir the chard leaves into the lentil mixture, adding one handful at a time, and allow them to cook in the residual heat until wilted, which should take about 5 minutes. Mix in the mustard, lemon zest, and lemon juice, then season with salt and pepper to taste. Transfer the lentils to a serving dish, drizzle with extra oil, and garnish with almonds and parsley. Serve immediately.

Per Serving:
calories: 190 | fat: 8g | protein: 9g | carbs: 23g | fiber: 6g | sodium: 470mg

Savory Herbed Wild Rice Pilaf

Prep time: 15 minutes | Cook time: 32 minutes | Serves 8

- 2 tablespoons extra-virgin olive oil
- 2 stalks celery, chopped
- 1 medium white onion, peeled and chopped
- 1 medium carrot, peeled and chopped
- 2 cups sliced baby bella mushrooms
- 2 cloves garlic, peeled and minced
- 1 tablespoon chopped fresh
- rosemary
- 1 tablespoon chopped fresh sage
- ¼ teaspoon salt
- ½ teaspoon ground black pepper
- 2 cups wild rice
- 2½ cups vegetable broth
- ½ cup dried cranberries
- ½ cup chopped toasted pecans

1. Press the Sauté button on the Instant Pot® and heat oil. Add celery, onion, carrot, and mushrooms. Cook until soft, about 10 minutes. Add garlic, rosemary, sage, salt, and pepper. Cook until fragrant, about 1 minute. Add rice and mix well. Press the Cancel button. 2. Stir in broth. Close lid, set steam release to Sealing, press the Manual button, and set time to 20 minutes. When the timer beeps, let pressure release naturally for 10 minutes, then quick-release the remaining pressure. Open lid and fold in cranberries and pecans. Serve warm.

Per Serving:
calories: 356 | fat: 13g | protein: 9g | carbs: 50g | fiber: 5g | sodium: 147mg

Farro and Mushroom Risotto

Prep time: 10 minutes | Cook time: 20 minutes | Serves 6

- 2 tablespoons olive oil
- 1 medium yellow onion, peeled and diced
- 16 ounces (454 g) sliced button mushrooms
- ½ teaspoon salt
- ½ teaspoon ground black pepper
- ½ teaspoon dried thyme
- ½ teaspoon dried oregano
- 1 clove garlic, peeled and minced
- 1 cup farro, rinsed and drained
- 1½ cups vegetable broth
- ¼ cup grated Parmesan cheese
- 2 tablespoons minced fresh flat-leaf parsley

1. Start by pressing the Sauté button on the Instant Pot® and heating the oil. Add the onion and mushrooms, sautéing for 8 minutes. Then, stir in the salt, pepper, thyme, and oregano, cooking for an additional 30 seconds. Add the garlic and continue to cook for another 30 seconds. Press the Cancel button to stop sautéing. 2. Mix in the farro and broth. Secure the lid, set the steam release to Sealing, press the Manual button, and set the timer for 10 minutes. Once the timer beeps, allow the pressure to release naturally for 10 minutes, then quick-release any remaining pressure until the float valve drops. 3. Before serving, top the dish with cheese and parsley.

Per Serving:
calories: 215 | fat: 8g | protein: 11g | carbs: 24g | fiber: 3g | sodium: 419mg

Mediterranean Pea and Potato Casserole

Prep time: 5 minutes | Cook time: 45 minutes | Serves 3

- ⅓ cup extra virgin olive oil
- 1 medium onion (any variety), diced
- 1 medium carrot, peeled and sliced
- 1 medium white potato, peeled and cut into bite-sized pieces
- 1 pound (454 g) peas (fresh or frozen)
- 3 tablespoons chopped fresh dill
- 2 medium tomatoes, grated, or 12 ounces (340 g) canned crushed tomatoes
- ½ teaspoon fine sea salt
- ¼ teaspoon freshly ground black pepper
- ½ cup hot water
- Salt to taste

1. Add the olive oil to a medium pot over medium heat. When the oil starts to shimmer, add the onions and sauté for 2 minutes. Add the carrots and potatoes, and sauté for 3 more minutes. 2. Add the peas and dill. Stir until the peas are coated in the olive oil. 3. Add the tomatoes, sea salt, black pepper, and hot water. Mix well.Bring to the mixture to a boil, then cover, reduce the heat to low, and simmer for 40 minutes or until the peas and carrots are soft and the casserole has thickened. (Check the water levels intermittently, adding more hot water if the mixture appears to be getting too dry.) 4. Remove the casserole from the heat, uncover, and set aside for 20 minutes. Add salt to taste before serving. Store covered in the refrigerator for up to 3 days.

Per Serving:
calories: 439 | fat: 26g | protein: 12g | carbs: 45g | fiber: 13g | sodium: 429mg

Rice Pilaf

Prep time: 5 minutes | Cook time: 30 minutes | Serves 6

- 2 tablespoons olive oil
- 1 medium onion, diced
- ¼ cup pine nuts
- 1½ cups long-grain brown rice
- 2 ½ cups hot chicken stock
- 1 cinnamon stick
- ¼ cup raisins
- Sea salt and freshly ground pepper, to taste

1. In a large saucepan, heat the olive oil over medium heat. 2. Add the onions and pine nuts, sautéing for 6 to 8 minutes until the pine nuts turn golden and the onions become translucent. 3. Stir in the rice and continue to sauté for 2 minutes until it is lightly browned. Then, pour the chicken stock into the pan and bring the mixture to a boil. 4. Incorporate the cinnamon and raisins into the pan. 5. Reduce the heat, cover the saucepan, and let it simmer for 15 to 20 minutes, or until the rice is tender and the liquid has been absorbed. 6. Once done, remove the pan from the heat and fluff the rice with a fork. Adjust the seasoning and serve.

Per Serving:
calories: 293 | fat: 10g | protein: 7g | carbs: 45g | fiber: 2g | sodium: 35mg

Quinoa with Kale, Carrots, and Walnuts

Prep time: 10 minutes | Cook time: 20 minutes | Serves 4

- 1 cup quinoa, rinsed and drained
- 2 cups water
- ¼ cup olive oil
- 2 tablespoons apple cider vinegar
- 1 clove garlic, peeled and minced
- ½ teaspoon ground black pepper
- ½ teaspoon salt
- 2 cups chopped kale
- 1 cup shredded carrot
- 1 cup toasted walnut pieces
- ½ cup crumbled feta cheese

1. Combine quinoa and water in the Instant Pot® and stir to mix thoroughly. Secure the lid, set the steam release to Sealing, press the Manual button, and adjust the timer to 20 minutes. Once the timer beeps, allow the pressure to release naturally for about 20 minutes, then open the lid. Use a fork to fluff the quinoa, then transfer it to a medium bowl and let it cool to room temperature for approximately 40 minutes. 2. Once cooled, add oil, vinegar, garlic, pepper, salt, kale, carrot, walnuts, and feta cheese to the quinoa and mix well. Cover and refrigerate for 4 hours before serving.

Per Serving:
calories: 625 | fat: 39g | protein: 19g | carbs: 47g | fiber: 10g | sodium: 738mg

Savory Tomato and Bulgur Pilaf

Prep time: 10 minutes | Cook time: 25 minutes | Serves 4

- 3 tablespoons olive oil
- 1 onion, diced
- 1 garlic clove, minced
- 1 tablespoon tomato paste
- ½ teaspoon paprika
- 3 Roma (plum) tomatoes, finely chopped, or 1 cup canned

- crushed tomatoes with their juices
- Juice of ½ lemon
- ¼ teaspoon sea salt, plus more as needed
- 1 cup dried bulgur
- 2 cups vegetable broth, chicken broth, or water

1. In a large saucepan, heat the olive oil over medium-high heat. Add the onion and garlic and sauté for 4 to 5 minutes, until the onion is soft. Add the tomato paste and paprika and stir for about 30 seconds. 2. Add the chopped tomatoes, lemon juice, and salt and cook for 1 to 2 minutes more. 3. Add the bulgur and stir for about 30 seconds. Add the broth, bring to a simmer, reduce the heat to low, cover, and simmer for 13 to 15 minutes, until the liquid has been absorbed. Uncover and stir, then remove from the heat, cover, and let stand for 5 minutes. 4. Taste and adjust the seasoning, then serve.

Per Serving:

calories: 243 | fat: 11g | protein: 6g | carbs: 34g | fiber: 6g | sodium: 92mg

Prassorizo (Leeks and Rice)

Prep time: 10 minutes | Cook time: 12 minutes | Serves 6

- 6 large leeks
- 5 cups water
- 4 scallions, chopped
- ⅓ cup minced fresh dill
- ¼ cup minced fresh mint
- ½ tablespoon dried thyme

- ½ teaspoon salt
- ¼ teaspoon ground black pepper
- 1 cup Arborio rice
- ⅓ cup extra-virgin olive oil
- 3 tablespoons lemon juice

1. Slice the white ends of the leeks into thick pieces and discard the green parts. 2. In the Instant Pot®, combine the leeks, water, scallions, dill, mint, thyme, salt, and pepper, stirring well. Add the rice and mix to combine. 3. Secure the lid, set the steam release to Sealing, press the Rice button, and set the timer for 12 minutes. Once the timer beeps, allow the pressure to release naturally for 10 minutes, then quick-release any remaining pressure. 4. After opening the lid, stir the mixture thoroughly. Drizzle in olive oil and lemon juice, then serve hot.

Per Serving:

calories: 224 | fat: 12g | protein: 4g | carbs: 28g | fiber: 4g | sodium: 408mg

Cilantro-Lime Green Lentil Medley

Prep time: 15 minutes | Cook time: 20 minutes | Serves 6

- 2 tablespoons olive oil
- 1 medium yellow onion, peeled and chopped
- 1 medium carrot, peeled and chopped
- ¼ cup chopped fresh cilantro
- ½ teaspoon ground cumin

- ½ teaspoon salt
- 2 cups dried green lentils, rinsed and drained
- 4 cups low-sodium chicken broth
- 2 tablespoons lime juice

1. Press the Sauté button on the Instant Pot® and heat oil. Add onion and carrot, and cook until just tender, about 3 minutes. Add cilantro, cumin, and salt, and cook until fragrant, about 30 seconds. Press the Cancel button. 2. Add lentils and broth to pot. Close lid, set steam release to Sealing, press the Manual button, and set time to 15 minutes. 3. When the timer beeps, let pressure release naturally, about 25 minutes. Open lid and stir in lime juice. Serve warm.

Per Serving:

calories: 316 | fat: 5g | protein: 20g | carbs: 44g | fiber: 21g | sodium: 349mg

Chapter 4

Vegetables and Sides

Chapter 4 Vegetables and Sides

Crispy Sweet Potato Pecan Tots

Prep time: 10 minutes | Cook time: 12 to 13 minutes per batch | Makes 18 to 24 tots

- 1 cup cooked mashed sweet potatoes
- 1 egg white, beaten
- ⅛ teaspoon ground cinnamon
- 1 dash nutmeg
- 2 tablespoons chopped
- pecans
- 1½ teaspoons honey
- Salt, to taste
- ½ cup panko bread crumbs
- Oil for misting or cooking spray

1. Preheat the air fryer to 390ºF (199ºC). 2. In a large bowl, mix together the potatoes, egg white, cinnamon, nutmeg, pecans, honey, and salt to taste. 3. Place panko crumbs on a sheet of wax paper. 4. For each tot, use about 2 teaspoons of sweet potato mixture. To shape, drop the measure of potato mixture onto panko crumbs and push crumbs up and around potatoes to coat edges. Then turn tot over to coat other side with crumbs. 5. Mist tots with oil or cooking spray and place in air fryer basket in single layer. 6. Air fry at 390ºF (199ºC) for 12 to 13 minutes, until browned and crispy. 7. Repeat steps 5 and 6 to cook remaining tots.

Per Serving:
calories: 51 | fat: 1g | protein: 1g | carbs: 9g | fiber: 1g | sodium: 45mg

Parsnip Fries with Romesco Sauce

Prep time: 20 minutes | Cook time: 24 minutes | Serves 4

Romesco Sauce:
- 1 red bell pepper, halved and seeded
- 1 (1-inch) thick slice of Italian bread, torn into pieces (about 1 to 1½ cups)
- 1 cup almonds, toasted
- Olive oil
- ½ Jalapeño pepper, seeded
- 1 tablespoon fresh parsley leaves
- 1 clove garlic
- 2 Roma tomatoes, peeled
- and seeded (or ⅓ cup canned crushed tomatoes)
- 1 tablespoon red wine vinegar
- ¼ teaspoon smoked paprika
- ½ teaspoon salt
- ¾ cup olive oil
- 3 parsnips, peeled and cut into long strips
- 2 teaspoons olive oil
- Salt and freshly ground black pepper, to taste

1. Begin by preheating the air fryer to 400ºF (204ºC). 2. Place the halved red peppers, cut side down, in the air fryer basket and cook for 8 to 10 minutes until the skin is blackened all over. Once done, remove the peppers from the air fryer and allow them to cool. When they are cool enough to handle, peel off the skin. 3. In a mixing bowl, combine the torn bread and almonds with a drizzle of olive oil, then air fry for 4 minutes, shaking the basket a few times during cooking to ensure even toasting. Once nicely browned, take them

out and let them cool for a minute or two. 4. In a food processor or blender, combine the toasted bread, almonds, roasted red pepper, jalapeño pepper, parsley, garlic, tomatoes, vinegar, smoked paprika, and salt. Blend until smooth. While the processor is running, slowly drizzle in olive oil through the feed tube until the mixture forms a smooth paste that is slightly pourable. 5. Toss the parsnip strips with olive oil, salt, and freshly ground black pepper. Air fry them at 400ºF (204ºC) for 10 minutes, shaking the basket a couple of times during cooking to ensure they brown and cook evenly. Serve the parsnip fries warm alongside the Romesco sauce for dipping.

Per Serving:
calories: 604 | fat: 55g | protein: 7g | carbs: 55g | fiber: 8g | sodium: 319mg

Citrus Beet and Watercress Salad with Dill

Prep time: 20 minutes | Cook time: 8 minutes | Serves 4

- 2 pounds (907 g) beets, scrubbed, trimmed, and cut into ¾-inch pieces
- ½ cup water
- 1 teaspoon caraway seeds
- ½ teaspoon table salt
- 1 cup plain Greek yogurt
- 1 small garlic clove, minced to paste
- 5 ounces (142 g) watercress, torn into bite-size pieces
- 1 tablespoon extra-virgin
- olive oil, divided, plus extra for drizzling
- 1 tablespoon white wine vinegar, divided
- 1 teaspoon grated orange zest plus 2 tablespoons juice
- ¼ cup hazelnuts, toasted, skinned, and chopped
- ¼ cup coarsely chopped fresh dill
- Coarse sea salt

1. Combine beets, water, caraway seeds, and table salt in Instant Pot. Lock lid in place and close pressure release valve. Select high pressure cook function and cook for 8 minutes. Turn off Instant Pot and quick-release pressure. Carefully remove lid, allowing steam to escape away from you. 2. Using slotted spoon, transfer beets to plate; set aside to cool slightly. Combine yogurt, garlic, and 3 tablespoons beet cooking liquid in bowl; discard remaining cooking liquid. In large bowl toss watercress with 2 teaspoons oil and 1 teaspoon vinegar. Season with table salt and pepper to taste. 3. Spread yogurt mixture over surface of serving dish. Arrange watercress on top of yogurt mixture, leaving 1-inch border of yogurt mixture. Add beets to now-empty large bowl and toss with orange zest and juice, remaining 2 teaspoons vinegar, and remaining 1 teaspoon oil. Season with table salt and pepper to taste. Arrange beets on top of watercress mixture. Drizzle with extra oil and sprinkle with hazelnuts, dill, and sea salt. Serve.

Per Serving:
calories: 240 | fat: 15g | protein: 9g | carbs: 19g | fiber: 5g | sodium: 440mg

Green Beans with Tomatoes and Potatoes

Prep time: 15 minutes | Cook time: 5 minutes | Serves 8

- 1 pound (454 g) small new potatoes
- 1 cup water
- 1 teaspoon salt
- 2 pounds (907 g) fresh green beans, trimmed
- 2 medium tomatoes, seeded and diced
- 2 tablespoons olive oil
- 1 tablespoon red wine vinegar
- 1 clove garlic, peeled and minced
- ½ teaspoon dry mustard powder
- ¼ teaspoon smoked paprika
- ¼ teaspoon ground black pepper

1. Start by placing the potatoes in a steamer basket. Set the rack inside the Instant Pot®, add water, and position the steamer basket on top. Secure the lid, set the steam release to Sealing, press the Manual button, and set the timer for 4 minutes. When the timer goes off, perform a quick release until the float valve drops. Press the Cancel button and carefully open the lid. 2. Next, add salt, green beans, and tomatoes to the Instant Pot®. Close the lid again, set the steam release to Sealing, press the Manual button, and set the timer for 1 minute. Once the timer beeps, quickly release the pressure until the float valve drops. Press the Cancel button and open the lid. Transfer the vegetable mixture to a serving platter or a large bowl. 3. In a small bowl, whisk together the oil, vinegar, garlic, mustard, paprika, and pepper. Drizzle the dressing over the vegetables and gently toss to coat evenly. Serve hot.

Per Serving:
calories: 112 | fat: 4g | protein: 2g | carbs: 20g | fiber: 5g | sodium: 368mg

Roasted Veggie Puff Pastry Turnovers

Prep time: 10 minutes | Cook time: 35 minutes | Serves 4 to 6

- Nonstick cooking spray
- 1 zucchini, cut in ¼-inch-thick slices
- ½ bunch asparagus, cut into quarters
- 1 package (6-inch) whole-
- grain pastry discs, in the freezer section (Goya brand preferred), at room temperature
- 1 large egg, beaten

1. Preheat the oven to 350°F(180°C). 2. Spray a baking sheet with cooking spray and arrange the zucchini and asparagus on it in a single layer. Roast for 15 to 20 minutes, until tender. Set aside to cool. 3. Allow the pastry dough to warm to room temperature. Place the discs on a floured surface. 4. Place a roasted zucchini slice on one half of each disc, then top with asparagus. Fold the empty side over the full side and pinch the turnover closed with a fork. 5. Once all discs are full and closed, brush the turnovers with the beaten egg and put them onto a baking sheet. Bake for 10 to 15 minutes, until golden brown. Let cool completely before eating.

Per Serving:
calories: 334 | fat: 15g | protein: 9g | carbs: 42g | fiber: 4g | sodium: 741mg

Spiced Braised Cauliflower with Potatoes

Prep time: 10 minutes | Cook time: 35 minutes | Serves 3

- ½ cup extra virgin olive oil
- 1 medium head cauliflower (about 2 pounds / 907 g), washed and cut into medium-sized florets
- 1 medium russet or white potato, cut into 1-inch pieces
- ¼ teaspoon freshly ground black pepper
- 3 allspice berries
- 1 cinnamon stick
- 3 cloves
- 2 tablespoons tomato paste
- 1 teaspoon fine sea salt
- ¾ cup hot water

1. Add the olive oil to a large pot over medium heat. When the oil begins to shimmer, add the cauliflower, potatoes, black pepper, allspice berries, cinnamon stick, and cloves. Sauté for 4 minutes or until the cauliflower begins to brown. 2. Add the tomato paste and sea salt. Continue heating, using a wooden spoon to swirl the tomato paste around the pan until the color changes to a brick red. 3. Add the hot water and stir gently. Reduce the heat to low, cover, and simmer for about 30 minutes or until the cauliflower is tender and the sauce has thickened. (If the sauce is still watery, remove the lid and simmer until the sauce has thickened.) Remove the allspice berries, cinnamon stick, and cloves. 4. Remove the cauliflower from the heat and set it aside to cool for at least 10 minutes before serving. When ready to serve, transfer the cauliflower to a large serving bowl and spoon the sauce over the top. Store covered in the refrigerator for up to 3 days.

Per Serving:
calories: 406 | fat: 36g | protein: 4g | carbs: 19g | fiber: 3g | sodium: 813mg

Lebanese Baba Ghanoush

Prep time: 15 minutes | Cook time: 20 minutes | Serves 4

- 1 medium eggplant
- 2 tablespoons vegetable oil
- 2 tablespoons tahini (sesame paste)
- 2 tablespoons fresh lemon juice
- ½ teaspoon kosher salt
- 1 tablespoon extra-virgin olive oil
- ½ teaspoon smoked paprika
- 2 tablespoons chopped fresh parsley

1. Begin by rubbing the eggplant thoroughly with vegetable oil. Place the eggplant in the air fryer basket and set the temperature to 400°F (204°C) for 20 minutes, or until the skin becomes blistered and charred. 2. Once cooked, transfer the eggplant to a resealable plastic bag, seal it, and let it sit for 15 minutes. This will allow the eggplant to continue cooking in the residual heat trapped inside the bag. 3. After 15 minutes, remove the eggplant from the bag and place it in a large bowl. Peel off and discard the charred skin, then roughly mash the eggplant flesh with a fork or potato masher. Stir in the tahini, lemon juice, and salt until well combined. 4. Spoon the eggplant mixture into a serving bowl. Drizzle with olive oil, then sprinkle paprika and chopped parsley on top before serving.

Per Serving:
calories: 171 | fat: 15g | protein: 3g | carbs: 10g | fiber: 5g | sodium: 303mg

Coriander-Cumin Roasted Carrots

Prep time: 10 minutes | Cook time: 20 minutes | Serves 2

- ½ pound (227 g) rainbow carrots (about 4)
- 2 tablespoons fresh orange juice
- 1 tablespoon honey
- ½ teaspoon coriander
- Pinch salt

1. Preheat the oven to 400°F (205ºC) and position the oven rack in the center. 2. Peel the carrots and slice them lengthwise into evenly thick strips. Place the sliced carrots in a large mixing bowl. 3. In a separate small bowl, combine the orange juice, honey, coriander, and salt, mixing until well combined. 4. Drizzle the orange juice mixture over the carrots and toss thoroughly to ensure they are well coated. 5. Arrange the carrots in a single layer on a baking dish. 6. Roast in the oven for 15 to 20 minutes, or until they are fork-tender.

Per Serving:
calories: 85 | fat: 0g | protein: 1g | carbs: 21g | fiber: 3g | sodium: 156mg

Garlic Tomato Green Beans

Prep time: 10 minutes | Cook time: 20 minutes | Serves 4

- ¼ cup extra-virgin olive oil
- 1 large onion, chopped
- 4 cloves garlic, finely chopped
- 1 pound (454 g) green beans, fresh or frozen,
- trimmed
- 1½ teaspoons salt, divided
- 1 (15-ounce / 425-g) can diced tomatoes
- ½ teaspoon freshly ground black pepper

1. In a large pot over medium heat, heat the olive oil, onion, and garlic; cook for 1 minute. 2. Cut the green beans into 2-inch pieces. 3. Add the green beans and 1 teaspoon of salt to the pot and toss everything together; cook for 3 minutes. 4. Add the diced tomatoes, remaining ½ teaspoon of salt, and black pepper to the pot; continue to cook for another 12 minutes, stirring occasionally. 5. Serve warm.

Per Serving:
calories: 200 | fat: 14g | protein: 4g | carbs: 18g | fiber: 6g | sodium: 844mg

Pur é ed Cauliflower Soup

Prep time: 15 minutes | Cook time: 11 minutes | Serves 6

- 2 tablespoons olive oil
- 1 medium onion, peeled and chopped
- 1 stalk celery, chopped
- 1 medium carrot, peeled and chopped
- 3 sprigs fresh thyme
- 4 cups cauliflower florets
- 2 cups vegetable stock
- ½ cup half-and-half
- ¼ cup low-fat plain Greek yogurt
- 2 tablespoons chopped fresh chives

1. Start by pressing the Sauté button on the Instant Pot® and adding oil. Once the oil is hot, add the onion, celery, and carrot, cooking until they are just tender, approximately 6 minutes. Then, add the thyme, cauliflower, and stock, stirring everything together before pressing the Cancel button. 2. Secure the lid on the Instant Pot, set the steam release to Sealing, press the Manual button, and set the timer for 5 minutes. Once the timer beeps, allow the pressure to release naturally for about 15 minutes. 3. Carefully open the lid, discard the thyme stems, and use an immersion blender to purée the soup until it reaches a smooth consistency. Stir in the half-and-half and yogurt until well combined. 4. Garnish the soup with chives and serve immediately.

Per Serving:
calories: 113 | fat: 7g | protein: 3g | carbs: 9g | fiber: 2g | sodium: 236mg

Dill-Scented Rice Pilaf with Leeks and Carrots

Prep time: 15 minutes | Cook time: 25 minutes | Serves 6

- 2 tablespoons olive oil
- 1 carrot, finely chopped (about ¾ cup)
- 2 leeks, halved lengthwise, washed, well drained, and sliced in half-moons
- ½ teaspoon salt
- ¼ teaspoon freshly ground black pepper
- 2 tablespoons chopped fresh dill
- 1 cup low-sodium vegetable broth or water
- ½ cup basmati rice

1. In a 2-or 3-quart saucepan, heat the olive oil over medium heat. Add the carrot, leeks, salt, pepper, and 1 tablespoon of the dill. Cover and cook for 6 to 8 minutes, stirring once, to soften all the vegetables but not brown them. 2. Add the broth or water and bring to a boil. Stir in the rice, reduce the heat to maintain a simmer, cover, and cook for 15 minutes. Remove from the heat; let stand, covered, for 10 minutes. 3. Fluff the rice with fork. Stir in the remaining 1 tablespoon dill and serve.

Per Serving:
1 cup: calories: 100 | fat: 7g | protein: 2g | carbs: 11g | fiber: 4g | sodium: 209mg

Spicy Wilted Greens with Garlic

Prep time: 10 minutes | Cook time: 5 minutes | Serves 2

- 1 tablespoon olive oil
- 2 garlic cloves, minced
- 3 cups sliced greens (kale, spinach, chard, beet greens, dandelion greens, or a
- combination)
- Pinch salt
- Pinch red pepper flakes (or more to taste)

1. In a sauté pan, heat the olive oil over medium-high heat. Once hot, add the garlic and sauté for about 30 seconds, just until it becomes fragrant. 2. Next, add the greens along with salt and pepper flakes, stirring to combine everything. Allow the greens to wilt, but be careful not to overcook them. Once they are wilted, remove the pan from the heat and serve immediately.

Per Serving:
calories: 91 | fat: 7g | protein: 1g | carbs: 7g | fiber: 3g | sodium: 111mg

Crispy Sesame-Ginger Broccoli

Prep time: 10 minutes | Cook time: 15 minutes | Serves 4

- 3 tablespoons toasted sesame oil
- 2 teaspoons sesame seeds
- 1 tablespoon chili-garlic sauce
- 2 teaspoons minced fresh
- ginger
- ½ teaspoon kosher salt
- ½ teaspoon black pepper
- 1 (16-ounce / 454-g) package frozen broccoli florets (do not thaw)

1. In a large bowl, combine the sesame oil, sesame seeds, chili-garlic sauce, ginger, salt, and pepper. Stir until well combined. Add the broccoli and toss until well coated. 2. Arrange the broccoli in the air fryer basket. Set the air fryer to 325°F (163°C) for 15 minutes, or until the broccoli is crisp, tender, and the edges are lightly browned, gently tossing halfway through the cooking time.

Per Serving:

calories: 143 | fat: 11g | protein: 4g | carbs: 9g | fiber: 4g | sodium: 385mg

Lightened-Up Eggplant Parmigiana

Prep time: 10 minutes | Cook time: 1 hour 20 minutes | Serves 3

- 2 medium globe eggplants, sliced into ¼-inch rounds
- 2 tablespoons extra virgin olive oil, divided
- 1 teaspoon fine sea salt, divided
- 1 medium onion (any variety), diced
- 1 garlic clove, finely chopped
- 20 ounces (567g) canned
- crushed tomatoes or tomato purée
- 3 tablespoons chopped fresh basil, divided
- ¼ teaspoon freshly ground black pepper
- 7 ounces (198 g) low-moisture mozzarella, thinly sliced or grated
- 2 ounces (57 g) grated Parmesan cheese

1. Begin by lining an oven rack with aluminum foil and preheating the oven to 350°F (180°C). 2. In a large bowl, toss the eggplant slices with 1 tablespoon of olive oil and ½ teaspoon of sea salt until well coated. Arrange the seasoned slices on the prepared oven rack. Place the rack in the middle position of the oven and roast the eggplant for 15 to 20 minutes, or until they are soft. 3. While the eggplant is roasting, heat the remaining tablespoon of olive oil in a medium pan over medium heat. Once the oil is shimmering, add the onions and sauté for 5 minutes. Then, add the garlic and sauté for an additional minute. Stir in the crushed tomatoes, 1½ tablespoons of basil, the remaining ½ teaspoon of sea salt, and black pepper. Lower the heat and let the mixture simmer for 15 minutes before removing it from the heat. 4. Once the eggplant slices are roasted, take them out of the oven. To assemble the dish, spread ½ cup of the tomato sauce on the bottom of an 11 × 7-inch (30 × 20 cm) casserole dish. Layer one-third of the eggplant rounds in a single layer in the dish, overlapping slightly if necessary. Add half of the mozzarella cheese on top of the eggplant, followed by ¾ cup of tomato sauce, and sprinkle 2½ tablespoons of grated Parmesan cheese over the top. Repeat this layering process with a second layer of eggplant, sauce, and cheese. Finally, add the remaining eggplant in a single layer on top, pour the remaining sauce over

it, and sprinkle with the remaining 1½ tablespoons of basil. 5. Bake the casserole for 40 to 45 minutes or until it is browned on top. After removing it from the oven, let it cool for 10 minutes before cutting it into 6 equal pieces for serving. Store any leftovers covered in the refrigerator for up to 3 days.

Per Serving:

calories: 453 | fat: 28g | protein: 28g | carbs: 26g | fiber: 4g | sodium: 842mg

Spicy Sesame Air-Fried Bok Choy

Prep time: 10 minutes | Cook time: 7 to 10 minutes | Serves 4

- 2 tablespoons olive oil
- 2 tablespoons reduced-sodium coconut aminos
- 2 teaspoons sesame oil
- 2 teaspoons chili-garlic sauce
- 2 cloves garlic, minced
- 1 head (about 1 pound / 454 g) bok choy, sliced lengthwise into quarters
- 2 teaspoons black sesame seeds

1. Preheat the air fryer to 400°F (204°C). 2. In a large bowl, combine the olive oil, coconut aminos, sesame oil, chili-garlic sauce, and garlic. Add the bok choy and toss, massaging the leaves with your hands if necessary, until thoroughly coated. 3. Arrange the bok choy in the basket of the air fryer. Pausing about halfway through the cooking time to shake the basket, air fry for 7 to 10 minutes until the bok choy is tender and the tips of the leaves begin to crisp. 4.Remove from the basket and let cool for a few minutes before coarsely chopping. Serve sprinkled with the sesame seeds.

Per Serving:

calories: 145 | fat: 13g | protein: 4g | carbs: 6g | fiber: 3g | sodium: 176mg

White Beans with Rosemary, Sage, and Garlic

Prep time: 10 minutes | Cook time: 10 minutes | Serves 2

- 1 tablespoon olive oil
- 2 garlic cloves, minced
- 1 (15-ounce / 425-g) can white cannellini beans, drained and rinsed
- ¼ teaspoon dried sage
- 1 teaspoon minced fresh
- rosemary (from 1 sprig) plus 1 whole fresh rosemary sprig
- ½ cup low-sodium chicken stock
- Salt

1. In a sauté pan, heat the olive oil over medium-high heat. Once hot, add the garlic and sauté for 30 seconds until fragrant. 2. Stir in the beans, sage, both minced and whole rosemary, and chicken stock, bringing the mixture to a boil. 3. Lower the heat to medium and let the beans simmer for 10 minutes, or until most of the liquid has evaporated. If you prefer a thicker consistency, use a fork to mash some of the beans. 4. Season the mixture with salt, and be sure to remove the whole rosemary sprig before serving.

Per Serving:

calories: 155 | fat: 7g | protein: 6g | carbs: 17g | fiber: 8g | sodium: 153mg

Spicy Creamer Potatoes

Prep time: 10 minutes | Cook time: 8 hours | Makes 7 (1-cup) servings

- 2 pounds (907 g) creamer potatoes
- 1 onion, chopped
- 3 garlic cloves, minced
- 1 chipotle chile in adobo sauce, minced
- 2 tablespoons freshly

- squeezed lemon juice
- 2 tablespoons water
- 1 tablespoon chili powder
- ½ teaspoon ground cumin
- ½ teaspoon salt
- ⅛ teaspoon freshly ground black pepper

1. In the slow cooker, mix together all the ingredients until well combined. 2. Cover the slow cooker and set it to cook on low for 7 to 8 hours, or until the potatoes are tender. Serve warm.

Per Serving:
calories: 113 | fat: 0g | protein: 3g | carbs: 25g | fiber: 4g | sodium: 208mg

Parmesan-Rosemary Radishes

Prep time: 5 minutes | Cook time: 15 to 20 minutes | Serves 4

- 1 bunch radishes, stemmed, trimmed, and quartered
- 1 tablespoon avocado oil
- 2 tablespoons finely grated fresh Parmesan cheese

- 1 tablespoon chopped fresh rosemary
- Sea salt and freshly ground black pepper, to taste

1. In a medium bowl, combine the radishes with avocado oil, Parmesan cheese, rosemary, salt, and pepper, tossing them until evenly coated. 2. Preheat the air fryer to 375ºF (191ºC). Arrange the seasoned radishes in a single layer in the air fryer basket. Roast for 15 to 20 minutes, or until they are golden brown and tender. Allow them to cool for 5 minutes before serving.

Per Serving:
calories: 58 | fat: 4g | protein: 1g | carbs: 4g | fiber: 2g | sodium: 63mg

Braised Greens with Olives and Walnut Vinaigrette

Prep time: 5 minutes | Cook time: 20 minutes | Serves 4

- 8 cups fresh greens (such as kale, mustard greens, spinach, or chard)
- 2 to 4 garlic cloves, finely minced
- ½ cup roughly chopped pitted green or black olives
- ½ cup roughly chopped

- shelled walnuts
- ¼ cup extra-virgin olive oil
- 2 tablespoons red wine vinegar
- 1 to 2 teaspoons freshly chopped herbs such as oregano, basil, rosemary, or thyme

1. Remove the tough stems from the greens and chop into bite-size pieces. Place in a large rimmed skillet or pot. 2. Turn the heat to high and add the minced garlic and enough water to just cover the greens. Bring to a boil, reduce the heat to low, and simmer until the greens are wilted and tender and most of the liquid has evaporated,

adding more if the greens start to burn. For more tender greens such as spinach, this may only take 5 minutes, while tougher greens such as chard may need up to 20 minutes. Once cooked, remove from the heat and add the chopped olives and walnuts. 3. In a small bowl, whisk together olive oil, vinegar, and herbs. Drizzle over the cooked greens and toss to coat. Serve warm.

Per Serving:
calories: 254 | fat: 25g | protein: 4g | carbs: 6g | fiber: 3g | sodium: 137mg

Rustic Vegetable Minestrone Soup

Prep time: 20 minutes | Cook time: 20 minutes | Serves 8

- 2 cups dried Great Northern beans, soaked overnight and drained
- 1 cup orzo
- 2 large carrots, peeled and diced
- 1 bunch Swiss chard, ribs removed and roughly chopped
- 1 medium zucchini, trimmed and diced
- 2 stalks celery, diced
- 1 medium onion, peeled and

- diced
- 1 teaspoon minced garlic
- 1 tablespoon Italian seasoning
- 1 teaspoon salt
- ½ teaspoon ground black pepper
- 2 bay leaves
- 1 (14½-ounce / 411-g) can diced tomatoes, including juice
- 4 cups vegetable broth
- 1 cup tomato juice

1. Place all ingredients in the Instant Pot® and stir to combine. Close lid, set steam release to Sealing, press the Soup button, and cook for the default time of 20 minutes. 2. When the timer beeps, let pressure release naturally for 10 minutes. Quick-release any remaining pressure until the float valve drops and open lid. Remove and discard bay leaves. 3. Ladle into bowls and serve warm.

Per Serving:
calories: 207 | fat: 1g | protein: 12g | carbs: 47g | fiber: 10g | sodium: 814mg

Mediterranean Zucchini Boats

Prep time: 5 minutes | Cook time: 10 minutes | Serves 4

- 1 large zucchini, ends removed, halved lengthwise
- 6 grape tomatoes, quartered
- ¼ teaspoon salt

- ¼ cup feta cheese
- 1 tablespoon balsamic vinegar
- 1 tablespoon olive oil

1. Using a spoon, scoop out 2 tablespoons from the center of each zucchini half, creating enough space to fill them with tomatoes and feta. 2. Evenly distribute the tomatoes in the centers of the zucchini halves and sprinkle with salt. Place the zucchini in an ungreased air fryer basket. Set the temperature to 350ºF (177ºC) and roast for 10 minutes, or until the zucchini is tender. 3. Once done, transfer the zucchini boats to a serving tray. Sprinkle with feta cheese and drizzle with vinegar and olive oil. Serve warm.

Per Serving:
calories: 92 | fat: 6g | protein: 3g | carbs: 8g | fiber: 2g | sodium: 242mg

Creamy Greek Garlic Potato Dip

Prep time: 10 minutes | Cook time: 30 minutes | Serves 4

- 2 potatoes (about 1 pound / 454 g), peeled and quartered
- ½ cup olive oil
- ¼ cup freshly squeezed
- lemon juice
- 4 garlic cloves, minced
- Sea salt
- Freshly ground black pepper

1. Place the potatoes in a large saucepan and fill the pan three-quarters full with water. Bring the water to a boil over medium-high heat, then reduce the heat to medium and cook the potatoes until fork-tender, 20 to 30 minutes. 2. While the potatoes are boiling, in a medium bowl, stir together the olive oil, lemon juice, and garlic; set aside. 3. Drain the potatoes and return them to the saucepan. Pour in the oil mixture and mash with a potato masher or a fork until well combined and smooth. Taste and season with salt and pepper. Serve.

Per Serving:
calories: 334 | fat: 27g | protein: 3g | carbs: 22g | fiber: 3g | sodium: 47mg

Zucchini Casserole

Prep time: 20 minutes | Cook time: 3 hours | Serves 4

- 1 medium red onion, sliced
- 1 green bell pepper, cut into thin strips
- 4 medium zucchini, sliced
- 1 (15-ounce / 425-g) can diced tomatoes, with the juice
- 1 teaspoon sea salt
- ½ teaspoon black pepper
- ½ teaspoon basil
- 1 tablespoon extra-virgin olive oil
- ¼ cup grated Parmesan cheese

1. In the slow cooker, combine the onion slices, bell pepper strips, zucchini slices, and tomatoes. Season the mixture with salt, pepper, and basil, stirring gently to combine. 2. Cover the slow cooker and set it to cook on low for 3 hours. 3. After 3 hours, drizzle olive oil over the casserole and sprinkle with Parmesan cheese. Cover again and continue cooking on low for an additional 1½ hours. Serve hot.

Per Serving:
calories: 124 | fat: 6g | protein: 6g | carbs: 15g | fiber: 5g | sodium: 723mg

Air-Fried Ratatouille Medley

Prep time: 15 minutes | Cook time: 20 minutes | Serves 2 to 3

- 2 cups ¾-inch cubed peeled eggplant
- 1 small red, yellow, or orange bell pepper, stemmed, seeded, and diced
- 1 cup cherry tomatoes
- 6 to 8 cloves garlic, peeled
- and halved lengthwise
- 3 tablespoons olive oil
- 1 teaspoon dried oregano
- ½ teaspoon dried thyme
- 1 teaspoon kosher salt
- ½ teaspoon black pepper

1. In a medium bowl, combine the eggplant, bell pepper, tomatoes, garlic, oil, oregano, thyme, salt, and pepper. Toss to combine. 2. Place the vegetables in the air fryer basket. Set the air fryer to 400°F (204°C) for 20 minutes, or until the vegetables are crisp-tender.

Per Serving:
calories: 161 | fat: 14g | protein: 2g | carbs: 9g | fiber: 3g | sodium: 781mg

Parmesan Roasted Fennel Wedges

Prep time: 5 minutes | Cook time: 30 minutes | Serves 4

- 2 fennel bulbs (about 2 pounds / 907 g), cored and cut into 8 wedges each (reserve fronds for garnish)
- ¼ cup olive oil
- Salt
- Freshly ground black pepper
- 1¼ teaspoons red pepper flakes
- ½ cup freshly grated Parmesan cheese

1. Preheat the oven to 350°F (180°C). 2. Arrange the fennel wedges on a large, rimmed baking sheet and drizzle the oil over the top. 3. Sprinkle each wedge with a pinch each of salt, black pepper, and red pepper flakes. Sprinkle the cheese over the top. 4. Bake in the preheated oven for about 30 minutes, until the fennel is tender and the cheese is golden brown. Remove from the oven and let cool in the oil until just warm. Using a slotted metal spatula, transfer the fennel to plates and garnish with the reserved fennel fronds.

Per Serving:
calories: 237 | fat: 19g | protein: 11g | carbs: 10g | fiber: 4g | sodium: 363mg

Garlicky Broccoli Rabe with Artichokes

Prep time: 5 minutes | Cook time: 10 minutes | Serves 4

- 2 pounds (907 g) fresh broccoli rabe
- ½ cup extra-virgin olive oil, divided
- 3 garlic cloves, finely minced
- 1 teaspoon salt
- 1 teaspoon red pepper flakes
- 1 (13¾-ounce / 390-g) can artichoke hearts, drained and quartered
- 1 tablespoon water
- 2 tablespoons red wine vinegar
- Freshly ground black pepper

1. Remove any thick lower stems and yellow leaves from the broccoli rabe and discard them. Cut the broccoli into individual florets, ensuring a couple of inches of the thin stem remains attached. 2. In a large skillet, heat ¼ cup of olive oil over medium-high heat. Add the trimmed broccoli rabe, garlic, salt, and red pepper flakes, and sauté for 5 minutes until the broccoli begins to soften. Then, add the artichoke hearts and continue sautéing for another 2 minutes. 3. Pour in the water and reduce the heat to low. Cover the skillet and simmer until the stems of the broccoli are tender, about 3 to 5 minutes. 4. In a small bowl, whisk together the remaining ¼ cup of olive oil and the vinegar. Drizzle this mixture over the sautéed broccoli and artichokes. Season with ground black pepper to taste, if desired.

Per Serving:
calories: 341 | fat: 28g | protein: 11g | carbs: 18g | fiber: 12g | sodium: 750mg

Cauliflower Tabbouleh with Avocado and Olives

Prep time: 15 minutes | Cook time: 5 minutes | Serves 6

- 6 tablespoons extra-virgin olive oil, divided
- 4 cups riced cauliflower
- 3 garlic cloves, finely minced
- 1½ teaspoons salt
- ½ teaspoon freshly ground black pepper
- ½ large cucumber, peeled, seeded, and chopped
- ½ cup chopped mint leaves
- ½ cup chopped Italian parsley
- ½ cup chopped pitted Kalamata olives
- 2 tablespoons minced red onion
- Juice of 1 lemon (about 2 tablespoons)
- 2 cups baby arugula or spinach leaves
- 2 medium avocados, peeled, pitted, and diced
- 1 cup quartered cherry tomatoes

1. In a large skillet, heat 2 tablespoons of olive oil over medium-high heat. Add the riced cauliflower, garlic, salt, and pepper and sauté until just tender but not mushy, 3 to 4 minutes. Remove from the heat and place in a large bowl. 2. Add the cucumber, mint, parsley, olives, red onion, lemon juice, and remaining 4 tablespoons olive oil and toss well. Place in the refrigerator, uncovered, and refrigerate for at least 30 minutes, or up to 2 hours. 3. Before serving, add the arugula, avocado, and tomatoes and toss to combine well. Season to taste with salt and pepper and serve cold or at room temperature.

Per Serving:
calories: 273 | fat: 25g | protein: 4g | carbs: 13g | fiber: 7g | sodium: 697mg

Cheesy Cauliflower Tots

Prep time: 15 minutes | Cook time: 12 minutes | Makes 16 tots

- 1 large head cauliflower
- 1 cup shredded Mozzarella cheese
- ½ cup grated Parmesan cheese
- 1 large egg
- ¼ teaspoon garlic powder
- ¼ teaspoon dried parsley
- ⅛ teaspoon onion powder

1. In a large pot on the stovetop, add 2 cups of water and insert a steamer basket. Bring the water to a boil. While waiting, cut the cauliflower into florets and place them in the steamer basket. Cover the pot with a lid. 2. Steam the cauliflower for about 7 minutes, or until it is fork-tender. Once done, carefully remove the florets from the steamer basket and transfer them to cheesecloth or a clean kitchen towel. Let them cool slightly, then squeeze out as much excess moisture as possible over the sink. It's crucial to remove enough moisture; otherwise, the mixture will be too soft to form into tots. After squeezing, mash the cauliflower with a fork until smooth. 3. Place the mashed cauliflower into a large mixing bowl and add Mozzarella, Parmesan, egg, garlic powder, parsley, and onion powder. Mix thoroughly until everything is well combined. The mixture should be wet yet easy to mold. 4. Take 2 tablespoons of the mixture and shape it into a tot. Repeat this process with the remaining mixture and place the formed tots into the air fryer basket. 5. Set the air fryer temperature to 320ºF (160ºC) and set the timer for 12 minutes. 6. Flip the tots halfway through the cooking time to ensure even cooking. The cauliflower tots should turn golden brown when they are fully cooked. Serve warm.

Per Serving:
2 tots: calories: 82 | fat: 3g | protein: 9g | carbs: 7g | fiber: 2g | sodium: 258mg

Walnut and Freekeh Pilaf

Prep time: 15 minutes | Cook time: 15 minutes | Serves 4

- 2½ cups freekeh
- 3 tablespoons extra-virgin olive oil, divided
- 2 medium onions, diced
- ¼ teaspoon ground cinnamon
- ¼ teaspoon ground allspice
- 5 cups chicken stock
- ½ cup chopped walnuts
- Salt
- Freshly ground black pepper
- ½ cup plain, unsweetened, full-fat Greek yogurt
- 1½ teaspoons freshly squeezed lemon juice
- ½ teaspoon garlic powder

1. In a small bowl, soak the freekeh in cold water for 5 minutes. After soaking, drain and rinse the freekeh, then rinse it once more to ensure it's clean. 2. In a large sauté pan or skillet, heat 2 tablespoons of oil over medium heat. Once hot, add the onions and cook until they become fragrant. Stir in the freekeh, cinnamon, and allspice, mixing well and stirring occasionally for about 1 minute. 3. Pour in the stock and add the walnuts, then season with salt and pepper. Bring the mixture to a simmer. 4. Cover the pan and reduce the heat to low. Allow it to cook for 15 minutes. Once the freekeh is tender, remove it from the heat and let it rest for 5 minutes. 5. In a small bowl, mix together the yogurt, lemon juice, and garlic powder. Adjust the seasoning with salt to enhance the flavors if necessary. Add the yogurt mixture to the cooked freekeh and serve immediately.

Per Serving:
calories: 653 | fat: 25g | protein: 23g | carbs: 91g | fiber: 12g | sodium: 575mg

Slow-Cooked Herb-Infused Vegetables

Prep time: 10 minutes | Cook time: 5 to 7 hours | Serves 6

- 2 pounds (907 g) fresh vegetables of your choice, sliced
- 1 teaspoon dried thyme
- 1 teaspoon dried rosemary
- 1 teaspoon sea salt
- ¼ teaspoon freshly ground black pepper
- 2 tablespoons extra-virgin olive oil

1. Put the vegetables in a slow cooker and season them with thyme, rosemary, salt, and pepper. 2. Drizzle the olive oil on top. 3. Cover the cooker and cook for 5 to 7 hours on Low heat, or until the vegetables are tender.

Per Serving:
calories: 85 | fat: 5g | protein: 1g | carbs: 11g | fiber: 3g | sodium: 442mg

Chapter 5

Vegetarian Mains

Chapter 5 Vegetarian Mains

Stuffed Pepper Stew

Prep time: 20 minutes | Cook time: 50 minutes | Serves 2

- 2 tablespoons olive oil
- 2 sweet peppers, diced (about 2 cups)
- ½ large onion, minced
- 1 garlic clove, minced
- 1 teaspoon oregano
- 1 tablespoon gluten-free vegetarian Worcestershire
- sauce
- 1 cup low-sodium vegetable stock
- 1 cup low-sodium tomato juice
- ¼ cup brown lentils
- ¼ cup brown rice
- Salt

1. In a Dutch oven, heat the olive oil over medium-high heat. Add the sweet peppers and onion, sautéing for about 10 minutes until the peppers are wilted and the onion begins to turn golden brown. 2. Stir in the garlic, oregano, and Worcestershire sauce, cooking for an additional 30 seconds. Then, add the vegetable stock, tomato juice, lentils, and rice to the pot. 3. Bring the mixture to a boil, then cover the pot and reduce the heat to medium-low. Let it simmer for 45 minutes, or until the rice is tender and the lentils are soft. Finally, season with salt to taste.

Per Serving:
calories: 379 | fat: 16g | protein: 11g | carbs: 53g | fiber: 7g | sodium: 392mg

Root Vegetable Soup with Garlic Aioli Drizzle

Prep time: 10 minutes | Cook time 25 minutes | Serves 4

For the Soup:
- 8 cups vegetable broth
- ½ teaspoon salt
- 1 medium leek, cut into thick rounds
- 1 pound (454 g) carrots, peeled and diced
- 1 pound (454 g) potatoes,

For the Aioli:
- 5 garlic cloves, minced
- ¼ teaspoon salt

- peeled and diced
- 1 pound (454 g) turnips, peeled and cut into 1-inch cubes
- 1 red bell pepper, cut into strips
- 2 tablespoons fresh oregano

- ⅔ cup olive oil
- 1 drop lemon juice

1. Bring the broth and salt to a boil and add the vegetables one at a time, letting the water return to a boil after each addition. Add the carrots first, then the leeks, potatoes, turnips, and finally the red bell peppers. Let the vegetables cook for about 3 minutes after adding the green beans and bringing to a boil. The process will take about 20 minutes in total. 2. Meanwhile, make the aioli. In a mortar and pestle, grind the garlic to a paste with the salt. Using a whisk and whisking constantly, add the olive oil in a thin stream.

Continue whisking until the mixture thickens to the consistency of mayonnaise. Add the lemon juice. 3. Serve the vegetables in the broth, dolloped with the aioli and garnished with the fresh oregano.

Per Serving:
calories: 538 | fat: 37g | protein: 5g | carbs: 50g | fiber: 9g | sodium: 773mg

Cheesy Zucchini Spinach Lasagna

Prep time: 15 minutes | Cook time: 1 hour | Serves 8

- ½ cup extra-virgin olive oil, divided
- 4 to 5 medium zucchini squash
- 1 teaspoon salt
- 8 ounces (227 g) frozen spinach, thawed and well drained (about 1 cup)
- 2 cups whole-milk ricotta cheese
- ¼ cup chopped fresh basil or 2 teaspoons dried basil
- 1 teaspoon garlic powder
- ½ teaspoon freshly ground black pepper
- 2 cups shredded fresh whole-milk mozzarella cheese
- 1¾ cups shredded Parmesan cheese
- ½ (24 ounces / 680 g) jar low-sugar marinara sauce (less than 5 grams sugar)

1. Preheat the oven to 425ºF (220ºC). 2. Line two baking sheets with parchment paper or aluminum foil and drizzle each with 2 tablespoons olive oil, spreading evenly. 3. Slice the zucchini lengthwise into ¼-inch-thick long slices and place on the prepared baking sheet in a single layer. Sprinkle with ½ teaspoon salt per sheet. Bake until softened, but not mushy, 15 to 18 minutes. Remove from the oven and allow to cool slightly before assembling the lasagna. 4. Reduce the oven temperature to 375ºF (190ºC). 5. While the zucchini cooks, prep the filling. In a large bowl, combine the spinach, ricotta, basil, garlic powder, and pepper. In a small bowl, mix together the mozzarella and Parmesan cheeses. In a medium bowl, combine the marinara sauce and remaining ¼ cup olive oil and stir to fully incorporate the oil into sauce. 6. To assemble the lasagna, spoon a third of the marinara sauce mixture into the bottom of a 9-by-13-inch glass baking dish and spread evenly. Place 1 layer of softened zucchini slices to fully cover the sauce, then add a third of the ricotta-spinach mixture and spread evenly on top of the zucchini. Sprinkle a third of the mozzarella-Parmesan mixture on top of the ricotta. Repeat with 2 more cycles of these layers: marinara, zucchini, ricotta-spinach, then cheese blend. 7. Bake until the cheese is bubbly and melted, 30 to 35 minutes. Turn the broiler to low and broil until the top is golden brown, about 5 minutes. Remove from the oven and allow to cool slightly before slicing.

Per Serving:
calories: 473 | fat: 36g | protein: 23g | carbs: 17g | fiber: 3g | sodium: 868mg

Crispy Eggplant Rounds

Prep time: 15 minutes | Cook time: 10 minutes | Serves 4

- 1 large eggplant, ends trimmed, cut into ½-inch slices
- ½ teaspoon salt
- 2 ounces (57 g) Parmesan
- 100% cheese crisps, finely ground
- ½ teaspoon paprika
- ¼ teaspoon garlic powder
- 1 large egg

1. Begin by sprinkling the eggplant rounds with salt. Lay the rounds on a kitchen towel and let them sit for 30 minutes to draw out excess moisture. Afterward, pat the rounds dry with a paper towel. 2. In a medium bowl, combine the cheese crisps, paprika, and garlic powder. In another medium bowl, whisk the egg. Dip each eggplant round into the egg, then gently press it into the cheese crisp mixture to coat both sides thoroughly. 3. Arrange the coated eggplant rounds in an ungreased air fryer basket. Set the temperature to 400°F (204°C) and air fry for 10 minutes, flipping the rounds halfway through the cooking time. The eggplant should be golden brown and crispy when finished. Serve warm.

Per Serving:
calories: 113 | fat: 5g | protein: 7g | carbs: 10g | fiber: 4g | sodium: 567mg

Hearty Moroccan Vegetable Tagine

Prep time: 20 minutes | Cook time: 1 hour | Serves 6

- ½ cup extra-virgin olive oil
- 2 medium yellow onions, sliced
- 6 celery stalks, sliced into ¼-inch crescents
- 6 garlic cloves, minced
- 1 teaspoon ground cumin
- 1 teaspoon ginger powder
- 1 teaspoon salt
- ½ teaspoon paprika
- ½ teaspoon ground cinnamon
- ¼ teaspoon freshly ground black pepper
- 2 cups vegetable stock
- 1 medium eggplant, cut into
- 1-inch cubes
- 2 medium zucchini, cut into ½-inch-thick semicircles
- 2 cups cauliflower florets
- 1 (13¾-ounce / 390-g) can artichoke hearts, drained and quartered
- 1 cup halved and pitted green olives
- ½ cup chopped fresh flat-leaf parsley, for garnish
- ½ cup chopped fresh cilantro leaves, for garnish
- Greek yogurt, for garnish (optional)

1. In a large, thick soup pot or Dutch oven, heat the olive oil over medium-high heat. Add the onion and celery and sauté until softened, 6 to 8 minutes. Add the garlic, cumin, ginger, salt, paprika, cinnamon, and pepper and sauté for another 2 minutes. 2. Add the stock and bring to a boil. Reduce the heat to low and add the eggplant, zucchini, and cauliflower. Simmer on low heat, covered, until the vegetables are tender, 30 to 35 minutes. Add the artichoke hearts and olives, cover, and simmer for another 15 minutes. 3. Serve garnished with parsley, cilantro, and Greek yogurt (if using).

Per Serving:
calories: 265 | fat: 21g | protein: 5g | carbs: 19g | fiber: 9g | sodium: 858mg

Pesto Spinach Flatbread

Prep time: 10 minutes | Cook time: 8 minutes | Serves 4

- 1 cup blanched finely ground almond flour
- 2 ounces (57 g) cream cheese
- 2 cups shredded Mozzarella
- cheese
- 1 cup chopped fresh spinach leaves
- 2 tablespoons basil pesto

1. In a large microwave-safe bowl, combine the flour, cream cheese, and Mozzarella. Microwave on high for 45 seconds, then stir the mixture. 2. Fold in the spinach and microwave for an additional 15 seconds. Stir until a soft dough ball forms. 3. Cut two pieces of parchment paper to fit the air fryer basket. Divide the dough into two sections and press each section out on the ungreased parchment to form 6-inch rounds. 4. Spread 1 tablespoon of pesto over each flatbread and carefully place the rounds, still on the parchment, into the ungreased air fryer basket. Set the air fryer to 350°F (177°C) and air fry for 8 minutes, flipping the crusts halfway through the cooking time. The flatbread should be golden when finished. 5. Allow the flatbreads to cool for 5 minutes before slicing and serving.

Per Serving:
calories: 387 | fat: 28g | protein: 28g | carbs: 10g | fiber: 5g | sodium: 556mg

Lemon-Parmesan Linguine with Brussels Sprouts

Prep time: 10 minutes | Cook time: 25 minutes | Serves 4

- 8 ounces (227 g) whole-wheat linguine
- ⅓ cup, plus 2 tablespoons extra-virgin olive oil, divided
- 1 medium sweet onion, diced
- 2 to 3 garlic cloves, smashed
- 8 ounces (227 g) Brussels sprouts, chopped
- ½ cup chicken stock, as needed
- ⅓ cup dry white wine
- ½ cup shredded Parmesan cheese
- 1 lemon, cut in quarters

1. Bring a large pot of water to a boil and cook the pasta according to package directions. Drain, reserving 1 cup of the pasta water. Mix the cooked pasta with 2 tablespoons of olive oil, then set aside. 2. In a large sauté pan or skillet, heat the remaining ⅓ cup of olive oil on medium heat. Add the onion to the pan and cook for about 5 minutes, until softened. Add the smashed garlic cloves and cook for 1 minute, until fragrant. 3. Add the Brussels sprouts and cook covered for 15 minutes. Add chicken stock as needed to prevent burning. Once Brussels sprouts have wilted and are fork-tender, add white wine and cook down for about 7 minutes, until reduced. 4. Add the pasta to the skillet and add the pasta water as needed. 5. Serve with the Parmesan cheese and lemon for squeezing over the dish right before eating.

Per Serving:
calories: 502 | fat: 31g | protein: 15g | carbs: 50g | fiber: 9g | sodium: 246mg

Broccoli Crust Pizza

Prep time: 15 minutes | Cook time: 12 minutes | Serves 4

- 3 cups riced broccoli, steamed and drained well
- 1 large egg
- ½ cup grated vegetarian Parmesan cheese
- 3 tablespoons low-carb Alfredo sauce
- ½ cup shredded Mozzarella cheese

1. In a large bowl, combine the broccoli, egg, and Parmesan cheese, mixing until well incorporated. 2. Cut a piece of parchment paper to fit your air fryer basket. Press the broccoli mixture onto the parchment to form a pizza shape, working in two batches if needed. Place the parchment into the air fryer basket. 3. Set the air fryer temperature to 370ºF (188ºC) and cook for 5 minutes. 4. Check the crust; it should be firm enough to flip. If it's not, cook for an additional 2 minutes. Once ready, carefully flip the crust. 5. Spread Alfredo sauce over the crust and top with Mozzarella cheese. Return the pizza to the air fryer basket and cook for another 7 minutes, or until the cheese is golden and bubbly. Serve warm.

Per Serving:
calories: 87 | fat: 2g | protein: 11g | carbs: 5g | fiber: 1g | sodium: 253mg

Quinoa Lentil Veggie Balls with Tomato Basil Sauce

Prep time: 25 minutes | Cook time: 45 minutes | Serves 4

For the Meatballs:
- Olive oil cooking spray
- 2 large eggs, beaten
- 1 tablespoon no-salt-added tomato paste
- ½ teaspoon kosher salt
- ½ cup grated Parmesan

- cheese
- ½ onion, roughly chopped
- ¼ cup fresh parsley
- 1 garlic clove, peeled
- 1½ cups cooked lentils
- 1 cup cooked quinoa

For the Tomato Sauce:
- 1 tablespoon extra-virgin olive oil
- 1 onion, minced
- ½ teaspoon dried oregano
- ½ teaspoon kosher salt

- 2 garlic cloves, minced
- 1 (28-ounce / 794-g) can no-salt-added crushed tomatoes
- ½ teaspoon honey
- ¼ cup fresh basil, chopped

Make the Meatballs: 1. Preheat the oven to 400ºF (205ºC). Lightly grease a 12-cup muffin pan with olive oil cooking spray. 2. In a large bowl, whisk together the eggs, tomato paste, and salt until fully combined. Mix in the Parmesan cheese. 3. In a food processor, add the onion, parsley, and garlic. Process until minced. Add to the egg mixture and stir together. Add the lentils to the food processor and process until puréed into a thick paste. Add to the large bowl and mix together. Add the quinoa and mix well. 4. Form balls, slightly larger than a golf ball, with ¼ cup of the quinoa mixture. Place each ball in a muffin pan cup. Note: The mixture will be somewhat soft but should hold together. 5. Bake 25 to 30 minutes, until golden brown. Make the Tomato Sauce: 6. Heat the olive oil in a large saucepan over medium heat. Add the onion, oregano, and salt and sauté until light golden brown, about 5 minutes. Add the garlic and cook for 30 seconds. 7. Stir in the tomatoes and honey. Increase the heat to high and cook, stirring often, until

simmering, then decrease the heat to medium-low and cook for 10 minutes. Remove from the heat and stir in the basil. Serve with the meatballs.

Per Serving:
3 meatballs: calories: 360 | fat: 10g | protein: 20g | carbs: 48g | fiber: 14g | sodium: 520mg

Moroccan Poached Eggs in Spiced Tomato Sauce

Prep time: 10 minutes | Cook time: 35 minutes | Serves 4

- 1 tablespoon olive oil
- 1 medium yellow onion, diced
- 2 red bell peppers, seeded and diced
- 1¾ teaspoons sweet paprika
- 1 teaspoon ras al hanout

- ½ teaspoon cayenne pepper
- 1 teaspoon salt
- ¼ cup tomato paste
- 1 (28-ounce / 794-g) can diced tomatoes, drained
- 8 eggs
- ¼ cup chopped cilantro

1. Heat the olive oil in a skillet over medium-high heat. Add the onion and bell peppers and cook, stirring frequently, until softened, about 5 minutes. Stir in the paprika, ras al hanout, cayenne, salt, and tomato paste and cook, stirring occasionally, for 5 minutes. 2. Stir in the diced tomatoes, reduce the heat to medium-low, and simmer for about 15 minutes, until the tomatoes break down and the sauce thickens. 3. Make 8 wells in the sauce and drop one egg into each. Cover the pan and cook for about 10 minutes, until the whites are fully set, but the yolks are still runny. 4. Spoon the sauce and eggs into serving bowls and serve hot, garnished with cilantro.

Per Serving:
calories: 238 | fat: 13g | protein: 15g | carbs: 18g | fiber: 5g | sodium: 735mg

Oven-Baked Falafel Sliders

Prep time: 10 minutes | Cook time: 30 minutes | Makes 6 sliders

- Olive oil cooking spray
- 1 (15-ounce / 425-g) can no-salt-added or low-sodium chickpeas, drained and rinsed
- 1 onion, roughly chopped
- 2 garlic cloves, peeled
- 2 tablespoons fresh parsley, chopped

- 2 tablespoons whole-wheat flour
- ½ teaspoon ground coriander
- ½ teaspoon ground cumin
- ½ teaspoon baking powder
- ½ teaspoon kosher salt
- ¼ teaspoon freshly ground black pepper

1. Preheat the oven to 350ºF (180ºC). Line a baking sheet with parchment paper or foil and lightly spray with olive oil cooking spray. 2. In a food processor, add the chickpeas, onion, garlic, parsley, flour, coriander, cumin, baking powder, salt, and black pepper. Process until smooth, stopping to scrape down the sides of the bowl. 3. Make 6 slider patties, each with a heaping ¼ cup of mixture, and arrange on the prepared baking sheet. Bake for 30 minutes, turning over halfway through.

Per Serving:
1 slider: calories: 90 | fat: 1g | protein: 4g | carbs:17 g | fiber: 3g | sodium: 110mg

Tortellini in Red Pepper Sauce

Prep time: 15 minutes | Cook time: 10 minutes | Serves 4

- 1 (16-ounce / 454-g) container fresh cheese tortellini (usually green and white pasta)
- 1 (16-ounce / 454-g) jar roasted red peppers, drained
- 1 teaspoon garlic powder
- ¼ cup tahini
- 1 tablespoon red pepper oil (optional)

1. Start by bringing a large pot of water to a boil, then cook the tortellini according to the package instructions. 2. While the tortellini is cooking, place the red peppers and garlic powder in a blender and blend until smooth. Once smooth, add the tahini and blend again until the sauce thickens. If the sauce becomes too thick, you can add up to 1 tablespoon of red pepper oil (if using) to achieve the desired consistency. 3. Once the tortellini is cooked, drain it and let it sit in the colander. In the empty pot, add the sauce and heat it over medium heat for 2 minutes. After that, return the tortellini to the pot and cook for an additional 2 minutes, stirring gently to combine. 4. Serve the dish warm and enjoy!

Per Serving:
calories: 350 | fat: 11g | protein: 12g | carbs: 46g | fiber: 4g | sodium: 192mg

Beet and Carrot Fritters with Lemon Yogurt Sauce

Prep time: 15 minutes | Cook time: 15 minutes | Serves 2

For the Yogurt Sauce:
- ⅓ cup plain Greek yogurt
- 1 tablespoon freshly squeezed lemon juice
- Zest of ½ lemon
- ¼ teaspoon garlic powder
- ¼ teaspoon salt

For the Fritters:
- 1 large carrot, peeled
- 1 small potato, peeled
- 1 medium golden or red beet, peeled
- 1 scallion, minced
- 2 tablespoons fresh minced parsley
- ¼ cup brown rice flour or
- unseasoned bread crumbs
- ¼ teaspoon garlic powder
- ¼ teaspoon salt
- 1 large egg, beaten
- ¼ cup feta cheese, crumbled
- 2 tablespoons olive oil (more if needed)

Make the Yogurt Sauce: 1. In a small bowl, mix together the yogurt, lemon juice and zest, garlic powder, and salt. Set aside. Make the Fritters: 1. Shred the carrot, potato, and beet in a food processor with the shredding blade. You can also use a mandoline with a julienne shredding blade or a vegetable peeler. Squeeze out any moisture from the vegetables and place them in a large bowl. 2. Add the scallion, parsley, rice flour, garlic powder, salt, and egg. Stir the mixture well to combine. Add the feta cheese and stir briefly, leaving chunks of feta cheese throughout. 3. Heat a large nonstick sauté pan over medium-high heat and add 1 tablespoon of the olive oil. 4. Make the fritters by scooping about 3 tablespoons of the vegetable mixture into your hands and flattening it into a firm disc about 3 inches in diameter. 5. Place 2 fritters at a time in the pan and let them cook for about two minutes. Check to see if the underside is golden, and then flip and repeat on the other side. Remove from the heat, add the rest of the olive oil to the pan, and repeat with the remaining vegetable mixture. 6. To serve, spoon about 1 tablespoon of the yogurt sauce on top of each fritter.

Per Serving:
calories: 295 | fat: 14g | protein: 6g | carbs: 44g | fiber: 5g | sodium: 482mg

Fava Bean Purée with Chicory

Prep time: 5 minutes | Cook time: 2 hours 10 minutes | Serves 4

- ½ pound (227 g) dried fava beans, soaked in water overnight and drained
- 1 pound (454 g) chicory leaves
- ¼ cup olive oil
- 1 small onion, chopped
- 1 clove garlic, minced
- Salt

1. In a saucepan, place the fava beans and cover them with at least an inch of water. Bring the mixture to a boil over medium-high heat. Once boiling, reduce the heat to low, cover the pot, and let it simmer until the beans are very tender, which should take about 2 hours. Check periodically to ensure there's enough water, adding more if necessary. 2. Once the beans are tender, drain any excess water and mash them using a potato masher until smooth. 3. While the beans are cooking, bring a large pot of salted water to a boil. Add the chicory and cook for about 3 minutes, or until tender. Drain the chicory and set aside. 4. In a medium skillet, heat the olive oil over medium-high heat. Add the onion and a pinch of salt, cooking while stirring frequently until the onion is softened and starts to brown, which should take about 5 minutes. Stir in the garlic and continue cooking for another minute. Transfer half of the onion mixture, along with the oil, into the bowl with the mashed beans and mix thoroughly. Taste the purée and adjust the salt as needed. 5. Serve the bean purée topped with the remaining onion mixture and oil, alongside the cooked chicory leaves.

Per Serving:
calories: 336 | fat: 14g | protein: 17g | carbs: 40g | fiber: 19g | sodium: 59mg

Pistachio Mint Pesto Pasta Delight

Prep time: 10 minutes | Cook time: 10 minutes | Serves 4

- 8 ounces (227 g) whole-wheat pasta
- 1 cup fresh mint
- ½ cup fresh basil
- ⅓ cup unsalted pistachios, shelled
- 1 garlic clove, peeled
- ½ teaspoon kosher salt
- Juice of ½ lime
- ⅓ cup extra-virgin olive oil

1. Cook the pasta according to the package directions. Drain, reserving ½ cup of the pasta water, and set aside. 2. In a food processor, add the mint, basil, pistachios, garlic, salt, and lime juice. Process until the pistachios are coarsely ground. Add the olive oil in a slow, steady stream and process until incorporated. 3. In a large bowl, mix the pasta with the pistachio pesto; toss well to incorporate. If a thinner, more saucy consistency is desired, add some of the reserved pasta water and toss well.

Per Serving:
calories: 420 | fat: 3g | protein: 11g | carbs: 48g | fiber: 2g | sodium: 150mg

Ricotta, Basil, and Pistachio-Stuffed Zucchini

Prep time: 15 minutes | Cook time: 25 minutes | Serves 4

- 2 medium zucchini, halved lengthwise
- 1 tablespoon extra-virgin olive oil
- 1 onion, diced
- 1 teaspoon kosher salt
- 2 garlic cloves, minced
- ¾ cup ricotta cheese
- ¼ cup unsalted pistachios, shelled and chopped
- ¼ cup fresh basil, chopped
- 1 large egg, beaten
- ¼ teaspoon freshly ground black pepper

1. Preheat the oven to 425°F (220°C) and line a baking sheet with parchment paper or foil. 2. Cut the zucchini in half lengthwise and scoop out the seeds and pulp, leaving about ¼ inch of flesh around the edges. Transfer the scooped pulp to a cutting board and chop it finely. 3. In a large skillet or sauté pan, heat the olive oil over medium heat. Add the chopped onion, zucchini pulp, and salt, sautéing for about 5 minutes until softened. Stir in the garlic and cook for an additional 30 seconds. 4. In a medium bowl, mix together the ricotta cheese, pistachios, basil, egg, and black pepper. Incorporate the sautéed onion mixture and stir until well combined. 5. Arrange the 4 zucchini halves on the prepared baking sheet and fill each half with the ricotta mixture. Bake for 20 minutes, or until the tops are golden brown.

Per Serving:
calories: 200 | fat: 12g | protein: 11g | carbs: 14g | fiber: 3g | sodium: 360mg

Crustless Spanakopita

Prep time: 15 minutes | Cook time: 45 minutes | Serves 6

- 12 tablespoons extra-virgin olive oil, divided
- 1 small yellow onion, diced
- 1 (32-ounce / 907-g) bag frozen chopped spinach, thawed, fully drained, and patted dry (about 4 cups)
- 4 garlic cloves, minced
- ½ teaspoon salt
- ½ teaspoon freshly ground black pepper
- 1 cup whole-milk ricotta cheese
- 4 large eggs
- ¾ cup crumbled traditional feta cheese
- ¼ cup pine nuts

1. Begin by preheating the oven to 375°F (190°C). 2. In a large skillet, heat 4 tablespoons of olive oil over medium-high heat. Add the onion and sauté for 6 to 8 minutes, or until it becomes softened. 3. Stir in the spinach, garlic, salt, and pepper, and continue to sauté for another 5 minutes. Once done, remove from the heat and let it cool slightly. 4. In a medium bowl, whisk together the ricotta cheese and eggs until well combined. Add this mixture to the cooled spinach and stir to combine thoroughly. 5. Pour 4 tablespoons of olive oil into the bottom of a 9-by-13-inch glass baking dish, swirling it to coat the bottom and sides. Pour the spinach-ricotta mixture into the dish and spread it into an even layer. 6. Bake for 20 minutes, or until the mixture starts to set. Remove from the oven and crumble feta cheese evenly over the top. Sprinkle with pine nuts and drizzle with the remaining 4 tablespoons of olive oil. Return the dish to the oven and bake for an additional 15 to 20 minutes, or until the spinach is fully set and the top is beginning to turn golden brown. Allow it to cool slightly before cutting into pieces to serve.

Per Serving:
calories: 497 | fat: 44g | protein: 18g | carbs: 11g | fiber: 5g | sodium: 561mg

Herb-Ricotta Stuffed Portobello Mushrooms

Prep time: 10 minutes | Cook time: 30 minutes | Serves 4

- 6 tablespoons extra-virgin olive oil, divided
- 4 portobello mushroom caps, cleaned and gills removed
- 1 cup whole-milk ricotta cheese
- ⅓ cup chopped fresh herbs
- (such as basil, parsley, rosemary, oregano, or thyme)
- 2 garlic cloves, finely minced
- ½ teaspoon salt
- ¼ teaspoon freshly ground black pepper

1. Preheat the oven to 400°F (205°C). 2. Line a baking sheet with parchment or foil and drizzle with 2 tablespoons olive oil, spreading evenly. Place the mushroom caps on the baking sheet, gill-side up. 3. In a medium bowl, mix together the ricotta, herbs, 2 tablespoons olive oil, garlic, salt, and pepper. Stuff each mushroom cap with one-quarter of the cheese mixture, pressing down if needed. Drizzle with remaining 2 tablespoons olive oil and bake until golden brown and the mushrooms are soft, 30 to 35 minutes, depending on the size of the mushrooms.

Per Serving:
calories: 308 | fat: 29g | protein: 9g | carbs: 6g | fiber: 1g | sodium: 351mg

Stuffed Portobellos

Prep time: 10 minutes | Cook time: 8 minutes | Serves 4

- 3 ounces (85 g) cream cheese, softened
- ½ medium zucchini, trimmed and chopped
- ¼ cup seeded and chopped red bell pepper
- 1½ cups chopped fresh
- spinach leaves
- 4 large portobello mushrooms, stems removed
- 2 tablespoons coconut oil, melted
- ½ teaspoon salt

1. In a medium bowl, combine the cream cheese, zucchini, pepper, and spinach, mixing until well blended. 2. Drizzle the mushrooms with coconut oil and sprinkle them with salt. Fill each mushroom cap with about ¼ of the zucchini mixture. 3. Arrange the stuffed mushrooms in an ungreased air fryer basket. Set the temperature to 400°F (204°C) and air fry for 8 minutes. The portobello mushrooms should be tender, and the tops should be nicely browned when finished. Serve warm.

Per Serving:
calories: 151 | fat: 13g | protein: 4g | carbs: 6g | fiber: 2g | sodium: 427mg

Roasted Ratatouille Farfalle

Prep time: 10 minutes | Cook time: 20 minutes | Serves 2

- 1 small eggplant (about 8 ounces / 227 g)
- 1 small zucchini
- 1 portobello mushroom
- 1 Roma tomato, halved
- ½ medium sweet red pepper, seeded
- ½ teaspoon salt, plus additional for the pasta water
- 1 teaspoon Italian herb seasoning
- 1 tablespoon olive oil
- 2 cups farfalle pasta (about 8 ounces / 227 g)
- 2 tablespoons minced sun-dried tomatoes in olive oil with herbs
- 2 tablespoons prepared pesto

1. Slice the ends off the eggplant and zucchini. Cut them lengthwise into ½-inch slices. 2. Place the eggplant, zucchini, mushroom, tomato, and red pepper in a large bowl and sprinkle with ½ teaspoon of salt. Using your hands, toss the vegetables well so that they're covered evenly with the salt. Let them rest for about 10 minutes. 3. While the vegetables are resting, preheat the oven to 400°F (205°C) and set the rack to the bottom position. Line a baking sheet with parchment paper. 4. When the oven is hot, drain off any liquid from the vegetables and pat them dry with a paper towel. Add the Italian herb seasoning and olive oil to the vegetables and toss well to coat both sides. 5. Lay the vegetables out in a single layer on the baking sheet. Roast them for 15 to 20 minutes, flipping them over after about 10 minutes or once they start to brown on the underside. When the vegetables are charred in spots, remove them from the oven. 6. While the vegetables are roasting, fill a large saucepan with water. Add salt and cook the pasta according to package directions. Drain the pasta, reserving ½ cup of the pasta water. 7. When cool enough to handle, cut the vegetables into large chunks (about 2 inches) and add them to the hot pasta. 8. Stir in the sun-dried tomatoes and pesto and toss everything well.

Per Serving:
calories: 612 | fat: 16g | protein: 23g | carbs: 110g | fiber: 23g | sodium: 776mg

Greek Frittata with Tomato-Olive Salad

Prep time: 10 minutes | Cook time: 25 minutes | Serves 4 to 6

Frittata:
- 2 tablespoons olive oil
- 6 scallions, thinly sliced
- 4 cups (about 5 ounces / 142 g) baby spinach leaves
- 8 eggs

Tomato-Olive Salad:
- 2 tablespoons olive oil
- 1 tablespoon lemon juice
- ¼ teaspoon dried oregano
- ½ teaspoon salt

- ¼ cup whole-wheat breadcrumbs, divided
- 1 cup (about 3 ounces / 85 g) crumbled feta cheese
- ¾ teaspoon salt
- ¼ teaspoon freshly ground black pepper

- ¼ teaspoon freshly ground black pepper
- 1 pint cherry, grape, or other small tomatoes, halved
- 3 pepperoncini, stemmed and chopped
- ½ cup coarsely chopped pitted Kalamata olives

1. Preheat the oven to 450°F (235°C). 2. In an oven-safe skillet over medium-high heat, heat the olive oil. Add the scallions and spinach, cooking while stirring frequently for about 4 minutes, or until the spinach is wilted. 3. In a medium bowl, whisk together the eggs, 2 tablespoons of breadcrumbs, cheese, ¾ cup of water, salt, and pepper. Pour this egg mixture into the skillet with the cooked spinach and scallions, stirring to combine. Evenly sprinkle the remaining 2 tablespoons of breadcrumbs over the top. Bake the frittata in the preheated oven for approximately 20 minutes, or until the eggs are set and the top is lightly browned. 4. While the frittata is baking, prepare the salad. In a medium bowl, whisk together olive oil, lemon juice, oregano, salt, and pepper. Add the tomatoes, pepperoncini, and olives, tossing everything to mix well. 5. Once the frittata is done, carefully invert it onto a serving platter and slice it into wedges. Serve warm or at room temperature alongside the tomato-olive salad.

Per Serving:
calories: 246 | fat: 19g | protein: 11g | carbs: 8g | fiber: 1g | sodium: 832mg

Chapter **6**

Salads

Chapter 6 Salads

Citrus Fennel Salad

Prep time: 15 minutes | Cook time: 0 minutes | Serves 2

For the Dressing:
- 2 tablespoons fresh orange juice
- 3 tablespoons olive oil
- 1 tablespoon blood orange vinegar, other orange
- vinegar, or cider vinegar
- 1 tablespoon honey
- Salt
- Freshly ground black pepper

For the Salad:
- 2 cups packed baby kale
- 1 medium navel or blood orange, segmented
- ½ small fennel bulb, stems and leaves removed, sliced
- into matchsticks
- 3 tablespoons toasted pecans, chopped
- 2 ounces (57 g) goat cheese, crumbled

Make the Dressing: In a small bowl, mix together the orange juice, olive oil, vinegar, and honey, whisking until well combined. Season with salt and pepper to taste, then set the dressing aside.
Make the Salad: 1. On two plates, evenly distribute the baby kale, orange segments, fennel, pecans, and goat cheese. 2. Drizzle half of the dressing over each salad.

Per Serving:
calories: 502 | fat: 39g | protein: 13g | carbs: 31g | fiber: 6g | sodium: 158mg

Classic Caprese Salad with Oregano and Olive Oil

Prep time: 5 minutes | Cook time: 0 minutes | Serves 2

- 2 firm medium tomatoes (any variety), cut into ¼-inch slices
- ¼ teaspoon kosher salt
- 8 fresh basil leaves
- 7 ounces (198 g) fresh
- mozzarella, cut into ¼-inch slices
- ¼ teaspoon dried oregano
- 3 teaspoons extra virgin olive oil

1. Place the sliced tomatoes on a cutting board and sprinkle them with the kosher salt. Set aside. 2. Arrange 4 basil leaves in a circular pattern on a large, round serving plate. (Tear the leaves into 2 pieces if they're large.) 3. Assemble the tomato slices and mozzarella slices on top of the basil leaves, alternating a tomato slice and then a mozzarella slice, adding a basil leaf between every 3–4 slices of tomato and mozzarella. 4. Sprinkle the oregano over the top and then drizzle the olive oil over the entire salad. Serve promptly. (This salad is best served fresh.)

Per Serving:
calories: 361 | fat: 24g | protein: 28g | carbs: 8g | fiber: 2g | sodium: 313mg

Turkish Shepherd's Salad with Feta and Herbs

Prep time: 15 minutes | Cook time: 0 minutes | Serves 6

- ¼ cup extra-virgin olive oil
- 2 tablespoons apple cider vinegar
- 2 tablespoons lemon juice
- ½ teaspoon kosher salt
- ¼ teaspoon ground black pepper
- 3 plum tomatoes, seeded and chopped
- 2 cucumbers, seeded and chopped
- 1 red bell pepper, seeded
- and chopped
- 1 green bell pepper, seeded and chopped
- 1 small red onion, chopped
- ⅓ cup pitted black olives (such as kalamata), halved
- ½ cup chopped fresh flat-leaf parsley
- ¼ cup chopped fresh mint
- ¼ cup chopped fresh dill
- 6 ounces (170 g) feta cheese, cubed

1. In a small bowl, whisk together the oil, vinegar, lemon juice, salt, and black pepper. 2. In a large serving bowl, combine the tomatoes, cucumber, bell peppers, onion, olives, parsley, mint, and dill. Pour the dressing over the salad, toss gently, and sprinkle with the cheese.

Per Serving:
calories: 238 | fat: 20g | protein: 6g | carbs: 10g | fiber: 2g | sodium: 806mg

Spanish Potato Salad

Prep time: 10 minutes | Cook time: 10 minutes | Serves 6 to 8

- 4 russet potatoes, peeled and chopped
- 3 large hard-boiled eggs, chopped
- 1 cup frozen mixed vegetables, thawed
- ½ cup plain, unsweetened, full-fat Greek yogurt
- 5 tablespoons pitted Spanish olives
- ½ teaspoon freshly ground black pepper
- ½ teaspoon dried mustard seed
- ½ tablespoon freshly squeezed lemon juice
- ½ teaspoon dried dill
- Salt
- Freshly ground black pepper

1. Begin by boiling the potatoes for 5 to 7 minutes, or until they are just fork-tender. Check them periodically to ensure they don't overcook. 2. While the potatoes are cooking, combine the eggs, vegetables, yogurt, olives, pepper, mustard, lemon juice, and dill in a large bowl. Season the mixture with salt and pepper to taste. Once the potatoes have cooled slightly, add them to the bowl and mix everything thoroughly. Serve immediately.

Per Serving:
calories: 192 | fat: 5g | protein: 9g | carbs: 30g | fiber: 2g | sodium: 59mg

Israeli Salad with Nuts and Seeds

Prep time: 15 minutes | Cook time: 0 minutes | Serves 4

- ¼ cup pine nuts
- ¼ cup shelled pistachios
- ¼ cup coarsely chopped walnuts
- ¼ cup shelled pumpkin seeds
- ¼ cup shelled sunflower seeds
- 2 large English cucumbers, unpeeled and finely chopped
- 1 pint cherry tomatoes, finely chopped
- ½ small red onion, finely chopped
- ½ cup finely chopped fresh flat-leaf Italian parsley
- ¼ cup extra-virgin olive oil
- 2 to 3 tablespoons freshly squeezed lemon juice (from 1 lemon)
- 1 teaspoon salt
- ¼ teaspoon freshly ground black pepper
- 4 cups baby arugula

1. Begin by toasting the pine nuts, pistachios, walnuts, pumpkin seeds, and sunflower seeds in a large dry skillet over medium-low heat. Cook for about 5 to 6 minutes, stirring frequently, until they turn golden and emit a fragrant aroma, taking care to avoid burning them. Once toasted, remove the skillet from the heat and set the mixture aside to cool. 2. In a spacious bowl, combine diced cucumber, chopped tomatoes, sliced red onion, and fresh parsley. 3. In a separate small bowl, whisk together olive oil, lemon juice, salt, and pepper to create a dressing. Drizzle this mixture over the vegetable medley and toss thoroughly to ensure everything is well coated. 4. Finally, add the toasted nuts and seeds along with a generous handful of arugula. Toss everything together to blend the flavors harmoniously. Serve the salad either at room temperature or chilled for a refreshing dish.

Per Serving:
calories: 404 | fat: 36g | protein: 10g | carbs: 16g | fiber: 5g | sodium: 601mg

Wild Greens Salad with Fresh Herbs

Prep time: 10 minutes | Cook time: 20 minutes | Serves 6 to 8

- ¼ cup olive oil
- 2 pounds (907 g) dandelion greens, tough stems removed and coarsely chopped
- 1 small bunch chicory, trimmed and coarsely chopped
- 1 cup chopped fresh flat-leaf parsley, divided
- 1 cup chopped fresh mint, divided
- ½ cup water
- 2 tablespoons red wine
- vinegar or apple cider vinegar
- 1 tablespoon fresh thyme, chopped
- 2 cloves garlic, minced
- ½ teaspoon kosher salt
- ½ teaspoon ground black pepper
- ¼ cup almonds or walnuts, coarsely chopped
- 2 tablespoons chopped fresh chives or scallion greens
- 1 tablespoon chopped fresh dill

1. In a large pot over medium heat, warm the oil. Add the greens along with half of the parsley, half of the mint, water, vinegar, thyme, garlic, salt, and pepper. Lower the heat and let it simmer until the greens are very tender, which should take about 20 minutes. 2. While the greens are cooking, toast the nuts in a small skillet over medium heat for 5 to 8 minutes until they are golden and fragrant. Remove the skillet from the heat once done. 3. If you plan to serve the dish immediately, stir in the chives or scallion greens, dill, and the remaining parsley and mint into the pot. If you prefer to serve it as a cool or cold salad, allow the mixture to reach room temperature or refrigerate it until cold, then stir in the fresh herbs. Top the dish with the toasted nuts before serving.

Per Serving:
calories: 190 | fat: 13g | protein: 6g | carbs: 17g | fiber: 7g | sodium: 279mg

Zesty Mediterranean Potato Salad with Olives and Herbs

Prep time: 10 minutes |Cook time: 20 minutes| Serves: 6

- 2 pounds (907 g) Yukon Gold baby potatoes, cut into 1-inch cubes
- 3 tablespoons freshly squeezed lemon juice (from about 1 medium lemon)
- 3 tablespoons extra-virgin olive oil
- 1 tablespoon olive brine
- ¼ teaspoon kosher or sea
- salt
- 1 (2¼-ounce / 35-g) can sliced olives (about ½ cup)
- 1 cup sliced celery (about 2 stalks) or fennel
- 2 tablespoons chopped fresh oregano
- 2 tablespoons torn fresh mint

1. In a medium saucepan, cover the potatoes with cold water until the waterline is one inch above the potatoes. Set over high heat, bring the potatoes to a boil, then turn down the heat to medium-low. Simmer for 12 to 15 minutes, until the potatoes are just fork tender. 2. While the potatoes are cooking, in a small bowl, whisk together the lemon juice, oil, olive brine, and salt. 3. Drain the potatoes in a colander and transfer to a serving bowl. Immediately pour about 3 tablespoons of the dressing over the potatoes. Gently mix in the olives and celery. 4. Before serving, gently mix in the oregano, mint, and the remaining dressing.

Per Serving:
calories: 192 | fat: 8g | protein: 3g | carbs: 28g | fiber: 4g | sodium: 195mg

Four-Bean Salad

Prep time: 20 minutes | Cook time: 0 minutes | Serves 4

- ½ cup white beans, cooked
- ½ cup black-eyed peas, cooked
- ½ cup fava beans, cooked
- ½ cup lima beans, cooked
- 1 red bell pepper, diced
- 1 small bunch flat-leaf
- parsley, chopped
- 2 tablespoons olive oil
- 1 teaspoon ground cumin
- Juice of 1 lemon
- Sea salt and freshly ground pepper, to taste

1. To save time, you can cook the beans a day or two in advance. 2. In a large bowl, combine all the ingredients and mix thoroughly. Adjust the seasoning to your taste. 3. Let the mixture sit for 30 minutes to allow the flavors to meld before serving.

Per Serving:
calories: 189 | fat: 7g | protein: 8g | carbs: 24g | fiber: 7g | sodium: 14mg

Classic Greek Salad with Feta and Kalamata Olives

Prep time: 10 minutes | Cook time: 0 minutes | Serves 4

- 2 large English cucumbers
- 4 Roma tomatoes, quartered
- 1 green bell pepper, cut into 1- to 1½-inch chunks
- ¼ small red onion, thinly sliced
- 4 ounces (113 g) pitted Kalamata olives
- ¼ cup extra-virgin olive oil
- 2 tablespoons freshly
- squeezed lemon juice
- 1 tablespoon red wine vinegar
- 1 tablespoon chopped fresh oregano or 1 teaspoon dried oregano
- ¼ teaspoon freshly ground black pepper
- 4 ounces (113 g) crumbled traditional feta cheese

1. Cut the cucumbers in half lengthwise and then into ½-inch-thick half-moons. Place in a large bowl. 2. Add the quartered tomatoes, bell pepper, red onion, and olives. 3. In a small bowl, whisk together the olive oil, lemon juice, vinegar, oregano, and pepper. Drizzle over the vegetables and toss to coat. 4. Divide between salad plates and top each with 1 ounce (28 g) of feta.

Per Serving:
calories: 256 | fat: 22g | protein: 6g | carbs: 11g | fiber: 3g | sodium: 476mg

Cranberry Apple Chicken Salad

Prep time: 10 minutes | Cook time: 0 minutes | Serves 2

- 2 cups chopped cooked chicken breast
- 2 Granny Smith apples, peeled, cored, and diced
- ½ cup dried cranberries
- ¼ cup diced red onion
- ¼ cup diced celery
- 2 tablespoons honey Dijon mustard
- 1 tablespoon olive oil mayonnaise
- ½ teaspoon salt
- ¼ teaspoon freshly ground black pepper

1. In a medium bowl, combine the chicken, apples, cranberries, onion, and celery and mix well. 2. In a small bowl, combine the mustard, mayonnaise, salt, and pepper and whisk together until well blended. 3. Stir the dressing into the chicken mixture until thoroughly combined.

Per Serving:
calories: 384 | fat: 9g | protein: 45g | carbs: 28g | fiber: 7g | sodium: 638mg

Tomato and Pepper Salad

Prep time: 10 minutes | Cook time: 0 minutes | Serves 6

- 3 large yellow peppers
- ¼ cup olive oil
- 1 small bunch fresh basil leaves
- 2 cloves garlic, minced
- 4 large tomatoes, seeded and diced
- Sea salt and freshly ground pepper, to taste

1. Preheat the broiler to high heat and place the peppers under it, broiling until they are blackened on all sides. 2. Once charred, remove the peppers from the heat and transfer them to a paper bag. Seal the bag and let the peppers cool down. 3. After they have cooled, peel off the skins, then remove the seeds and chop the peppers into pieces. 4. In a food processor, add half of the chopped peppers along with the olive oil, basil, and garlic. Pulse several times until the mixture becomes a smooth dressing. 5. In a large bowl, combine the remaining chopped peppers with the tomatoes and toss them with the prepared dressing. 6. Season the salad with sea salt and freshly ground black pepper. Let the salad sit at room temperature for a while before serving.

Per Serving:
calories: 129 | fat: 9g | protein: 2g | carbs: 11g | fiber: 2g | sodium: 8mg

Raw Zucchini Salad

Prep time: 15 minutes | Cook time: 0 minutes | Serves 2

- 1 medium zucchini, shredded or sliced paper thin
- 6 cherry tomatoes, halved
- 3 tablespoons olive oil
- Juice of 1 lemon
- Sea salt and freshly ground pepper, to taste
- 3–4 basil leaves, thinly sliced
- 2 tablespoons freshly grated, low-fat Parmesan cheese

1. Arrange the zucchini slices in even layers on two plates and top them with the tomatoes. 2. Drizzle the olive oil and lemon juice over the vegetables, then season to taste with salt and pepper. 3. Finish by adding the basil on top and sprinkling with cheese before serving.

Per Serving:
calories: 256 | fat: 21g | protein: 2g | carbs: 19g | fiber: 3g | sodium: 3mg

Riviera Tuna Salad

Prep time: 15 minutes | Cook time: 0 minutes | Serves 4

- ¼ cup olive oil
- ¼ cup balsamic vinegar
- ½ teaspoon minced garlic
- ¼ teaspoon dried oregano
- Sea salt and freshly ground pepper, to taste
- 2 tablespoons capers, drained
- 4–6 cups baby greens
- 1 (6-ounce / 170-g) can solid white albacore tuna, drained
- 1 cup canned garbanzo beans, rinsed and drained
- ¼ cup low-salt olives, pitted and quartered
- 2 Roma tomatoes, chopped

1. For the vinaigrette, whisk together the olive oil, balsamic vinegar, garlic, oregano, sea salt, and pepper until the mixture is well emulsified. 2. Fold in the capers and refrigerate the vinaigrette for up to 6 hours before serving. 3. In a salad bowl or on individual plates, arrange the baby greens and top them with tuna, beans, olives, and tomatoes. 4. Drizzle the vinaigrette over the salad and serve immediately.

Per Serving:
calories: 300 | fat: 19g | protein: 16g | carbs: 17g | fiber: 5g | sodium: 438mg

Grilled Sourdough Panzanella with Fresh Mozzarella

Prep time: 10 minutes | Cook time: 20 minutes | Serves 6

- 4 ounces (113 g) sourdough bread, cut into 1' slices
- 3 tablespoons extra-virgin olive oil, divided
- 2 tablespoons red wine vinegar
- 2 cloves garlic, mashed to a paste
- 1 teaspoon finely chopped fresh oregano or ½ teaspoon dried
- 1 teaspoon fresh thyme leaves
- ½ teaspoon Dijon mustard
- Pinch of kosher salt
- Few grinds of ground black pepper
- 2 pounds (907 g) ripe tomatoes (mixed colors)
- 6 ounces (170 g) fresh mozzarella pearls
- 1 cucumber, cut into ½'-thick half-moons
- 1 small red onion, thinly sliced
- 1 cup baby arugula
- ½ cup torn fresh basil

1. Coat a grill rack or grill pan with olive oil and prepare to medium-high heat. 2. Brush 1 tablespoon of the oil all over the bread slices. Grill the bread on both sides until grill marks appear, about 2 minutes per side. Cut the bread into 1' cubes. 3. In a large bowl, whisk together the vinegar, garlic, oregano, thyme, mustard, salt, pepper, and the remaining 2 tablespoons oil until emulsified. 4. Add the bread, tomatoes, mozzarella, cucumber, onion, arugula, and basil. Toss to combine and let sit for 10 minutes to soak up the flavors.

Per Serving:
calories: 219 | fat: 12g | protein: 10g | carbs: 19g | fiber: 3g | sodium: 222mg

Moroccan Tomato and Roasted Chile Salad

Prep time: 15 minutes | Cook time: 0 minutes | Serves 6

- 2 large green bell peppers
- 1 hot red chili Fresno or jalapeño pepper
- 4 large tomatoes, peeled, seeded, and diced
- 1 large cucumber, peeled and diced
- 1 small bunch flat-leaf parsley, chopped
- 4 tablespoons olive oil
- 1 teaspoon ground cumin
- Juice of 1 lemon
- Sea salt and freshly ground pepper, to taste

1. Begin by preheating the broiler on high. Place all the peppers and chilies on a baking sheet and broil them until the skins are blackened and blistered. 2. Once charred, transfer the peppers and chilies into a paper bag. Seal the bag and set it aside to cool, allowing the steam to help loosen the skins. In the meantime, combine the remaining ingredients in a medium bowl and mix thoroughly. 3. After the peppers and chilies have cooled, remove them from the bag and peel off the skins. Seed and chop the peppers, then add them to the salad mixture. 4. Season the salad with sea salt and freshly ground black pepper to taste. 5. Gently toss all the ingredients together and let the salad sit for 15 to 20 minutes before serving to allow the flavors to meld.

Per Serving:
calories: 128 | fat: 10g | protein: 2g | carbs: 10g | fiber: 3g | sodium: 16mg

Simple Insalata Mista (Mixed Salad) with Honey Balsamic Dressing

Prep time: 15 minutes | Cook time: 0 minutes | Serves 2

For the Dressing:
- ¼ cup balsamic vinegar
- ¼ cup olive oil
- 1 tablespoon honey
- 1 teaspoon Dijon mustard
- ¼ teaspoon salt, plus more

For the Salad:
- 4 cups chopped red leaf lettuce
- ½ cup cherry or grape tomatoes, halved
- ½ English cucumber, sliced in quarters lengthwise and

- to taste
- ¼ teaspoon garlic powder
- Pinch freshly ground black pepper

- then cut into bite-size pieces
- Any combination fresh, torn herbs (parsley, oregano, basil, chives, etc.)
- 1 tablespoon roasted sunflower seeds

Make the Dressing: In a jar with a lid, combine the vinegar, olive oil, honey, mustard, salt, garlic powder, and pepper. Secure the lid and shake vigorously until well mixed.
Make the Salad: 1. In a large bowl, combine the lettuce, tomatoes, cucumber, and fresh herbs. 2. Toss the ingredients together until evenly mixed. 3. Drizzle the desired amount of dressing over the salad and toss again to ensure the salad is well coated. 4. Finish by sprinkling the sunflower seeds on top.

Per Serving:
calories: 339 | fat: 26g | protein: 4g | carbs: 24g | fiber: 3g | sodium: 171mg

Lemon Quinoa Salad with Zucchini, Mint, and Pistachios

Prep time: 20 to 30 minutes | Cook time: 20 minutes | Serves 4

For the Quinoa:
- 1½ cups water
- 1 cup quinoa

For the Salad:
- 2 tablespoons extra-virgin olive oil
- 1 zucchini, thinly sliced into rounds
- 6 small radishes, sliced
- 1 shallot, julienned
- ¾ teaspoon kosher salt
- ¼ teaspoon freshly ground

- ¼ teaspoon kosher salt

- black pepper
- 2 garlic cloves, sliced
- Zest of 1 lemon
- 2 tablespoons lemon juice
- ¼ cup fresh mint, chopped
- ¼ cup fresh basil, chopped
- ¼ cup pistachios, shelled and toasted

Make the Quinoa: Bring the water, quinoa, and salt to a boil in a medium saucepan. Reduce to a simmer, cover, and cook for 10 to 12 minutes. Fluff with a fork. Make the Salad: 1. Heat the olive oil in a large skillet or sauté pan over medium-high heat. Add the zucchini, radishes, shallot, salt, and black pepper, and sauté for 7 to 8 minutes. Add the garlic and cook 30 seconds to 1 minute more. 2. In a large bowl, combine the lemon zest and lemon juice. Add the quinoa and mix well. Add the cooked zucchini mixture and mix well. Add the mint, basil, and pistachios and gently mix.

Per Serving:
calories: 220 | fat: 12g | protein: 6g | carbs: 25g | fiber: 5g | sodium: 295mg

Chilled Watermelon and Burrata Salad with Basil

Prep time: 10 minutes | Cook time: 0 minutes | Serves 4

- 2 cups cubes or chunks watermelon
- 1½ cups small burrata cheese balls, cut into medium chunks
- 1 small red onion or 2 shallots, thinly sliced into half-moons
- ¼ cup olive oil
- ¼ cup balsamic vinegar
- 4 fresh basil leaves, sliced chiffonade-style (roll up leaves of basil, and slice into thin strips)
- 1 tablespoon lemon zest
- Salt and freshly ground black pepper, to taste

1. In a large bowl, mix all the ingredients. Refrigerate until chilled before serving.

Per Serving:
1 cup: calories: 224 | fat: 14g | protein: 14g | carbs: 12g | fiber: 1g | sodium: 560mg

Lemon Balsamic Spinach Salad

Prep time: 10 minutes | Cook time: 5 minutes | Serves 4

- 1 large ripe tomato
- 1 medium red onion
- ½ teaspoon fresh lemon zest
- 3 tablespoons balsamic vinegar
- ¼ cup extra-virgin olive oil
- ½ teaspoon salt
- 1 pound (454 g) baby spinach, washed, stems removed

1. Dice the tomato into ¼-inch pieces and slice the onion into long slivers. 2. In a small bowl, whisk together the lemon zest, balsamic vinegar, olive oil, and salt. 3. Put the spinach, tomatoes, and onions in a large bowl. Pour the dressing over the salad and lightly toss to coat.

Per Serving:
calories: 172 | fat: 14g | protein: 4g | carbs: 10g | fiber: 4g | sodium: 389mg

Greek Black-Eyed Pea Salad

Prep time: 10 minutes | Cook time: 0 minutes | Serves 4

- 2 tablespoons olive oil
- Juice of 1 lemon (about 2 tablespoons)
- 1 garlic clove, minced
- 1 teaspoon ground cumin
- 1 (15½-ounce / 439-g) can no-salt-added black-eyed peas, drained and rinsed
- 1 red bell pepper, seeded and chopped
- 1 shallot, finely chopped
- 2 scallions (green onions), chopped
- 2 tablespoons chopped fresh dill
- ¼ cup chopped fresh parsley
- ½ cup pitted Kalamata olives, sliced
- ½ cup crumbled feta cheese (optional)

1. In a large bowl, combine the olive oil, lemon juice, garlic, and cumin, whisking until well blended. 2. Incorporate the black-eyed peas, diced bell pepper, shallot, scallions, dill, parsley, olives, and feta (if desired). Toss everything together until evenly mixed. Serve immediately.

Per Serving:
calories: 213 | fat: 14g | protein: 7g | carbs: 16g | fiber: 5g | sodium: 426mg

Orange-Tarragon Chicken Lettuce Wraps

Prep time: 15 minutes | Cook time: 0 minutes | Serves 4

- ½ cup plain whole-milk Greek yogurt
- 2 tablespoons Dijon mustard
- 2 tablespoons extra-virgin olive oil
- 2 tablespoons chopped fresh tarragon or 1 teaspoon dried tarragon
- ½ teaspoon salt
- ¼ teaspoon freshly ground black pepper
- 2 cups cooked shredded chicken
- ½ cup slivered almonds
- 4 to 8 large Bibb lettuce leaves, tough stem removed
- 2 small ripe avocados, peeled and thinly sliced
- Zest of 1 clementine, or ½ small orange (about 1 tablespoon)

1. In a medium bowl, combine the yogurt, mustard, olive oil, tarragon, orange zest, salt, and pepper and whisk until creamy. 2. Add the shredded chicken and almonds and stir to coat. 3. To assemble the wraps, place about ½ cup chicken salad mixture in the center of each lettuce leaf and top with sliced avocados.

Per Serving:
calories: 491 | fat: 38g | protein: 28g | carbs: 14g | fiber: 9g | sodium: 454mg

Arugula Spinach Salad with Shaved Parmesan

Prep time: 10 minutes | Cook time: 2 minutes | Serves 3

- 3 tablespoons raw pine nuts
- 3 cups arugula
- 3 cups baby leaf spinach
- 5 dried figs, pitted and

For the Dressing:
- 4 teaspoons balsamic vinegar
- 1 teaspoon Dijon mustard
- chopped
- 2½ ounces (71 g) shaved Parmesan cheese

- 1 teaspoon honey
- 5 tablespoons extra virgin olive oil

1. In a small pan over low heat, toast the pine nuts for about 2 minutes, or until they start to brown. Remove them from the heat immediately and transfer to a small bowl to cool. 2. To prepare the dressing, combine balsamic vinegar, Dijon mustard, and honey in a small bowl. Using a fork, whisk the mixture together while gradually adding the olive oil until well blended. 3. In a large bowl, combine the arugula and baby spinach, then layer on the figs, Parmesan cheese, and toasted pine nuts. Drizzle the dressing over the salad and toss everything together until the ingredients are evenly coated. Serve immediately for the best flavor and freshness.

Per Serving:
calories: 416 | fat: 35g | protein: 10g | carbs: 18g | fiber: 3g | sodium: 478mg

Ras el Hanout Chickpea and Green Bean Salad

Prep time: 10 minutes | Cook time: 10 minutes | Serves 6 to 8

- 1 pound (454 g) green beans, trimmed
- 2 tablespoons olive oil
- 2 tablespoons red wine vinegar
- 1 garlic clove, minced
- 2 teaspoons ras el hanout
- 1 (15½-ounce / 439-g) can no-salt-added chickpeas, drained and rinsed
- 1 shallot, finely chopped
- 3 tablespoons chopped fresh parsley

1. Bring a large saucepan of water to a boil. Add the green beans and cook just until crisp-tender. Drain the green beans into a colander and rinse under cool running water to stop the cooking. 2. In a large bowl, whisk together the olive oil, vinegar, garlic, and ras el hanout. 3. Add the chickpeas, green beans, shallot, and parsley and toss to combine. Serve.

Per Serving:
1 cup: calories: 68 | fat: 4g | protein: 2g | carbs: 7g | fiber: 3g | sodium: 16mg

Pickled Radish and Wild Rice Chickpea Salad

Prep time: 20 minutes | Cook time: 45 minutes | Serves 6

For the Rice:
- 1 cup water
- 4 ounces (113 g) wild rice
- ¼ teaspoon kosher salt
- For the Pickled Radish:

For the Dressing:
- 2 tablespoons extra-virgin olive oil
- 2 tablespoons white wine vinegar
- ½ teaspoon pure maple

For the Salad:
- 1 (15-ounce / 425-g) can no-salt-added or low-sodium chickpeas, rinsed and drained
- 1 bulb fennel, diced
- ¼ cup walnuts, chopped and

- 1 bunch radishes (6 to 8 small), thinly sliced
- ½ cup white wine vinegar
- ½ teaspoon kosher salt

syrup
- ½ teaspoon kosher salt
- ¼ teaspoon freshly ground black pepper

toasted
- ¼ cup crumbled feta cheese
- ¼ cup currants
- 2 tablespoons fresh dill, chopped

Make the Rice: 1. Bring the water, rice, and salt to a boil in a medium saucepan. Cover, reduce the heat, and simmer for 45 minutes. Make the Pickled Radish: 1. In a medium bowl, combine the radishes, vinegar, and salt. Let sit for 15 to 30 minutes. Make the Dressing: 1. In a large bowl, whisk together the olive oil, vinegar, maple syrup, salt, and black pepper. Make the Salad: 1. While still warm, add the rice to the bowl with the dressing and mix well. 2. Add the chickpeas, fennel, walnuts, feta, currants, and dill. Mix well. 3. Garnish with the pickled radishes before serving.

Per Serving:
calories: 310 | fat: 16g | protein: 10g | carbs: 36g | fiber: 7g | sodium: 400mg

Roasted Golden Beet, Avocado, and Watercress Salad

Prep time: 15 minutes | Cook time: 1 hour | Serves 4

- 1 bunch (about 1½ pounds / 680 g) golden beets
- 1 tablespoon extra-virgin olive oil
- 1 tablespoon white wine vinegar
- ½ teaspoon kosher salt
- ¼ teaspoon freshly ground black pepper
- 1 bunch (about 4 ounces / 113 g) watercress
- 1 avocado, peeled, pitted, and diced
- ¼ cup crumbled feta cheese
- ¼ cup walnuts, toasted
- 1 tablespoon fresh chives, chopped

1. Preheat your oven to 425ºF (220ºC). Rinse and trim the beets, cutting an inch above the root while leaving the long tail intact if you prefer. Wrap each beet in aluminum foil and arrange them on a baking sheet. Roast the beets until they are tender, which will take about 45 to 60 minutes depending on their size. Begin checking for doneness at the 45-minute mark; they should be easily pierced with a fork when done. 2. Once roasted, take the beets out of the oven and let them cool slightly. Rinse them under cold running water to remove the skins easily. Cut the beets into bite-sized cubes or wedges. 3. In a large mixing bowl, whisk together olive oil, vinegar, salt, and black pepper to create a dressing. Add the watercress and roasted beets, tossing to combine. Gently fold in the avocado, feta, walnuts, and chives, mixing carefully to avoid mashing the ingredients.

Per Serving:
calories: 235 | fat: 16g | protein: 6g | carbs: 21g | fiber: 8g | sodium: 365mg

Classic Tuna Niçoise Salad

Prep time: 15 minutes | Cook time: 20 minutes | Serves 4

- 1 pound (454 g) small red or fingerling potatoes, halved
- 1 pound (454 g) green beans or haricots verts, trimmed
- 1 head romaine lettuce, chopped or torn into bite-size pieces
- ½ pint cherry tomatoes,

halved
- 8 radishes, thinly sliced
- ½ cup olives, pitted (any kind you like)
- 2 (5-ounce / 142-g) cans no-salt-added tuna packed in olive oil, drained
- 8 anchovies (optional)

1. Fill a large pot fitted with a steamer basket with 2 to 3 inches of water. Put the potatoes in the steamer basket and lay the green beans on top of the potatoes. Bring the water to a boil over high heat, lower the heat to low and simmer, cover, and cook for 7 minutes, or until the green beans are tender but crisp. Remove the green beans and continue to steam the potatoes for an additional 10 minutes. 2. Place the romaine lettuce on a serving platter. Group the potatoes, green beans, tomatoes, radishes, olives, and tuna in different areas of the platter. If using the anchovies, place them around the platter.

Per Serving:
calories: 315 | fat: 9g | protein: 28g | carbs: 33g | fiber: 9g | sodium: 420mg

Chapter **7**

Poultry

Easy Turkey Tenderloin

Prep time: 20 minutes | Cook time: 30 minutes | Serves 4

- Olive oil
- ½ teaspoon paprika
- ½ teaspoon garlic powder
- ½ teaspoon salt
- ½ teaspoon freshly ground

- black pepper
- Pinch cayenne pepper
- 1½ pounds (680 g) turkey breast tenderloin

1. Begin by lightly spraying the air fryer basket with olive oil to prevent sticking. 2. In a small bowl, mix together paprika, garlic powder, salt, black pepper, and cayenne pepper. Use this spice blend to rub all over the turkey, ensuring it's well coated. 3. Place the seasoned turkey into the air fryer basket and give it another light spray with olive oil. 4. Set the air fryer to 370ºF (188ºC) and cook the turkey for 15 minutes. After this initial cooking time, flip the turkey and lightly spray it again with olive oil. Continue air frying until the internal temperature reaches at least 170ºF (77ºC), which will take an additional 10 to 15 minutes. 5. Once cooked, allow the turkey to rest for 10 minutes before slicing and serving.

Per Serving:

calories: 196 | fat: 3g | protein: 40g | carbs: 1g | fiber: 0g | sodium: 483mg

Pomegranate-Glazed Chicken Breasts with Fresh Seeds

Prep time: 10 minutes | Cook time: 30 minutes | Serves 6

- 1 teaspoon cumin
- 1 clove garlic, minced
- Sea salt and freshly ground pepper, to taste
- 6 tablespoons olive oil, divided
- 6 boneless, skinless chicken breasts

- 1 cup pomegranate juice (no sugar added)
- 2 tablespoons honey
- 1 tablespoon Dijon mustard
- ½ teaspoon dried thyme
- 1 fresh pomegranate, seeds removed

1. Mix the cumin, garlic, sea salt, and freshly ground pepper with 2 tablespoons of olive oil, and rub into the chicken. 2. Heat the remaining olive oil in a large skillet over medium heat. 3. Add the chicken breasts and sauté for 10 minutes, turning halfway through the cooking time, so the chicken breasts are golden brown on each side. 4. Add the pomegranate juice, honey, Dijon mustard, and thyme. 5. Lower the heat and simmer for 20 minutes, or until the chicken is cooked through and the sauce reduces by half. 6. Transfer the chicken and sauce to a serving platter, and top with fresh pomegranate seeds.

Per Serving:

calories: 532 | fat: 21g | protein: 62g | carbs: 20g | fiber: 2g | sodium: 157mg

Slow-Cooked Pesto Chicken with Red Potatoes

Prep time: 15 minutes | Cook time: 6 to 8 hours | Serves 6

For the Pesto:
- 1 cup fresh basil leaves
- 1 garlic clove, crushed
- ¼ cup pine nuts
- ¼ cup grated Parmesan cheese
- 2 tablespoons extra-virgin

- olive oil, plus more as needed
- 1 teaspoon sea salt
- ½ teaspoon freshly ground black pepper

For the Chicken:
- Nonstick cooking spray
- 2 pounds (907 g) red potatoes, quartered
- 3 pounds (1.4 kg) boneless,

- skinless chicken thighs
- ½ cup low-sodium chicken broth

Make the Pesto: 1. In a food processor, combine the basil, garlic, pine nuts, Parmesan cheese, olive oil, salt, and pepper. Pulse until smooth, adding more olive oil ½ teaspoon at a time if needed until any clumps are gone. Set aside. Make the Chicken: 1. Coat a slow-cooker insert with cooking spray and put the potatoes into the prepared slow cooker. 2. Place the chicken on top of the potatoes. 3. In a medium bowl, whisk together the pesto and broth until combined and pour the mixture over the chicken. 4. Cover the cooker and cook for 6 to 8 hours on Low heat.

Per Serving:

calories: 467 | fat: 24g | protein: 38g | carbs: 25g | fiber: 3g | sodium: 819mg

Garlic Dill Wings

Prep time: 5 minutes | Cook time: 25 minutes | Serves 4

- 2 pounds (907 g) bone-in chicken wings, separated at joints
- ½ teaspoon salt
- ½ teaspoon ground black

- pepper
- ½ teaspoon onion powder
- ½ teaspoon garlic powder
- 1 teaspoon dried dill

1. In a large bowl, combine the wings with salt, pepper, onion powder, garlic powder, and dill, tossing until they are evenly coated. Arrange the wings in a single layer in the ungreased air fryer basket, working in batches if necessary. 2. Set the air fryer temperature to 400ºF (204ºC) and cook the wings for 25 minutes, shaking the basket every 7 minutes to ensure even cooking. The wings should reach an internal temperature of at least 165ºF (74ºC) and have a golden brown color when finished. Serve them warm.

Per Serving:

calories: 290 | fat: 8g | protein: 50g | carbs: 1g | fiber: 0g | sodium: 475mg

Slow-Cooked Chicken Caprese Bake

Prep time: 10 minutes | Cook time: 6 to 8 hours | Serves 4

- 2 pounds (907 g) boneless, skinless chicken thighs, cut into 1-inch cubes
- 1 (15-ounce / 425-g) can no-salt-added diced tomatoes
- 2 cups fresh basil leaves (about 1 large bunch)
- ¼ cup extra-virgin olive oil
- 2½ tablespoons balsamic vinegar
- ½ teaspoon sea salt
- ⅛ teaspoon freshly ground black pepper
- 2 cups shredded mozzarella cheese

1. In a slow cooker, layer the chicken, tomatoes, and basil. 2. In a small bowl, whisk together the olive oil, vinegar, salt, and pepper until blended. Pour the dressing into the slow cooker. Stir to mix well. 3. Cover the cooker and cook for 6 to 8 hours on Low heat. 4. Sprinkle the mozzarella cheese on top. Replace the cover on the cooker and cook for 10 to 20 minutes on Low heat, or until the cheese melts.

Per Serving:
calories: 805 | fat: 61g | protein: 54g | carbs: 8g | fiber: 2g | sodium: 497mg

Personal Cauliflower Pizzas

Prep time: 10 minutes | Cook time: 25 minutes | Serves 2

- 1 (12-ounce / 340-g) bag frozen riced cauliflower
- ⅓ cup shredded Mozzarella cheese
- ¼ cup almond flour
- ¼ grated Parmesan cheese
- 1 large egg
- ½ teaspoon salt
- 1 teaspoon garlic powder
- 1 teaspoon dried oregano
- 4 tablespoons no-sugar-
- added marinara sauce, divided
- 4 ounces (113 g) fresh Mozzarella, chopped, divided
- 1 cup cooked chicken breast, chopped, divided
- ½ cup chopped cherry tomatoes, divided
- ¼ cup fresh baby arugula, divided

1. Begin by preheating the air fryer to 400ºF (204ºC). Cut 4 sheets of parchment paper to fit the air fryer basket, then brush each sheet lightly with olive oil and set them aside. 2. In a large glass bowl, microwave the cauliflower according to the package instructions. Once cooked, transfer the cauliflower to a clean towel, gather the sides, and squeeze firmly over the sink to remove any excess moisture. Return the drained cauliflower to the bowl, then mix in the shredded Mozzarella, almond flour, Parmesan cheese, egg, salt, garlic powder, and oregano. Stir until everything is well combined. 3. Divide the dough into two equal portions. Take one portion and place it on one of the prepared parchment sheets, gently pressing it into a thin, flat disk about 7 to 8 inches in diameter. Air fry for 15 minutes, or until the crust starts to brown slightly. Let it cool for 5 minutes afterward. 4. Carefully transfer the parchment with the crust to a baking sheet. Place another sheet of parchment over the crust. Holding the edges of both sheets, flip the crust over and return it to the air fryer basket, with the new sheet of parchment on the bottom. Remove the top sheet of parchment and air fry the crust for an additional 15 minutes, or until the top is golden brown. Remove the basket from the air fryer when done. 5. Spread 2 tablespoons of marinara sauce evenly over the crust, then top with half of the fresh Mozzarella, chicken, cherry tomatoes, and arugula. Air fry for another 5 to 10 minutes, or until the cheese is melted and starting to brown. Once finished, let the pizza sit for 10 minutes before serving. Repeat the process with the remaining ingredients to make a second pizza.

Per Serving:
calories: 655 | fat: 35g | protein: 67g | carbs: 20g | fiber: 7g | sodium: 741mg

Provencal Chicken with Niçoise Olives

Prep time: 20 minutes | Cook time: 50 minutes | Serves 6

- ¼ cup olive oil
- 3 medium onions, coarsely chopped
- 3 cloves garlic, minced
- 4 pounds (1.8 kg) chicken breast from 1 cut-up chicken
- 5 Roma tomatoes, peeled and chopped
- ½ cup white wine
- 1 (14½-ounce / 411-g) can chicken broth
- ½ cup black Niçoise olives, pitted
- Juice of 1 lemon
- ¼ cup flat-leaf parsley, chopped
- 1 tablespoon fresh tarragon leaves, chopped
- Sea salt and freshly ground pepper, to taste

1. Heat the olive oil in a deep saucepan or stew pot over medium heat. Cook the onions and garlic 5 minutes, or until tender and translucent. 2. Add the chicken and cook an additional 5 minutes to brown slightly. 3. Add the tomatoes, white wine, and chicken broth, cover, and simmer 30–45 minutes on medium-low heat, or until the chicken is tender and the sauce is thickened slightly. 4. Remove the lid and add the olives and lemon juice. 5. Cook an additional 10–15 minutes to thicken the sauce further. 6. Stir in the parsley and tarragon, and season to taste. Serve immediately with noodles or potatoes and a dark leafy salad.

Per Serving:
calories: 501 | fat: 15g | protein: 74g | carbs: 11g | fiber: 2g | sodium: 451mg

Mozzarella Chicken Nuggets

Prep time: 10 minutes | Cook time: 15 minutes | Serves 4

- 1 pound (454 g) ground chicken thighs
- ½ cup shredded Mozzarella cheese
- 1 large egg, whisked
- ½ teaspoon salt
- ¼ teaspoon dried oregano
- ¼ teaspoon garlic powder

1. In a large bowl, combine all ingredients. Form mixture into twenty nugget shapes, about 2 tablespoons each. 2. Place nuggets into ungreased air fryer basket, working in batches if needed. Adjust the temperature to 375ºF (191ºC) and air fry for 15 minutes, turning nuggets halfway through cooking. Let cool 5 minutes before serving.

Per Serving:
calories: 195 | fat: 8g | protein: 28g | carbs: 1g | fiber: 0g | sodium: 419mg

Skillet Parsley Chicken with Golden Potatoes

Prep time: 5 minutes |Cook time: 25 minutes| Serves: 6

- 1½ pounds (680 g) boneless, skinless chicken thighs, cut into 1-inch cubes
- 1 tablespoon extra-virgin olive oil
- 1½ pounds (680 g) Yukon Gold potatoes, unpeeled, cut into ½-inch cubes (about 6 small potatoes)
- 2 garlic cloves, minced (about 1 teaspoon)
- ¼ cup dry white wine or apple cider vinegar
- 1 cup low-sodium or no-salt-added chicken broth
- 1 tablespoon Dijon mustard
- ¼ teaspoon kosher or sea salt
- ¼ teaspoon freshly ground black pepper
- 1 cup chopped fresh flat-leaf (Italian) parsley, including stems
- 1 tablespoon freshly squeezed lemon juice (½ small lemon)

1. Pat the chicken dry with a few paper towels. In a large skillet over medium-high heat, heat the oil. Add the chicken and cook for 5 minutes, stirring only after the chicken has browned on one side. Remove the chicken from the pan with a slotted spoon, and put it on a plate; it will not yet be fully cooked. Leave the skillet on the stove. 2. Add the potatoes to the skillet and cook for 5 minutes, stirring only after the potatoes have become golden and crispy on one side. Push the potatoes to the side of the skillet, add the garlic, and cook, stirring constantly, for 1 minute. Add the wine and cook for 1 minute, until nearly evaporated. Add the chicken broth, mustard, salt, pepper, and reserved chicken pieces. Turn the heat up to high, and bring to a boil. 3. Once boiling, cover the skillet, reduce the heat to medium-low, and cook for 10 to 12 minutes, until the potatoes are tender and the internal temperature of the chicken measures 165°F (74ºC) on a meat thermometer and any juices run clear. 4. During the last minute of cooking, stir in the parsley. Remove from the heat, stir in the lemon juice, and serve.

Per Serving:
calories: 266 | fat: 7g | protein: 26g | carbs: 22g | fiber: 3g | sodium: 258mg

Balsamic Chicken Thighs with Tomato and Basil

Prep time: 15 minutes | Cook time: 17 minutes | Serves 6

- 1 pound (454 g) boneless, skinless chicken thighs
- ¼ teaspoon salt
- ¼ teaspoon ground black pepper
- ¼ teaspoon Italian seasoning
- 3 tablespoons olive oil
- 1 medium white onion, peeled and chopped
- 1 medium red bell pepper, seeded and chopped
- 2 cloves garlic, peeled and minced
- 4 medium tomatoes, seeded and diced
- ½ cup red wine
- ¼ cup balsamic vinegar
- ½ cup grated Parmesan cheese
- ¼ cup chopped fresh basil

1. Season the chicken on both sides with salt, black pepper, and Italian seasoning. Press the Sauté button on the Instant Pot® and add the oil. Once hot, add the chicken and brown it well on each side, approximately 4 minutes per side. After browning, transfer the chicken to a plate and set it aside. 2. In the same pot, add the onion and bell pepper. Sauté for about 2 minutes, or until they are just tender. Add the garlic and cook for another 30 seconds until fragrant. Stir in the tomatoes and wine, scraping up any browned bits from the bottom of the pot. Then, press the Cancel button. 3. Return the chicken to the pot and drizzle in the balsamic vinegar. Secure the lid, set the steam release to Sealing, press the Manual button, and set the timer for 6 minutes. Once the timer beeps, allow the pressure to release naturally for about 15 minutes. Press the Cancel button and carefully open the lid. 4. Top the dish with cheese and fresh basil before serving it hot.

Per Serving:
calories: 239 | fat: 13g | protein: 20g | carbs: 8g | fiber: 1g | sodium: 447mg

Marinated Chicken

Prep time: 5 minutes | Cook time: 16 minutes | Serves 4

- ½ cup olive oil
- 2 tablespoon fresh rosemary
- 1 teaspoon minced garlic
- Juice and zest of 1 lemon
- ¼ cup chopped flat-leaf
- parsley
- Sea salt and freshly ground pepper, to taste
- 4 boneless, skinless chicken breasts

1. In a plastic bag or bowl, combine all the ingredients except the chicken. 2. Add the chicken to the container and shake or stir to ensure that the marinade thoroughly coats the chicken pieces. 3. Cover and refrigerate for up to 24 hours to let the flavors meld. 4. Preheat a grill to medium heat and cook the chicken for 6 to 8 minutes on each side, turning it only once during the cooking process for even grilling. 5. Serve the grilled chicken alongside a Greek salad and brown rice for a complete meal.

Per Serving:
calories: 571 | fat: 34g | protein: 61g | carbs: 1g | fiber: 0g | sodium: 126mg

Caribbean Jerk Chicken Skewers

Prep time: 10 minutes | Cook time: 14 minutes | Serves 4

- 8 ounces (227 g) boneless, skinless chicken thighs, cut into 1-inch cubes
- 2 tablespoons jerk seasoning
- 2 tablespoons coconut oil
- ½ medium red bell pepper,
- seeded and cut into 1-inch pieces
- ¼ medium red onion, peeled and cut into 1-inch pieces
- ½ teaspoon salt

1. Place chicken in a medium bowl and sprinkle with jerk seasoning and coconut oil. Toss to coat on all sides. 2. Using eight (6-inch) skewers, build skewers by alternating chicken, pepper, and onion pieces, about three repetitions per skewer. 3. Sprinkle salt over skewers and place into ungreased air fryer basket. Adjust the temperature to 370ºF (188ºC) and air fry for 14 minutes, turning skewers halfway through cooking. Chicken will be golden and have an internal temperature of at least 165ºF (74ºC) when done. Serve warm.

Per Serving:
calories: 142 | fat: 9g | protein: 12g | carbs: 4g | fiber: 1g | sodium: 348mg

Baked Chicken Caprese

Prep time: 5minutes |Cook time: 25 minutes| Serves: 4

- Nonstick cooking spray
- 1 pound (454 g) boneless, skinless chicken breasts
- 2 tablespoons extra-virgin olive oil
- ¼ teaspoon freshly ground black pepper
- ¼ teaspoon kosher or sea salt
- 1 large tomato, sliced thinly
- 1 cup shredded mozzarella or 4 ounces (113 g) fresh mozzarella cheese, diced
- 1 (14½-ounce / 411-g) can low-sodium or no-salt-added crushed tomatoes
- 2 tablespoons fresh torn basil leaves
- 4 teaspoons balsamic vinegar

1. Position one oven rack about 4 inches below the broiler element and preheat the oven to 450°F (235ºC). Line a large, rimmed baking sheet with aluminum foil and place a wire cooling rack on top. Lightly spray the rack with nonstick cooking spray and set it aside. 2. If the chicken isn't already cut, divide it into 4 pieces. Place the chicken breasts in a large zip-top plastic bag. Using a rolling pin or meat mallet, pound the chicken until it is evenly flattened to about ¼ inch thick. Add oil, pepper, and salt to the bag, reseal it, and massage the ingredients into the chicken. Remove the chicken from the bag and place it on the prepared wire rack. 3. Bake the chicken for 15 to 18 minutes, or until its internal temperature reaches 165°F (74ºC) on a meat thermometer and the juices run clear. Switch the oven to the high broiler setting. Layer tomato slices on top of each chicken breast, then add the mozzarella cheese. Broil the chicken for an additional 2 to 3 minutes, or until the cheese is melted and bubbly, taking care not to let the edges burn. Remove the chicken from the oven. 4. While the chicken cooks, pour the crushed tomatoes into a small microwave-safe bowl. Cover with a paper towel and microwave on high for about 1 minute, or until heated through. When ready to serve, divide the warm tomatoes among four dinner plates and place a chicken breast on top of each. Finish by garnishing with fresh basil and a drizzle of balsamic vinegar.

Per Serving:
calories: 304 | fat: 15g | protein: 34g | carbs: 7g | fiber: 3g | sodium: 215mg

Slow-Cooked Fenugreek Spiced Chicken

Prep time: 15 minutes | Cook time: 6½ hours | Serves 6

- 1 tablespoon vegetable oil
- 2 teaspoons cumin seeds
- 2 onions, finely diced
- 2 tablespoons freshly grated ginger
- 3 garlic cloves, finely chopped
- 1 teaspoon turmeric
- 2 tomatoes, puréed
- 1 teaspoon chili powder
- 1 teaspoon coriander seeds, ground
- 1 teaspoon salt
- 1 or 2 fresh green chiles, chopped
- 8 boneless chicken thighs, skinned, trimmed, and cut into chunks
- 2 bunches fresh fenugreek leaves, washed and finely chopped (or 3 tablespoons dried fenugreek leaves)
- 2 tablespoons yogurt
- 2 teaspoons garam masala

1. Heat the oil in a frying pan (or in the slow cooker if you have a sear setting). Add the cumin seeds. Once fragrant, add the onions and cook until they begin to brown, about 10 minutes. Add the ginger, garlic, and turmeric, and cook for a few minutes. 2. Stir in the puréed tomatoes, chili powder, ground coriander seeds, salt, and green chiles. Put everything in the slow cooker and set the cooker to high. 3. Stir in the chicken pieces. Cover and cook on high for 4 hours, or on low for 6 hours. 4. Add the fenugreek leaves and stir into the sauce. Leave the cover off and cook for another half hour on high. This will also reduce the sauce and thicken it slightly. 5. Turn the cooker to low and stir in the yogurt, 1 tablespoon at a time, until it's fully incorporated into the sauce. 6. Turn off the heat, stir in the garam masala, and serve.

Per Serving:
calories: 405 | fat: 14g | protein: 54g | carbs: 15g | fiber: 3g | sodium: 664mg

Spicy Harissa Yogurt-Roasted Chicken Thighs

Prep time: 5 minutes | Cook time: 25 minutes | Serves 4

- ½ cup plain Greek yogurt
- 2 tablespoons harissa
- 1 tablespoon lemon juice
- ½ teaspoon kosher salt
- ¼ teaspoon freshly ground black pepper
- 1½ pounds (680 g) boneless, skinless chicken thighs

1. In a bowl, combine the yogurt, harissa, lemon juice, salt, and black pepper. Add the chicken and mix together. Marinate for at least 15 minutes, and up to 4 hours in the refrigerator. 2. Preheat the oven to 425ºF (220ºC). Line a baking sheet with parchment paper or foil. Remove the chicken thighs from the marinade and arrange in a single layer on the baking sheet. Roast for 20 minutes, turning the chicken over halfway. 3. Change the oven temperature to broil. Broil the chicken until golden brown in spots, 2 to 3 minutes.

Per Serving:
calories: 190 | fat: 10g | protein: 24g | carbs: 1g | fiber: 0g | sodium: 230mg

Crispy Za' atar-Spiced Chicken Tenders

Prep time: 5 minutes | Cook time: 15 minutes | Serves 4

- Olive oil cooking spray
- 1 pound (454 g) chicken tenders
- 1½ tablespoons za'atar
- ½ teaspoon kosher salt
- ¼ teaspoon freshly ground black pepper

1. Preheat the oven to 450ºF (235ºC). Line a baking sheet with parchment paper or foil and lightly spray with olive oil cooking spray. 2. In a large bowl, combine the chicken, za'atar, salt, and black pepper. Mix together well, covering the chicken tenders fully. Arrange in a single layer on the baking sheet and bake for 15 minutes, turning the chicken over once halfway through the cooking time.

Per Serving:
calories: 145 | fat: 4g | protein: 26g | carbs: 0g | fiber: 0g | sodium: 190mg

Coconut Curry Chicken

Prep time: 15 minutes | Cook time: 3 to 4 hours | Serves 6

- 1 tablespoon coconut oil
- 1 teaspoon cumin seeds
- 2 medium onions, grated
- 7 to 8 ounces (198 to 227 g) canned plum tomatoes
- 1 teaspoon salt
- 1 teaspoon turmeric
- ½ to 1 teaspoon Kashmiri chili powder (optional)
- 2 to 3 fresh green chiles, chopped
- 1 cup coconut cream
- 12 chicken thighs, skinned, trimmed, and cut into bite-size chunks
- 1 teaspoon garam masala
- Handful fresh coriander leaves, chopped

1. In a frying pan or the slow cooker if it has a sear setting, heat the oil over medium heat. Once hot, add the cumin seeds and cook until they are sizzling and fragrant. Then, add the onions and sauté until they turn golden brown, approximately 5 to 7 minutes. 2. While the onions are cooking, purée the tomatoes in a blender and then add them to the pan along with salt, turmeric, chili powder (if using), and fresh green chiles. 3. Mix everything together and transfer the contents to the slow cooker. Pour in the coconut cream and add the meat, stirring well to coat it in the sauce. 4. Cover the slow cooker and set it to cook on low for 4 hours or on high for 3 hours. 5. After the cooking time, taste the sauce and adjust the seasoning as needed. If the sauce appears too watery, switch the cooker to high and cook uncovered for an additional 30 minutes. 6. Before serving, stir in the garam masala and toss in fresh coriander leaves for garnish.

Per Serving:

calories: 648 | fat: 32g | protein: 78g | carbs: 9g | fiber: 2g | sodium: 761mg

Chicken and Chickpea Skillet with Berbere Spice

Prep time: 15 minutes | Cook time: 45 minutes | Serves 6

- 2 tablespoons olive oil
- 1 (3-to 4-pound / 1.4-to 1.8-kg) whole chicken, cut into 8 pieces
- 3 teaspoons Berbere or baharat spice blend
- 1 large onion, preferably Spanish, thinly sliced into half-moons
- 2 garlic cloves, minced
- 2 cups 1-inch cubes peeled butternut squash, or 1 (12-ounce / 340-g) bag pre-cut squash
- 1 (15-ounce / 425-g) can no-salt-added chickpeas, undrained
- ½ cup golden raisins
- Hot cooked rice, for serving

1. In a 12-inch skillet, heat 1 tablespoon of olive oil over medium-high heat. Season the chicken with 2 teaspoons of Berbere spice and add half of it to the skillet. Sear the chicken until it's golden brown, approximately 4 to 6 minutes on each side. Once browned, remove the chicken to a plate and repeat the process with the remaining chicken. Set aside all the chicken pieces. 2. Using the same skillet, pour in the remaining 1 tablespoon of olive oil. Add the chopped onion and sauté for about 5 minutes, stirring until it becomes soft. Then, incorporate the rest of the Berbere spice, garlic, squash, chickpeas, and raisins, stirring well to combine. Return the browned chicken to the skillet, placing it among the vegetables. Bring the mixture to a boil. Once boiling, reduce the heat to a simmer, cover the skillet tightly, and let it cook for 20 to 25 minutes. The chicken should be fully cooked, registering an internal temperature of 165°F (74°C), and the squash should be tender. 3. Serve the flavorful mixture over hot cooked rice.

Per Serving:

1 cup: calories: 507 | fat: 26g | protein: 42g | carbs: 33g | fiber: 9g | sodium: 218mg

Pork Rind Fried Chicken

Prep time: 30 minutes | Cook time: 20 minutes | Serves 4

- ¼ cup buffalo sauce
- 4 (4-ounce / 113-g) boneless, skinless chicken breasts
- ½ teaspoon paprika
- ½ teaspoon garlic powder
- ¼ teaspoon ground black pepper
- 2 ounces (57 g) plain pork rinds, finely crushed

1. In a large sealable bowl or bag, pour in the buffalo sauce. Add the chicken and toss it well to ensure it's fully coated. Seal the bowl or bag and refrigerate for at least 30 minutes, or up to overnight for maximum flavor. 2. After marinating, take the chicken out of the marinade, ensuring not to shake off the excess sauce. Season both sides of the thighs with paprika, garlic powder, and pepper. 3. In a large bowl, place the pork rinds and press each chicken piece into them, coating both sides evenly. 4. Arrange the coated chicken in an ungreased air fryer basket. Set the temperature to 400°F (204°C) and cook for 20 minutes, turning the chicken halfway through to ensure even cooking. The chicken should be golden brown and reach an internal temperature of at least 165°F (74°C) when fully cooked. Serve warm.

Per Serving:

calories: 217 | fat: 8g | protein: 35g | carbs: 1g | fiber: 0g | sodium: 400mg

Deconstructed Greek Chicken Kebabs

Prep time: 20 minutes | Cook time: 6 to 8 hours | Serves 4

- 2 pounds (907 g) boneless, skinless chicken thighs, cut into 1-inch cubes
- 2 zucchini (nearly 1 pound / 454 g), cut into 1-inch pieces
- 1 green bell pepper, seeded and cut into 1-inch pieces
- 1 red bell pepper, seeded and cut into 1-inch pieces
- 1 large red onion, chopped
- 2 tablespoons extra-virgin
- olive oil
- 2 tablespoons freshly squeezed lemon juice
- 1 tablespoon red wine vinegar
- 2 garlic cloves, minced
- 1 teaspoon sea salt
- 1 teaspoon dried oregano
- ½ teaspoon dried basil
- ½ teaspoon dried thyme
- ¼ teaspoon freshly ground black pepper

1. In a slow cooker, add the chicken, zucchini, green and red bell peppers, onion, olive oil, lemon juice, vinegar, garlic, salt, oregano, basil, thyme, and black pepper. Stir everything together until well combined. 2. Cover the slow cooker and set it to cook on low heat for 6 to 8 hours.

Per Serving:

calories: 372 | fat: 17g | protein: 47g | carbs: 8g | fiber: 2g | sodium: 808mg

Chapter **8**

Beef, Pork, and Lamb

Chapter 8 Beef, Pork, and Lamb

Italian Marinated Cube Steak Roll-Ups with Peppers and Mushrooms

Prep time: 30 minutes | Cook time: 8 to 10 minutes | Serves 4

- 4 cube steaks (6 ounces / 170 g each)
- 1 (16-ounce / 454-g) bottle Italian dressing
- 1 teaspoon salt
- ½ teaspoon freshly ground black pepper
- ½ cup finely chopped yellow onion
- ½ cup finely chopped green bell pepper
- ½ cup finely chopped mushrooms
- 1 to 2 tablespoons oil

1. In a large resealable bag or airtight storage container, combine the steaks and Italian dressing. Seal the bag and refrigerate to marinate for 2 hours. 2. Remove the steaks from the marinade and place them on a cutting board. Discard the marinade. Evenly season the steaks with salt and pepper. 3. In a small bowl, stir together the onion, bell pepper, and mushrooms. Sprinkle the onion mixture evenly over the steaks. Roll up the steaks, jelly roll-style, and secure with toothpicks. 4. Preheat the air fryer to 400°F (204°C). 5. Place the steaks in the air fryer basket. 6. Cook for 4 minutes. Flip the steaks and spritz them with oil. Cook for 4 to 6 minutes more until the internal temperature reaches 145°F (63°C). Let rest for 5 minutes before serving.

Per Serving:
calories: 364 | fat: 20g | protein: 37g | carbs: 7g | fiber: 1g | sodium: 715mg

Ground Beef Taco Rolls

Prep time: 20 minutes | Cook time: 10 minutes | Serves 4

- ½ pound (227 g) ground beef
- ⅓ cup water
- 1 tablespoon chili powder
- 2 teaspoons cumin
- ½ teaspoon garlic powder
- ¼ teaspoon dried oregano
- ¼ cup canned diced tomatoes and chiles, drained
- 2 tablespoons chopped cilantro
- 1½ cups shredded Mozzarella cheese
- ½ cup blanched finely ground almond flour
- 2 ounces (57 g) full-fat cream cheese
- 1 large egg

1. In a medium skillet over medium heat, brown the ground beef for about 7 to 10 minutes, stirring occasionally. Once the meat is fully cooked, drain off any excess fat. 2. Add water to the skillet along with chili powder, cumin, garlic powder, oregano, and the tomatoes with chiles. Stir in chopped cilantro, then bring the mixture to a boil. Once boiling, reduce the heat and let it simmer for 3 minutes. 3. In a large microwave-safe bowl, combine the Mozzarella cheese, almond flour, cream cheese, and egg. Microwave the mixture for 1 minute, then stir quickly until a smooth ball of dough forms.

4. Cut a piece of parchment paper to use as your work surface. Transfer the dough onto the parchment and press it out into a large rectangle, wetting your hands as needed to prevent sticking. Cut the dough into eight equal rectangles. 5. Spoon a few portions of the meat mixture onto each rectangle. Fold the short ends toward the center, then roll up the dough from the longer side, similar to how you would roll a burrito. 6. Cut another piece of parchment paper to fit your air fryer basket. Arrange the taco rolls on the parchment and then place it into the air fryer basket. 7. Set the air fryer temperature to 360°F (182°C) and air fry for 10 minutes. 8. Flip the rolls halfway through the cooking time for even crispiness. 9. After cooking, allow the taco rolls to cool for 10 minutes before serving.

Per Serving:
calories: 411 | fat: 31g | protein: 27g | carbs: 7g | fiber: 3g | sodium: 176mg

Italian Braised Pork

Prep time: 10 minutes | Cook time: 4⅓ hours | Serves 4

- 2½ pounds (1.1 kg) boneless pork shoulder
- Coarse sea salt
- Black pepper
- 2 tablespoons olive oil
- 1 large yellow onion, finely diced
- 3 cloves garlic, minced
- 1 stalk celery, finely diced
- ¾ teaspoon fennel seeds
- ½ cup dry red wine
- 1 (28-ounce / 794-g) can crushed tomatoes
- 4 cups prepared hot couscous, for serving

1. Begin by seasoning the pork with salt and pepper on all sides. 2. In a large skillet, heat the olive oil over medium-high heat. Add the seasoned pork and cook, turning it occasionally, until it's browned on all sides, which should take about 8 minutes. Once browned, transfer the pork to the slow cooker. 3. Lower the heat to medium under the skillet and add the chopped onion, minced garlic, celery, and fennel seeds. Sauté the mixture, stirring frequently, until the onion becomes soft, approximately 4 minutes. 4. Pour in the wine, using a wooden spoon to scrape up any flavorful browned bits stuck to the bottom of the pan. Cook until the liquid is reduced by half, which should take about 2 minutes. Transfer this wine mixture to the slow cooker, and stir in the tomatoes. 5. Cover the slow cooker and set it to cook on high for 4 hours, or on low for 8 hours, until the pork is very tender. 6. Once cooked, remove the pork from the slow cooker and place it on a cutting board. Shred the meat into bite-sized pieces, discarding any fat. 7. Skim off any excess fat from the sauce in the slow cooker and discard it. Return the shredded pork to the slow cooker and stir to combine with the sauce. Cook for an additional 5 minutes to reheat everything thoroughly. 8. Serve the warm pork mixture over couscous for a hearty meal.

Per Serving:
calories: 669 | fat: 17g | protein: 72g | carbs: 49g | fiber: 7g | sodium: 187mg

Slow-Cooked Greek Lemon Lamb Chops

Prep time: 10 minutes | Cook time: 6 to 8 hours | Serves 6

- 3 pounds (1.4 kg) lamb chops
- ½ cup low-sodium beef broth
- Juice of 1 lemon
- 1 tablespoon extra-virgin
- olive oil
- 2 garlic cloves, minced
- 1 teaspoon dried oregano
- 1 teaspoon sea salt
- ½ teaspoon freshly ground black pepper

1. Put the lamb chops in a slow cooker. 2. In a small bowl, whisk together the beef broth, lemon juice, olive oil, garlic, oregano, salt, and pepper until blended. Pour the sauce over the lamb chops. 3. Cover the cooker and cook for 6 to 8 hours on Low heat.

Per Serving:
calories: 325 | fat: 13g | protein: 47g | carbs: 1g | fiber: 0g | sodium: 551mg

Bulgur and Beef-Stuffed Peppers

Prep time: 15 minutes | Cook time: 26 minutes | Serves 4

- ½ cup bulgur wheat
- 1 cup vegetable broth
- 2 tablespoons olive oil
- 1 medium white onion, peeled and diced
- 1 clove garlic, peeled and minced
- 1 medium Roma tomato, seeded and chopped
- 1 teaspoon minced fresh rosemary
- 1 teaspoon fresh thyme
- leaves
- ½ teaspoon salt
- ½ teaspoon ground black pepper
- ½ pound (227 g) 90% lean ground beef
- 4 large red bell peppers, tops removed and seeded
- ½ cup marinara sauce
- 1 cup water
- ½ cup grated Parmesan cheese

1. Begin by adding bulgur and broth to the Instant Pot®. Stir the mixture well, then close the lid, setting the steam release to Sealing. Press the Rice button, adjust the pressure to Low, and set the timer for 12 minutes. Once the timer beeps, perform a quick release of the pressure until the float valve drops. Open the lid and fluff the bulgur with a fork, then transfer it to a medium bowl and set aside to cool. 2. Next, press the Sauté button and add oil to the pot. Once heated, add the onion and sauté until tender, which should take about 5 minutes. Then, stir in the garlic, tomato, rosemary, thyme, salt, and pepper, cooking until fragrant, about 1 minute. 3. Add the ground beef to the skillet, breaking it apart with a spatula as it cooks, until it's no longer pink, approximately 5 minutes. Press the Cancel button to stop sautéing. 4. Combine the beef mixture with the cooled bulgur and mix thoroughly. Stuff this mixture into the bell peppers, taking care not to pack it too tightly. Top each stuffed pepper with marinara sauce. 5. Clean out the pot, add water, and place the rack inside. Carefully position the stuffed peppers upright on the rack. Close the lid, set the steam release to Sealing, press the Manual button, and set the timer for 3 minutes. Once the timer goes off, quickly release the pressure until the float valve drops. Open the lid and, using tongs, carefully transfer the peppers to plates. 6. Top the stuffed peppers with cheese and serve immediately for a delicious meal.

Per Serving:
calories: 363 | fat: 17g | protein: 21g | carbs: 31g | fiber: 7g | sodium: 594mg

Savory Pork and Leek Stew with Vegetables

Prep time: 15 minutes | Cook time: 55 minutes | Serves 4

- 2 tablespoons olive oil
- 2 leeks, white parts only, chopped and rinsed well
- 1 onion, chopped
- 2 garlic cloves, minced
- 1 carrot, chopped
- 1 celery stalk, chopped
- 2 pounds (907 g) boneless pork loin chops, cut into
- 2-inch pieces
- 4 cups beef broth
- 2 cups water
- 3 potatoes, peeled and chopped
- 1 tablespoon tomato paste
- Sea salt
- Freshly ground black pepper

1. In a large skillet, heat the olive oil over medium-high heat. Add the leeks, onion, and garlic and sauté for 5 minutes, or until softened. Add the carrot and celery and cook for 3 minutes. Add the pork, broth, water, potatoes, and tomato paste and bring to a boil. 2. Reduce the heat to low, cover, and simmer for 45 minutes, or until the pork is cooked through. Season to taste with salt and pepper and serve.

Per Serving:
calories: 623 | fat: 16g | protein: 57g | carbs: 60g | fiber: 8g | sodium: 193mg

Spicy Dijon Marinated Steak Tips with Mushrooms

Prep time: 30 minutes | Cook time: 10 minutes | Serves 4

- 1½ pounds (680 g) sirloin, trimmed and cut into 1-inch pieces
- 8 ounces (227 g) brown mushrooms, halved
- ¼ cup Worcestershire sauce
- 1 tablespoon Dijon mustard
- 1 tablespoon olive oil
- 1 teaspoon paprika
- 1 teaspoon crushed red pepper flakes
- 2 tablespoons chopped fresh parsley (optional)

1. Place the beef and mushrooms in a gallon-size resealable bag. In a small bowl, whisk together the Worcestershire, mustard, olive oil, paprika, and red pepper flakes. Pour the marinade into the bag and massage gently to ensure the beef and mushrooms are evenly coated. Seal the bag and refrigerate for at least 4 hours, preferably overnight. Remove from the refrigerator 30 minutes before cooking. 2. Preheat the air fryer to 400ºF (204ºC). 3. Drain and discard the marinade. Arrange the steak and mushrooms in the air fryer basket. Air fry for 10 minutes, pausing halfway through the baking time to shake the basket. Transfer to a serving plate and top with the parsley, if desired.

Per Serving:
calories: 383 | fat: 23g | protein: 37g | carbs: 7g | fiber: 1g | sodium: 307mg

Braised Short Ribs with Red Wine

Prep time: 10 minutes | Cook time: 1 hour 30 minutes to 2 hours| Serves 4

- 1½ pounds (680 g) boneless beef short ribs (if using bone-in, use 3½ pounds)
- 1 teaspoon salt
- ½ teaspoon freshly ground black pepper
- ½ teaspoon garlic powder
- ¼ cup extra-virgin olive oil
- 1 cup dry red wine (such as cabernet sauvignon or merlot)
- 2 to 3 cups beef broth, divided
- 4 sprigs rosemary

1. Begin by preheating your oven to 350°F (180°C). 2. Season the short ribs generously with salt, pepper, and garlic powder. Allow them to rest for 10 minutes to absorb the flavors. 3. In a Dutch oven or a deep skillet suitable for the oven, heat olive oil over medium-high heat until it is shimmering hot. 4. Once the oil is adequately heated, add the short ribs to the pot, browning them for 2 to 3 minutes on each side until they achieve a dark, rich color. Once browned, remove the short ribs from the oil and keep them warm. 5. Pour in the red wine and 2 cups of beef broth into the Dutch oven. Whisk the mixture together and bring it to a boil. After boiling, lower the heat to a simmer and let it cook until the liquid reduces to about 2 cups, which should take around 10 minutes. 6. Return the browned short ribs to the pot, ensuring that the liquid comes about halfway up the meat. If necessary, add up to 1 cup of the remaining broth. Cover the pot and braise the ribs in the oven until they are fork-tender, which will take approximately 1½ to 2 hours. 7. Once done, remove the pot from the oven and allow it to sit, covered, for 10 minutes before serving. Serve the short ribs warm, drizzled with the flavorful cooking liquid for added richness.

Per Serving:
calories: 525 | fat: 37g | protein: 34g | carbs: 5g | fiber: 1g | sodium: 720mg

Meatballs in Creamy Almond Sauce

Prep time: 15 minutes | Cook time: 35 minutes | Serves 4 to 6

- 8 ounces (227 g) ground veal or pork
- 8 ounces (227 g) ground beef
- ½ cup finely minced onion, divided
- 1 large egg, beaten
- ¼ cup almond flour
- 1½ teaspoons salt, divided
- 1 teaspoon garlic powder
- ½ teaspoon freshly ground black pepper
- ½ teaspoon ground nutmeg
- 2 teaspoons chopped fresh flat-leaf Italian parsley, plus ¼ cup, divided
- ½ cup extra-virgin olive oil, divided
- ¼ cup slivered almonds
- 1 cup dry white wine or chicken broth
- ¼ cup unsweetened almond butter

1. Start by mixing the ground veal and beef in a spacious bowl. Add in ¼ cup of finely chopped onion and the egg, then use a fork to thoroughly blend all the ingredients together. In a separate small bowl, combine the almond flour, 1 teaspoon of salt, garlic powder, pepper, and nutmeg. Gradually mix this dry blend into the meat mixture along with 2 teaspoons of chopped parsley until everything is well incorporated. Shape this mixture into small meatballs, roughly 1 inch in diameter, and place them on a plate. Let the meatballs rest at room temperature for about 10 minutes to firm up slightly. 2. In a large skillet, heat ¼ cup of oil over medium-high heat. Once hot, carefully add the meatballs to the skillet, browning them on all sides. This should take about 2 to 3 minutes per side, and you may need to do this in batches to avoid overcrowding the pan. Once browned, remove the meatballs and keep them warm on a plate. 3. In the same skillet, add the remaining ¼ cup of minced onion and the other ¼ cup of olive oil. Sauté for 5 minutes, stirring occasionally until the onion becomes translucent. Next, reduce the heat to medium-low and introduce the slivered almonds, cooking them until they are golden brown, about 3 to 5 minutes. 4. In a small bowl, whisk together the white wine, almond butter, and the remaining ½ teaspoon of salt until smooth. Pour this mixture into the skillet, stirring continuously until it reaches a boil. Lower the heat again, return the meatballs to the skillet, and cover. Allow everything to simmer together for 8 to 10 minutes, or until the meatballs are fully cooked through. 5. Once cooked, take the skillet off the heat and stir in the remaining ¼ cup of chopped parsley for a fresh touch. Serve the meatballs warm, generously drizzled with the flavorful almond sauce. Enjoy this hearty dish with a side of your choice!

Per Serving:
calories: 447 | fat: 36g | protein: 20g | carbs: 7g | fiber: 2g | sodium: 659mg

Spanish Meatballs

Prep time: 10 minutes | Cook time: 5 hours 10 minutes | Serves 8

- 2 pounds (907 g) ground pork
- 1 medium yellow onion, finely chopped
- 1½ teaspoons ground cumin
- 1½ teaspoons hot smoked paprika
- 5 tablespoons plain dried bread crumbs
- 2 large eggs, lightly beaten
- 3 tablespoons chopped fresh
- parsley
- Coarse sea salt
- Black pepper
- 3 tablespoons extra-virgin olive oil
- 1 (28-ounce / 794-g) can diced tomatoes, with the juice
- Rustic bread, for serving (optional)

1. In a large bowl, mix together the ground pork, ¼ cup of chopped onion, cumin, ½ teaspoon of paprika, breadcrumbs, eggs, and parsley. Season the mixture with salt and pepper, and mix thoroughly until well combined. 2. Shape the meat mixture into 25 meatballs, each approximately 1½ inches in diameter, and place them on a plate. 3. In a large nonstick skillet, heat 1½ tablespoons of olive oil over medium-high heat. Brown the meatballs on all sides, cooking for about 8 minutes per batch, and then transfer the browned meatballs to the slow cooker. 4. In the same skillet, add the remaining chopped onion and sauté until fragrant, stirring frequently for about 2 minutes. Transfer the cooked onion to the slow cooker. Sprinkle in the remaining 1 teaspoon of paprika and add the tomatoes. Season the mixture with salt and pepper. 5. Cover the slow cooker and cook on low heat for 5 hours, or until the meatballs are tender. Serve the meatballs with slices of rustic bread, if desired.

Per Serving:
calories: 241 | fat: 11g | protein: 27g | carbs: 9g | fiber: 3g | sodium: 137mg

Rosemary Pork Shoulder with Apple Wine Sauce

Prep time: 15 minutes | Cook time: 52 minutes | Serves 8

- 1 (3½-pound / 1.6-kg) pork shoulder roast
- 3 tablespoons Dijon mustard
- 1 tablespoon olive oil
- ½ cup dry white wine
- 2 medium tart apples, peeled, cored, and quartered
- 3 cloves garlic, peeled and minced
- ½ teaspoon salt
- ½ teaspoon ground black pepper
- 1 teaspoon dried rosemary

1. Coat all sides of roast with mustard. Press the Sauté button on the Instant Pot® and heat oil. Add pork roast and brown on all sides, about 3 minutes per side. 2. Add wine and scrape up any browned bits sticking to the bottom of the pot. Add apples, garlic, salt, pepper, and rosemary. Press the Cancel button. 3. Close lid, set steam release to Sealing, press the Manual button, and set time to 45 minutes. When the timer beeps, let pressure release naturally, about 25 minutes. 4. Open the lid. Transfer roast to a serving platter. Tent and keep warm while you use an immersion blender to purée sauce in pot. Slice roast and pour the puréed juices over the slices. Serve.

Per Serving:
calories: 394 | fat: 25g | protein: 33g | carbs: 5g | fiber: 1g | sodium: 393mg

Lemon-Rosemary Lamb with Olives and Potatoes

Prep time: 20 minutes | Cook time: 4 hours | Serves 4

- 1¼ pounds (567 g) small potatoes, halved
- 4 large shallots, cut into ½-inch wedges
- 3 cloves garlic, minced
- 1 tablespoon lemon zest
- 3 sprigs fresh rosemary
- Coarse sea salt
- Black pepper
- 4 tablespoons all-purpose flour
- ¾ cup chicken stock
- 3½ pounds (1.6 kg) lamb shanks, cut crosswise into 1½-inch pieces and fat trimmed
- 2 tablespoons extra-virgin olive oil
- ½ cup dry white wine
- 1 cup pitted green olives, halved
- 2 tablespoons lemon juice

1. Combine the potatoes, shallots, garlic, lemon zest, and rosemary sprigs in the slow cooker. Season with salt and pepper. 2. In a small bowl, whisk together 1 tablespoon of the flour and the stock. Add to the slow cooker. 3. Place the remaining 3 tablespoons flour on a plate. Season the lamb with salt and pepper; then coat in the flour, shaking off any excess. 4. In a large skillet over medium-high, heat the olive oil. In batches, cook the lamb until browned on all sides, about 10 minutes. Transfer to the slow cooker. 5. Add the wine to the skillet and cook, stirring with a wooden spoon and scraping up the flavorful browned bits from the bottom of the pan, until reduced by half, about 2 minutes. Then add to the slow cooker. 6. Cover and cook until the lamb is tender, on high for about 3½ hours, or on low for 7 hours. 7. Stir in olive halves, then cover, and cook 20

additional minutes. 8. To serve, transfer the lamb and vegetables to warm plates. 9. Skim the fat from the cooking liquid, then stir in the lemon juice, and season the sauce with salt and pepper. 10. Serve the sauce with the lamb and vegetables.

Per Serving:
calories: 765 | fat: 26g | protein: 93g | carbs: 38g | fiber: 5g | sodium: 596mg

Herb-Rubbed Pork Loin with Dried Fig and White Wine Sauce

Prep time: 10 minutes | Cook time: 55 minutes | Serves 6

- 3 teaspoon fresh rosemary
- 1 tablespoon fresh thyme
- Sea salt and freshly ground pepper, to taste
- 1 (3-pound / 1.4-kg) pork loin
- ½ cup olive oil
- 3 carrots, peeled and sliced
- 1 onion, diced
- 1 garlic clove, minced
- 1 cup dried figs, cut into small pieces
- 1 cup white wine
- Juice of 1 lemon

1. Preheat the oven to 300°F (150°C). 2. Mix the rosemary, thyme, sea salt, and freshly ground pepper together to make a dry rub. Press the rub into the pork loin. 3. Heat the olive oil in a skillet. 4. Add the pork loin, carrots, onion, and garlic, and cook for 15 minutes, or until the pork is browned. 5. Transfer all to a shallow roasting pan. 6. Add the figs, white wine, and lemon juice. 7. Cover with aluminum foil and bake for 40–50 minutes, or until the meat is tender and internal temperature is about 145°F (63°C). 8. Transfer the meat to a serving dish, and cover with aluminum foil. Wait 15 minutes before slicing. 9. In the meantime, pour the vegetables, figs, and liquids into a blender. Process until smooth and strain through a sieve or strainer. 10. Transfer to a gravy dish, or pour directly over the sliced meat.

Per Serving:
calories: 546 | fat: 28g | protein: 52g | carbs: 22g | fiber: 4g | sodium: 139mg

Zesty Serrano Pork Kebabs

Prep time: 22 minutes | Cook time: 18 minutes | Serves 3

- 2 tablespoons tomato purée
- ½ fresh serrano, minced
- ⅓ teaspoon paprika
- 1 pound (454 g) pork, ground
- ½ cup green onions, finely chopped
- 3 cloves garlic, peeled and finely minced
- 1 teaspoon ground black pepper, or more to taste
- 1 teaspoon salt, or more to taste

1. Thoroughly combine all ingredients in a mixing dish. Then form your mixture into sausage shapes. 2. Cook for 18 minutes at 355°F (179°C). Mound salad on a serving platter, top with air-fried kebabs and serve warm. Bon appétit!

Per Serving:
calories: 216 | fat: 6g | protein: 35g | carbs: 4g | fiber: 1g | sodium: 855mg

Spiced Lamb Burgers with Harissa Mayo

Prep timePrep Time: 15 minutes | Cook Time: 10 minutes | Serves 2

- ½ small onion, minced
- 1 garlic clove, minced
- 2 teaspoons minced fresh parsley
- 2 teaspoons minced fresh mint
- ¼ teaspoon salt
- Pinch freshly ground black pepper
- 1 teaspoon cumin
- 1 teaspoon smoked paprika
- ¼ teaspoon coriander
- 8 ounces (227 g) lean ground lamb
- 2 tablespoons olive oil mayonnaise
- ½ teaspoon harissa paste (more or less to taste)
- 2 hamburger buns or pitas, fresh greens, tomato slices (optional, for serving)

1. Preheat the grill to medium-high and oil the grill grate. Alternatively, you can cook these in a heavy pan (cast iron is best) on the stovetop. 2. In a large bowl, combine the onion, garlic, parsley, mint, salt, pepper, cumin, paprika, and coriander. Add the lamb and, using your hands, combine the meat with the spices so they are evenly distributed. Form meat mixture into 2 patties. 3. Grill the burgers for 4 minutes per side, or until the internal temperature registers 160°F (71°C) for medium. 4. If cooking on the stovetop, heat the pan to medium-high and oil the pan. Cook the burgers for 5 to 6 minutes per side, or until the internal temperature registers 160°F(71°C). 5. While the burgers are cooking, combine the mayonnaise and harissa in a small bowl. 6. Serve the burgers with the harissa mayonnaise and slices of tomato and fresh greens on a bun or pita—or skip the bun altogether.

Per Serving:
calories: 381 | fat: 20g | protein: 22g | carbs: 27g | fiber: 2g | sodium: 653mg

Kheema Meatloaf

Prep time: 10 minutes | Cook time: 15 minutes | Serves 4

- 1 pound (454 g) 85% lean ground beef
- 2 large eggs, lightly beaten
- 1 cup diced yellow onion
- ¼ cup chopped fresh cilantro
- 1 tablespoon minced fresh ginger
- 1 tablespoon minced garlic
- 2 teaspoons garam masala
- 1 teaspoon kosher salt
- 1 teaspoon ground turmeric
- 1 teaspoon cayenne pepper
- ½ teaspoon ground cinnamon
- ⅛ teaspoon ground cardamom

1. In a spacious mixing bowl, carefully combine the ground beef with eggs, finely chopped onion, cilantro, ginger, minced garlic, garam masala, salt, turmeric, cayenne pepper, cinnamon, and cardamom. Mix until all ingredients are well integrated. 2. Transfer the seasoned mixture into a baking dish and position it in the air fryer basket. Adjust the air fryer settings to 350°F (177°C) and cook for 15 minutes. Utilize a meat thermometer to verify that the meatloaf has reached an internal temperature of 160°F (71°C), indicating it is cooked to medium. 3. Once cooking is complete, carefully drain any excess fat and liquid from the dish, allowing the meatloaf to rest for 5 minutes before slicing. 4. After resting, slice the meatloaf and serve it while hot for optimal flavor.

Per Serving:
calories: 205 | fat: 8g | protein: 28g | carbs: 5g | fiber: 1g | sodium: 696mg

Smoked Paprika and Lemon Marinated Pork Kabobs

Prep time: 10 minutes | Cook time: 10 minutes | Serves 4

- ⅓ cup finely chopped flat-leaf parsley
- ¼ cup olive oil
- 2 tablespoons minced red onion
- 1 tablespoon lemon juice
- 1 tablespoon smoked paprika
- 2 teaspoons ground cumin
- 1 clove garlic, minced
- ¼ teaspoon cayenne pepper
- ½ teaspoon salt
- 2 pork tenderloins, each about 1 pound (454 g), trimmed of silver skin and any excess fat, cut into 1¼-inch cubes
- 1 lemon, cut into wedges, for serving

1. In a spacious mixing bowl, combine the parsley, olive oil, chopped onion, lemon juice, smoked paprika, cumin, minced garlic, cayenne pepper, and salt, whisking until well blended. Incorporate the pork into the mixture, ensuring it is thoroughly coated. Cover the bowl and let it marinate in the refrigerator for at least 4 hours, or preferably overnight, stirring occasionally to enhance the flavor absorption. 2. Immerse bamboo skewers in water for 30 minutes to prevent burning during grilling. 3. Set your grill to high heat to prepare for cooking. 4. Take the marinated pork out of the bowl, discarding the excess marinade. Skewer the meat onto the pre-soaked bamboo sticks and arrange them on the grill. Close the grill lid and cook, turning the skewers occasionally, until the pork is fully cooked and has a golden-brown exterior, approximately 8 to 10 minutes in total. 5. Once cooked, carefully place the skewers on a serving platter. Serve them hot, accompanied by fresh lemon wedges for an extra burst of flavor.

Per Serving:
calories: 447 | fat: 21g | protein: 60g | carbs: 3g | fiber: 1g | sodium: 426mg

Mediterranean Chimichurri Skirt Steak

Prep time: 10 minutes | Cook time: 15 minutes | Serves 4

- ¾ cup fresh mint
- ¾ cup fresh parsley
- ⅔ cup extra-virgin olive oil
- ⅓ cup lemon juice
- Zest of 1 lemon
- 2 tablespoons dried oregano
- 4 garlic cloves, peeled
- ½ teaspoon red pepper flakes
- ½ teaspoon kosher salt
- 1 to 1½ pounds (454 to 680 g) skirt steak, cut in half if longer than grill pan

1. In a food processor or blender, combine the mint, parsley, olive oil, lemon juice, lemon zest, oregano, garlic, red pepper flakes, and salt. Blend until you reach your desired consistency, whether slightly chunky or a smooth purée. Set aside half a cup of the chimichurri mixture for later use. 2. Pour the remaining chimichurri mixture into a medium bowl or a zip-top bag. Add the steak, ensuring it's well coated, and marinate for at least 30 minutes or up to 8 hours in the refrigerator for maximum flavor. 3. Preheat a grill pan over medium-high heat. Add the marinated steak to the pan and cook for 4 minutes on each side for medium rare. If you prefer medium, cook for an additional 1 to 2 minutes per side. 4. Once cooked, transfer the steak to a cutting board, cover it loosely with foil to keep warm, and let it rest for 10 minutes. After resting, thinly slice the steak against the grain and serve it with the reserved chimichurri sauce on the side.

Per Serving:
calories: 460 | fat: 38g | protein: 28g | carbs: 5g | fiber: 2g | sodium: 241mg

Giouvarlakia Soup

Prep time: 10 minutes | Cook time: 5 minutes | Serves 6

- 1 pound (454 g) lean ground beef
- 1 medium onion, peeled and grated
- 3 large eggs, divided
- ⅓ cup plus ½ cup Arborio rice, divided
- 1 teaspoon ground allspice
- ⅛ teaspoon ground nutmeg
- ¾ teaspoon salt, divided
- ¾ teaspoon ground black pepper, divided
- 8 cups low-sodium chicken broth
- 1 tablespoon all-purpose flour
- 2 tablespoons water
- 3 tablespoons lemon juice

1. In a sizable mixing bowl, blend together the ground beef, chopped onion, 1 egg, ⅓ cup of rice, allspice, nutmeg, ¼ teaspoon of salt, and ¼ teaspoon of pepper until well mixed. Form the mixture into 1-inch meatballs and set them aside. 2. Pour the broth into the Instant Pot®, then add the meatballs, the remaining ½ cup of rice, and the additional ½ teaspoon of salt and pepper. Secure the lid, ensure the steam release valve is set to Sealing, press the Manual button, and adjust the cooking time to 5 minutes. When the timer goes off, allow the pressure to release naturally for 10 minutes, then quick-release any remaining pressure until the float valve drops. Press the Cancel button and carefully open the lid. 3. In a separate large bowl, create a slurry by whisking together flour and water until smooth. Incorporate lemon juice and the remaining 2 eggs into the mixture. While whisking vigorously, gradually add a ladleful of soup liquid to the egg mixture. Continue whisking and slowly incorporate another 3–4 ladles of soup, one at a time. 4. Gently stir the egg mixture back into the soup, ensuring a smooth blend. 5. Let the soup cool for 5 minutes, then serve it hot for the best flavor experience.

Per Serving:
calories: 262 | fat: 5g | protein: 25g | carbs: 18g | fiber: 0g | sodium: 670mg

Lemon-Mint Grilled Lamb Loin Chops

Prep time: 5 minutes | Cook time: 10 to 12 minutes | Serves 4 to 6

- 3 tablespoons olive oil
- Zest and juice of 1 lemon
- 2 tablespoons pomegranate molasses
- 1 cup finely chopped fresh mint
- ½ cup finely chopped fresh
- cilantro or parsley
- 2 scallions (green onions), finely chopped
- 6 lamb loin chops
- Freshly ground black pepper, to taste

1. In a small bowl, whisk together the olive oil, lemon zest, lemon juice, pomegranate molasses, mint, parsley, and scallions until well combined. Put the lamb in a large zip-top plastic bag. Add the marinade, seal the bag, and massage the marinade onto all sides of the chops. Refrigerate for at least 1 hour or up to overnight. 2. When ready to cook, heat a grill to medium. 3. Remove the chops from the marinade; discard the marinade. Season with pepper, if desired. Grill the chops for 10 to 12 minutes, turning once, for medium. Let rest for 10 minutes before serving.

Per Serving:
1 cup: calories: 182 | fat: 11g | protein: 10g | carbs: 10g | fiber: 0g | sodium: 46mg

Chapter **9**

Fish and Seafood

Chapter 9 Fish and Seafood

Sherry-Braised Monkfish with Almond Sauce

Prep time: 10 minutes | Cook time: 25 minutes | Serves 4

- 2 tablespoons olive oil
- 1 medium onion, diced
- 2 red bell peppers, diced
- 1½ teaspoons salt
- ½ teaspoon freshly ground black pepper
- 3 cloves garlic, minced
- ⅓ cup dry sherry
- 1 cup bottled clam juice
- ¼ cup blanched slivered almonds
- 4 monkfish fillets, about 6 ounces (170 g) each
- 2 tablespoons chopped flat-leaf parsley

1. Heat the olive oil in a large saucepan over medium heat. Add the onion, peppers, salt, and pepper and cook, stirring frequently, for about 5 minutes, until the vegetables are softened. Add the garlic and sherry and cook for 1 more minute. Stir in the clam juice and bring to a simmer. Reduce the heat to low, cover, and simmer for 10 minutes. 2. Transfer the onion mixture to a food processor or blender and process to a smooth purée. Add the almonds and pulse until they are finely ground. Pour the sauce back into the saucepan and return to a simmer over medium heat. 3. Add the fish to the sauce, cover the pan, and simmer for 10 to 12 minutes, until the fish is just cooked through. Slice the fish into ¼-inch thick slices and serve immediately, garnished with parsley.

Per Serving:
calories: 291 | fat: 13g | protein: 28g | carbs: 15g | fiber: 3g | sodium: 877mg

Slow-Cooked Citrus-Seasoned Sole

Prep time: 5 minutes | Cook time: 2 to 4 hours | Serves 4

Nonstick cooking spray
- 2 pounds (907 g) fresh sole fillets
- 3 tablespoons freshly squeezed lime juice
- 2 tablespoons extra-virgin olive oil
- 2 garlic cloves, minced
- 1 tablespoon ground cumin
- 1½ teaspoons paprika
- 1 teaspoon sea salt
- ¼ cup fresh cilantro

1. Coat a slow-cooker insert with cooking spray, or line the bottom and sides with parchment paper or aluminum foil. 2. Place the sole in the prepared slow cooker in a single layer, cutting it into pieces to fit if needed. 3. In a small bowl, whisk together the lime juice, olive oil, garlic, cumin, paprika, and salt until blended. Pour the sauce over the fish. 4. Cover the cooker and cook for 2 to 4 hours on Low heat. 5. Garnish with fresh cilantro for serving.

Per Serving:
calories: 234 | fat: 12g | protein: 29g | carbs: 2g | fiber: 1g | sodium: 713mg

Salmon with Tarragon-Dijon Sauce

Prep time: 5 minutes | Cook time: 15 minutes | Serves 4

- 1¼ pounds (567 g) salmon fillet (skin on or removed), cut into 4 equal pieces
- ¼ cup avocado oil mayonnaise
- ¼ cup Dijon or stone-ground mustard
- Zest and juice of ½ lemon
- 2 tablespoons chopped fresh tarragon or 1 to 2 teaspoons dried tarragon
- ½ teaspoon salt
- ¼ teaspoon freshly ground black pepper
- 4 tablespoons extra-virgin olive oil, for serving

1. Preheat your oven to 425°F (220°C) and line a baking sheet with parchment paper for easy cleanup. 2. Arrange the salmon fillets skin-side down on the prepared baking sheet, ensuring they're spaced evenly. 3. In a small bowl, whisk together the mayonnaise, mustard, lemon zest, lemon juice, tarragon, salt, and pepper until well combined. Spread the sauce mixture evenly over the top of each salmon fillet, coating them generously. 4. Bake the salmon for 10 to 12 minutes, or until the top is slightly golden and the center is still a bit translucent, adjusting the time based on the thickness of the fillets. Once done, remove the salmon from the oven and allow it to rest on the baking sheet for 10 minutes. Just before serving, drizzle each fillet with 1 tablespoon of olive oil for added richness.

Per Serving:
calories: 343 | fat: 23g | protein: 30g | carbs: 4g | fiber: 1g | sodium: 585mg

Tomato-Basil Salmon

Prep time: 10 minutes | Cook time: 4 to 6 hours | Serves 4

- 1 (15-ounce / 425-g) can no-salt-added crushed tomatoes
- ½ cup chopped onion
- 4 teaspoons dried basil
- 3 garlic cloves, minced
- 2 pounds (907 g) fresh
- salmon fillets, skin on or off as preferred
- 1 teaspoon sea salt
- ¼ teaspoon freshly ground black pepper
- ¼ cup chopped fresh basil

1. In the slow cooker, combine tomatoes, onion, basil, and garlic, stirring thoroughly to ensure everything is well mixed. 2. Season the salmon generously on all sides with salt and pepper. Place the salmon into the slow cooker, cutting it into smaller portions if necessary to fit, and gently spoon some of the tomato mixture over the top of the fish. 3. Cover the slow cooker and let it cook on Low heat for 4 to 6 hours, allowing the flavors to blend and the salmon to become tender. 4. For a fresh touch, garnish the dish with fresh basil right before serving.

Per Serving:
calories: 471 | fat: 24g | protein: 58g | carbs: 9g | fiber: 3g | sodium: 733mg

Cod with Warm Tabbouleh Salad

Prep time: 10 minutes | Cook time: 6 minutes | Serves 4

- 1 cup medium-grind bulgur, rinsed
- 1 teaspoon table salt, divided
- 1 lemon, sliced ¼ inch thick, plus 2 tablespoons juice
- 4 (6-ounce / 170-g) skinless cod fillets, 1½ inches thick
- 3 tablespoons extra-virgin olive oil, divided, plus extra for drizzling
- ¼ teaspoon pepper
- 1 small shallot, minced
- 10 ounces (283 g) cherry tomatoes, halved
- 1 cup chopped fresh parsley
- ½ cup chopped fresh mint

1. Place the trivet that comes with your Instant Pot at the bottom of the insert and add ½ cup of water. Fold a sheet of aluminum foil into a 16 by 6-inch sling and position a 1½-quart round soufflé dish in the center of the sling. In the dish, combine 1 cup of water, bulgur, and ½ teaspoon of salt. Using the sling, carefully lower the soufflé dish into the pot, resting it on the trivet, with the narrow ends of the sling resting along the sides of the insert. 2. Secure the lid, close the pressure release valve, and select the high-pressure cook function, setting the timer for 3 minutes. Once the cooking is done, turn off the Instant Pot and perform a quick pressure release. Carefully remove the lid, letting the steam escape away from you. Use the sling to transfer the soufflé dish to a wire rack to cool. Remove the trivet, but keep the sling and water inside the pot. 3. Lay lemon slices in two rows across the center of the sling. Brush the cod with 1 tablespoon of oil and season it with the remaining ½ teaspoon of salt and pepper. Arrange the cod, skin side down, in an even layer over the lemon slices. Use the sling to lower the cod into the Instant Pot, letting the edges of the sling rest along the sides of the insert. Secure the lid, close the pressure release valve, and set the high-pressure cook function for another 3 minutes. 4. Meanwhile, in a large bowl, whisk together the remaining 2 tablespoons of oil, lemon juice, and shallot. Add the bulgur, tomatoes, parsley, and mint, gently tossing everything together. Season the salad with salt and pepper to taste. 5. Turn off the Instant Pot and quick-release the pressure. Carefully remove the lid, allowing steam to escape away from you. Using the sling, lift the cod onto a large plate. Gently tilt and use a spatula to remove the lemon slices from beneath the fillets. Serve the cod alongside the salad, drizzling each portion with extra oil for added flavor.

Per Serving:
calories: 380 | fat: 12g | protein: 36g | carbs: 32g | fiber: 6g | sodium: 690mg

Fiery Steamed Chili Crab

Prep time: 10 minutes | Cook time: 3 minutes | Serves 2

- 2 tablespoons garlic chili sauce
- 1 tablespoon hoisin sauce
- 1 tablespoon minced fresh ginger
- 1 teaspoon fish sauce
- 2 cloves garlic, peeled and
- minced
- 2 small bird's eye chilies, minced
- 2 (2-pound / 907-g) Dungeness crabs
- 1 cup water

1. In a medium bowl, combine garlic chili sauce, hoisin sauce,

ginger, fish sauce, garlic, and chilies. Mix well. Coat crabs in chili mixture. 2. Add water to the Instant Pot® and insert steamer basket. Add crabs to basket. Close lid, set steam release to Sealing, press the Manual button, and set time to 3 minutes. 3. When the timer beeps, quick-release the pressure until the float valve drops. Press the Cancel button and open lid. Transfer crabs to a serving platter. Serve hot.

Per Serving:
calories: 128 | fat: 1g | protein: 25g | carbs: 1g | fiber: 0g | sodium: 619mg

Moroccan-Style Grilled Tuna

Prep time: 10 minutes | Cook time: 6 to 8 minutes | Serves 4

- 2 tablespoons finely chopped cilantro
- 2 tablespoons finely chopped parsley
- 6 cloves garlic, minced
- ½ teaspoon unrefined sea salt or salt
- ½ teaspoon paprika
- 1 lemon, juiced and zested
- 3 tablespoons extra-virgin olive oil
- 4 tuna steaks (4 ounces / 113 g each)

1. In a medium-sized bowl, combine cilantro, parsley, garlic, salt, paprika, lemon juice, and lemon zest, mixing until well incorporated. Gradually whisk in the olive oil until the mixture forms a smooth chermoula sauce. 2. Arrange the fish in a glass baking dish and drizzle half of the prepared chermoula sauce over the top. Cover the dish tightly with plastic wrap and let the fish marinate in the refrigerator for 1 hour to fully infuse the flavors. 3. Preheat the grill to medium-high heat for cooking. 4. Place the fish on the grill, turning it only once, and cook until it becomes firm, about 6 to 8 minutes. Once cooked, transfer the fish to a serving platter, generously spread the remaining chermoula sauce over it, and let it rest for 5 minutes to soak up the flavors before serving.

Per Serving:
calories: 217 | fat: 11g | protein: 25g | carbs: 3g | fiber: 0g | sodium: 335mg

Herb-Infused Baked Flounder

Prep time: 5 minutes | Cook time: 10 minutes | Serves 4

- ½ cup lightly packed flatleaf parsley
- ¼ cup olive oil
- 4 garlic cloves, peeled and halved
- 2 tablespoons fresh rosemary
- 2 tablespoons fresh thyme leaves
- 2 tablespoons fresh sage
- 2 tablespoons lemon zest
- Sea salt and freshly ground pepper, to taste
- 4 flounder fillets

1. Preheat the oven to 350ºF (180ºC). 2. Place all the ingredients except the fish in a food processor. Blend to form a thick paste. 3. Place the fillets on a baking sheet, and brush this paste on them. Refrigerate for at least 1 hour. 4. Bake for 8–10 minutes, or until the flounder is slightly firm and opaque. Season with sea salt and freshly ground pepper.

Per Serving:
calories: 283 | fat: 18g | protein: 27g | carbs: 3g | fiber: 1g | sodium: 322mg

Swordfish in Tarragon-Citrus Butter

Prep time: 5 minutes | Cook time: 20 minutes | Serves 4

- 1 pound (454 g) swordfish steaks, cut into 2-inch pieces
- 1 teaspoon salt
- ¼ teaspoon freshly ground black pepper
- ¼ cup extra-virgin olive oil, plus 2 tablespoons, divided
- 2 tablespoons unsalted

- butter
- Zest and juice of 2 clementines
- Zest and juice of 1 lemon
- 2 tablespoons chopped fresh tarragon
- Sautéed greens, riced cauliflower, or zucchini noodles, for serving

1. In a bowl, season the swordfish chunks with salt and pepper, tossing to ensure they are evenly coated. 2. Heat ¼ cup of olive oil in a large skillet over medium-high heat. Once the oil is hot, add the swordfish and sear for 2 to 3 minutes on each side, until all sides are lightly golden brown. Using a slotted spoon, carefully remove the fish from the skillet and keep it warm. 3. Lower the heat to medium-low and add the remaining 2 tablespoons of olive oil and the butter to the same skillet. Once the butter has melted, whisk in the clementine and lemon zests, their juices, and the tarragon. Season with a pinch of salt. Return the swordfish to the pan, tossing to coat the pieces in the citrus butter sauce. Serve the fish with the sauce drizzled on top, accompanied by sautéed greens, riced cauliflower, or zucchini noodles for a complete meal.

Per Serving:
calories: 330 | fat: 26g | protein: 23g | carbs: 1g | fiber: 0g | sodium: 585mg

Mediterranean Poached Octopus Salad

Prep time: 10 minutes | Cook time: 16 minutes | Serves 8

- 2 pounds (907 g) potatoes (about 6 medium)
- 3 teaspoons salt, divided
- 1 (2-pound / 907-g) frozen octopus, thawed, cleaned, and rinsed
- 3 cloves garlic, peeled, divided

- 1 bay leaf
- 2 teaspoons whole peppercorns
- ½ cup olive oil
- ¼ cup white wine vinegar
- ½ teaspoon ground black pepper
- ½ cup chopped fresh parsley

1. Place potatoes in the Instant Pot® with 2 teaspoons salt and enough water to just cover the potatoes halfway. Close lid, set steam release to Sealing, press the Manual button, and set time to 6 minutes. When the timer beeps, quick-release the pressure until the float valve drops and open lid. Press the Cancel button. 2. Remove potatoes with tongs (reserve the cooking water), and peel them as soon as you can handle them. Dice potatoes into bite-sized pieces. Set aside. 3. Add octopus to potato cooking water in the pot and add more water to cover if needed. Add 1 garlic clove, bay leaf, and peppercorns. Close lid, set steam release to Sealing, press the Manual button, and set time to 10 minutes. When the timer beeps, quick-release the pressure until the float valve drops and open lid. Remove and discard bay leaf. 4. Check octopus for tenderness by seeing if a fork will sink easily into the thickest part of the flesh. If not, close the top and bring it to pressure for another minute or two and check again. 5. Remove octopus and drain. Chop head and tentacles into small, bite-sized chunks. 6. Crush remaining 2 garlic cloves and place in a small jar or plastic container. Add olive oil, vinegar, remaining 1 teaspoon salt, and pepper. Close the lid and shake well. 7. In a large serving bowl, mix potatoes with octopus, cover with vinaigrette, and sprinkle with parsley.

Per Serving:
calories: 301 | fat: 15g | protein: 15g | carbs: 30g | fiber: 2g | sodium: 883mg

Roasted Branzino with Lemon and Herbs

Prep time: 10 minutes | Cook time: 20 minutes | Serves 2

- 1 to 1½ pounds (454 to 680 g) branzino, scaled and gutted
- Salt
- Freshly ground black pepper
- 1 tablespoon olive oil

- 1 lemon, sliced
- 3 garlic cloves, minced
- ¼ cup chopped fresh herbs (any mixture of oregano, thyme, parsley, and rosemary)

1. Preheat your oven to 425ºF (220ºC) and position the oven rack in the center. 2. Place the cleaned branzino in a baking dish, making 4 to 5 slits across the top of the fish, spaced about 1½ inches apart. 3. Generously season the inside of the fish with salt and pepper, then drizzle it with olive oil to enhance the flavor. 4. Stuff the fish cavity with lemon slices, sprinkle the chopped garlic and herbs over the lemon, and gently close the fish. 5. Roast the branzino for 15 to 20 minutes, or until the flesh is fully cooked, opaque, and easily flakes when tested with a fork. 6. Before serving, carefully open the fish, remove the lemon slices, and gently pull out the bone to enjoy a clean, tender bite.

Per Serving:
calories: 287 | fat: 12g | protein: 42g | carbs: 2g | fiber: 0g | sodium: 151mg

Paprika-Spiced Fish

Prep time: 5 minutes | Cook time: 10 minutes | Serves 4

- 4 (5-ounce / 142-g) sea bass fillets
- ½ teaspoon salt
- 1 tablespoon smoked

- paprika
- 3 tablespoons unsalted butter
- Lemon wedges

1. Generously season both sides of the fish with salt, ensuring an even coating. Follow by sprinkling paprika over both sides for an extra layer of flavor. 2. Heat a skillet over high heat until hot, then melt the butter in the pan, allowing it to coat the surface. 3. When the butter is fully melted and begins to sizzle, place the seasoned fish in the skillet. Cook for approximately 4 minutes on each side, flipping once, until the fish is golden and cooked through. 4. After cooking, transfer the fish to a serving plate and finish by squeezing fresh lemon juice over the top for a burst of brightness. Serve immediately.

Per Serving:
calories: 257 | fat: 34g | protein: 34g | carbs: 1g | fiber: 1g | sodium: 416mg

Mediterranean Mussels with Potatoes

Prep time: 15 minutes | Cook time: 12 minutes | Serves 6

- 2 pounds (907 g) baby Yukon Gold potatoes, cut in half
- ½ cup water
- 2 tablespoons olive oil, divided
- 1 medium yellow onion, peeled and diced
- 1 tablespoon chopped fresh oregano
- ½ teaspoon paprika
- 4 cloves garlic, peeled and minced
- ¼ teaspoon salt
- ¼ teaspoon ground black pepper
- 1 (15-ounce / 425-g) can diced tomatoes
- 1½ cups water
- 2 pounds (907 g) mussels, scrubbed and beards removed
- ½ cup sliced green olives
- 2 tablespoons chopped fresh parsley

1. Place potatoes, water, and 1 tablespoon oil in the Instant Pot®. Close lid, set steam release to Sealing, press the Manual button, and set time to 2 minutes. When the timer beeps, quick-release the pressure until the float valve drops. Press the Cancel button. Open lid and drain potatoes. Set aside. Wash and dry pot. 2. Press the Sauté button and heat remaining 1 tablespoon oil. Add onion and cook until tender, about 4 minutes. Add oregano, paprika, garlic, salt, and pepper, and cook until very fragrant, about 30 seconds. Add tomatoes and water, and stir well. Press the Cancel button. 3. Stir in mussels, olives, and potatoes. Close lid, set steam release to Sealing, press the Manual button, and set time to 5 minutes. When the timer beeps, quick-release the pressure until the float valve drops and open lid. Discard any mussels that haven't opened. Garnish with parsley and serve immediately.

Per Serving:
calories: 272 | fat: 8g | protein: 15g | carbs: 35g | fiber: 4g | sodium: 560mg

Shrimp Foil Packets

Prep time: 15 minutes | Cook time: 4 to 6 hours | Serves 4

- 1½ pounds (680 g) whole raw medium shrimp, peeled, deveined, and divided into 4 (6-ounce / 170-g) portions
- Sea salt
- Freshly ground black pepper
- 2 teaspoons extra-virgin olive oil, divided
- 4 teaspoons balsamic
- vinegar, divided
- 4 garlic cloves, minced
- 1 red onion, cut into chunks
- 1 large zucchini, sliced
- 4 Roma tomatoes, chopped
- 4 teaspoons dried oregano, divided
- Juice of 1 lemon

1. Spread out a large sheet of aluminum foil on a flat surface. Arrange one-quarter of the shrimp in the middle of the foil, then season with salt and pepper to taste. Drizzle over ½ teaspoon of olive oil and 1 teaspoon of vinegar to enhance the flavor. 2. Layer one-quarter each of the garlic, onion, and zucchini over the shrimp, followed by adding 1 chopped tomato and sprinkling 1 teaspoon of oregano on top. Place another sheet of foil over the ingredients and tightly fold the edges together to seal the packet securely. 3. Repeat this process to create 3 additional foil packets, making a total of 4.

Arrange the packets in a single layer in the slow cooker, or stack them if space is limited. 4. Cover the slow cooker and cook on Low heat for 4 to 6 hours until the shrimp and vegetables are perfectly tender. 5. Be cautious when opening the foil packets, as hot steam will escape. Once opened, drizzle each packet with fresh lemon juice for added brightness before serving.

Per Serving:
calories: 210 | fat: 5g | protein: 30g | carbs: 17g | fiber: 3g | sodium: 187mg

Zesty Lemon-Dill Mahi-Mahi

Prep time: 5 minutes | Cook time: 14 minutes | Serves 2

- Oil, for spraying
- 2 (6-ounce / 170-g) mahi-mahi fillets
- 1 tablespoon lemon juice
- 1 tablespoon olive oil
- ¼ teaspoon salt
- ¼ teaspoon freshly ground black pepper
- 1 tablespoon chopped fresh dill
- 2 lemon slices

1. Line the air fryer basket with parchment and spray lightly with oil. 2. Place the mahi-mahi in the prepared basket. 3. In a small bowl, whisk together the lemon juice and olive oil. Brush the mixture evenly over the mahi-mahi. 4. Sprinkle the mahi-mahi with the salt and black pepper and top with the dill. 5. Air fry at 400°F (204°C) for 12 to 14 minutes, depending on the thickness of the fillets, until they flake easily. 6. Transfer to plates, top each with a lemon slice, and serve.

Per Serving:
calories: 218 | fat: 8g | protein: 32g | carbs: 3g | fiber: 1g | sodium: 441mg

Fresh Cucumber and Salmon Salad with Capers

Prep time: 10 minutes | Cook time: 8 to 10 minutes | Serves 2

- 1 pound (454 g) salmon fillet
- 1½ tablespoons olive oil, divided
- 1 tablespoon sherry vinegar
- 1 tablespoon capers, rinsed and drained
- 1 seedless cucumber, thinly
- sliced
- ¼ Vidalia onion, thinly sliced
- 2 tablespoons chopped fresh parsley
- Salt and freshly ground black pepper, to taste

1. Preheat the air fryer to 400°F (204°C). 2. Lightly coat the salmon with ½ tablespoon of the olive oil. Place skin-side down in the air fryer basket and air fry for 8 to 10 minutes until the fish is opaque and flakes easily with a fork. Transfer the salmon to a plate and let cool to room temperature. Remove the skin and carefully flake the fish into bite-size chunks. 3. In a small bowl, whisk the remaining 1 tablespoon olive oil and the vinegar until thoroughly combined. Add the flaked fish, capers, cucumber, onion, and parsley. Season to taste with salt and freshly ground black pepper. Toss gently to coat. Serve immediately or cover and refrigerate for up to 4 hours.

Per Serving:
calories: 399 | fat: 20g | protein: 47g | carbs: 4g | fiber: 1g | sodium: 276mg

South Indian Fried Fish

Prep time: 20 minutes | Cook time: 8 minutes | Serves 4

- 2 tablespoons olive oil
- 2 tablespoons fresh lime or lemon juice
- 1 teaspoon minced fresh ginger
- 1 clove garlic, minced
- 1 teaspoon ground turmeric
- ½ teaspoon kosher salt
- ¼ to ½ teaspoon cayenne pepper
- 1 pound (454 g) tilapia fillets (2 to 3 fillets)
- Olive oil spray
- Lime or lemon wedges (optional)

1. In a large bowl, mix together the oil, lime juice, ginger, garlic, turmeric, salt, and cayenne pepper until everything is well blended. Set the mixture aside. 2. Cut each tilapia fillet into three or four evenly-sized pieces. Add the fish to the bowl with the marinade, gently tossing to coat each piece thoroughly. Let the fish marinate at room temperature for 10 to 15 minutes, but avoid marinating for longer as the lime juice can start to "cook" the fish. 3. Lightly spray the air fryer basket with olive oil spray. Arrange the marinated fish in the basket in a single layer, and then spray the tops of the fish as well. Set the air fryer to 325°F (163°C) and cook for 3 minutes to start the cooking process. Increase the temperature to 400°F (204°C) and cook for an additional 5 minutes to fully cook and crisp the fish. For thinner pieces, check at the 3-minute mark of the second cooking phase and remove any pieces that are done, adding them back for the last minute to ensure crispness. 4. Carefully take the fish out of the air fryer basket and serve immediately. Garnish with lemon wedges if desired for a bright, citrusy finish.

Per Serving:

calories: 175 | fat: 9g | protein: 23g | carbs: 2g | fiber: 0g | sodium: 350mg

Slow-Cooked Moroccan-Spiced Fish

Prep time: 10 minutes | Cook time: 2 to 4 hours | Serves 4

Ras Al-Hanout:
- ¼ teaspoon ground cumin
- ¼ teaspoon ground ginger
- ¼ teaspoon ground turmeric
- ¼ teaspoon paprika
- ¼ teaspoon garlic powder
- ¼ teaspoon red pepper flakes
- ⅛ teaspoon ground
- cinnamon
- ⅛ teaspoon ground coriander
- ⅛ teaspoon ground nutmeg
- ⅛ teaspoon ground cloves
- ⅛ teaspoon sea salt
- ⅛ teaspoon freshly ground black pepper

Fish:
- Nonstick cooking spray
- 2 pounds (907 g) fresh white-fleshed fish fillets of
- your choice
- 2 garlic cloves, minced

Make the Ras Al-Hanout: In a small bowl, stir together the cumin, ginger, turmeric, paprika, garlic powder, red pepper flakes, cinnamon, coriander, nutmeg, cloves, salt, and pepper. Make the Fish: 1. Coat a slow-cooker insert with cooking spray, or line the bottom and sides with parchment paper or aluminum foil. 2. Season the fish all over with the ras al-hanout and garlic. Place the fish in the prepared slow cooker in a single layer, cutting it into pieces to fit if needed. 3. Cover the cooker and cook for 2 to 4 hours on Low heat.

Per Serving:

calories: 243 | fat: 2g | protein: 51g | carbs: 1g | fiber: 0g | sodium: 216mg

Italian Fish

Prep time: 10 minutes | Cook time: 3 minutes | Serves 4

- 1 (14½-ounce / 411-g) can diced tomatoes
- ¼ teaspoon dried minced onion
- ¼ teaspoon onion powder
- ¼ teaspoon dried minced garlic
- ¼ teaspoon garlic powder
- ¼ teaspoon dried basil
- ¼ teaspoon dried parsley
- ⅛ teaspoon dried oregano
- ¼ teaspoon sugar
- ⅛ teaspoon dried lemon granules, crushed
- ⅛ teaspoon chili powder
- ⅛ teaspoon dried red pepper flakes
- 1 tablespoon grated Parmesan cheese
- 4 (4-ounce / 113-g) cod fillets, rinsed and patted dry

1. Begin by combining tomatoes, finely chopped onion, onion powder, minced garlic, garlic powder, basil, parsley, oregano, sugar, lemon granules, chili powder, red pepper flakes, and cheese directly into the Instant Pot®. Stir the mixture until well blended. Lay the fillets on top of the tomato mixture, tucking in the thinner tail ends to ensure the fillets are of equal thickness. Gently ladle some of the tomato mixture over the fillets to coat them evenly. 2. Secure the lid, switch the steam release to Sealing, press the Manual button, and set the cooking time for 3 minutes. Once the timer sounds, perform a quick pressure release until the float valve lowers, then carefully open the lid. Serve the dish immediately for best results.

Per Serving:

calories: 116 | fat: 3g | protein: 20g | carbs: 5g | fiber: 2g | sodium: 400mg

Salmon Fritters with Zucchini

Prep time: 15 minutes | Cook time: 12 minutes | Serves 4

- 2 tablespoons almond flour
- 1 zucchini, grated
- 1 egg, beaten
- 6 ounces (170 g) salmon
- fillet, diced
- 1 teaspoon avocado oil
- ½ teaspoon ground black pepper

1. In a bowl, combine almond flour, grated zucchini, egg, salmon, and ground black pepper, mixing until all ingredients are well incorporated. 2. Shape the mixture into small fritters, ensuring they are evenly sized. 3. Lightly spray or brush the air fryer basket with avocado oil, then carefully place the fritters inside, making sure they do not overlap. 4. Set the air fryer to 375°F (191°C) and cook the fritters for 6 minutes on each side, flipping halfway through to ensure even cooking and a crispy texture.

Per Serving:

calories: 102 | fat: 4g | protein: 11g | carbs: 4g | fiber: 1g | sodium: 52mg

Crispy Parmesan-Crusted Cod: A Friday Night Fish Fry

Prep time: 10 minutes | Cook time: 10 minutes | Serves 4

- 1 large egg
- ½ cup powdered Parmesan cheese (about 1½ ounces / 43 g)
- 1 teaspoon smoked paprika
- ¼ teaspoon celery salt
- ¼ teaspoon ground black pepper
- 4 (4-ounce / 113-g) cod fillets
- Chopped fresh oregano or parsley, for garnish (optional)
- Lemon slices, for serving (optional)

1. Spray the air fryer basket with avocado oil. Preheat the air fryer to 400ºF (204ºC). 2. Crack the egg in a shallow bowl and beat it lightly with a fork. Combine the Parmesan cheese, paprika, celery salt, and pepper in a separate shallow bowl. 3. One at a time, dip the fillets into the egg, then dredge them in the Parmesan mixture. Using your hands, press the Parmesan onto the fillets to form a nice crust. As you finish, place the fish in the air fryer basket. 4. Air fry the fish in the air fryer for 10 minutes, or until it is cooked through and flakes easily with a fork. Garnish with fresh oregano or parsley and serve with lemon slices, if desired. 5. Store leftovers in an airtight container in the refrigerator for up to 3 days. Reheat in a preheated 400ºF (204ºC) air fryer for 5 minutes, or until warmed through.

Per Serving:
calories: 165 | fat: 6g | protein: 25g | carbs: 2g | fiber: 0g | sodium: 392mg

Italian Baccalà

Prep time: 2 to 3 hours | Cook time: 4 to 6 hours | Serves 4

- 1½ pounds (680 g) salt cod
- 1 (15-ounce / 425-g) can no-salt-added diced tomatoes
- ½ onion, chopped
- 2 garlic cloves, minced
- ½ teaspoon red pepper flakes
- ¼ cup chopped fresh parsley, plus more for garnish
- Juice of ½ lemon

1. Rinse the salt cod thoroughly under cold water to remove any visible salt. Place the cod in a large bowl and fully submerge it in water, allowing it to soak for at least 2 to 3 hours. If soaking for more than 24 hours, be sure to change the water after 12 hours to maintain freshness. 2. In the slow cooker, combine the tomatoes, onion, garlic, red pepper flakes, parsley, and lemon juice, stirring until everything is well mixed. Drain the soaked cod, and break it into pieces as needed to fit it into the slow cooker. 3. Cover the slow cooker and cook the cod mixture on Low heat for 4 to 6 hours, letting the flavors meld together as the cod tenderizes. 4. When ready to serve, garnish the dish with a sprinkle of fresh parsley for added brightness and flavor.

Per Serving:
calories: 211 | fat: 2g | protein: 39g | carbs: 8g | fiber: 2g | sodium: 179mg

Marinated Swordfish Skewers

Prep time: 30 minutes | Cook time: 6 to 8 minutes | Serves 4

- 1 pound (454 g) filleted swordfish
- ¼ cup avocado oil
- 2 tablespoons freshly squeezed lemon juice
- 1 tablespoon minced fresh parsley
- 2 teaspoons Dijon mustard
- Sea salt and freshly ground black pepper, to taste
- 3 ounces (85 g) cherry tomatoes

1. Cut the fish into 1½-inch chunks, making sure to remove any remaining bones for a smooth texture. 2. In a large bowl, whisk together the olive oil, lemon juice, parsley, and Dijon mustard until well blended. Season the mixture with salt and pepper to taste. Add the fish chunks and gently toss them in the marinade, ensuring each piece is well coated. Cover the bowl and marinate the fish in the refrigerator for 30 minutes to allow the flavors to develop. 3. After marinating, remove the fish from the marinade. Thread the fish chunks and cherry tomatoes onto 4 skewers, alternating between them for a balanced presentation. 4. Preheat the air fryer to 400ºF (204ºC). Place the skewers in the air fryer basket and cook for 3 minutes. Flip the skewers and air fry for an additional 3 to 5 minutes, or until the fish is fully cooked and reaches an internal temperature of 140ºF (60ºC) when checked with an instant-read thermometer. Serve hot.

Per Serving:
calories: 291 | fat: 21g | protein: 23g | carbs: 2g | fiber: 0g | sodium: 121mg

Zesty Basil Cod Kebabs

Prep time: 15 minutes | Cook time: 2 minutes | Serves 4

- 1 cup water
- 4 (4-ounce / 113-g) cod or other white fish fillets, cut into 1" pieces
- ½ medium onion, peeled and cut into 1" pieces
- ½ medium red bell pepper, seeded and cut into 1" pieces
- 2 tablespoons extra-virgin olive oil
- 2 tablespoons chopped fresh basil
- ½ teaspoon salt
- ½ teaspoon ground black pepper
- 1 small lemon, cut into wedges

1. Place rack inside the Instant Pot® and add water. 2. Thread fish, onion, and bell pepper alternately onto four wooden skewers. Brush skewers with olive oil, then top with basil, salt, and black pepper. Place skewers on rack. Close lid, set steam release to Sealing, press Steam, and set time to 2 minutes. 3. When the timer beeps, quick-release the pressure until the float valve drops. Press the Cancel button and open lid. Serve with lemon.

Per Serving:
calories: 93 | fat: 7g | protein: 5g | carbs: 2g | fiber: 1g | sodium: 312mg

Garlic Lemon Baked Halibut with Roasted Cherry Tomatoes

Prep time: 5 minutes | Cook time: 15 minutes | Serves 4

- 4 (5-ounce / 142-g) pieces of boneless halibut, skin on
- 1 pint (2 cups) cherry tomatoes
- 3 tablespoons garlic, minced
- ½ cup lemon juice
- ¼ cup extra-virgin olive oil
- 1 teaspoon salt

1. Preheat the oven to 425°F(220ºC). 2. Put the halibut in a large baking dish; place the tomatoes around the halibut. 3. In a small bowl, combine the garlic, lemon juice, olive oil, and salt. 4. Pour the sauce over the halibut and tomatoes. Put the baking dish in the oven and bake for 15 minutes. Serve immediately.

Per Serving:
calories: 350 | fat: 18g | protein: 39g | carbs: 8g | fiber: 1g | sodium: 687mg

Olive Oil Poached Fish over Citrus Salad

Prep time: 10 minutes | Cook time: 25 minutes | Serves 4

Fish
- 4 skinless white fish fillets (1¼ to 1½ pounds / 567 to 680 g total), such as halibut, sole, or cod, ¾'–1' thick
- ¼ teaspoon kosher salt

Salad
- ¼ cup white wine vinegar
- 1 Earl Grey tea bag
- 2 blood oranges or tangerines
- 1 ruby red grapefruit or pomelo
- 6 kumquats, thinly sliced, or 2 clementines, peeled and sectioned

- ¼ teaspoon ground black pepper
- 5–7 cups olive oil
- 1 lemon, thinly sliced

- 4 cups baby arugula
- ½ cup pomegranate seeds
- ¼ cup extra-virgin olive oil
- 2 teaspoons minced shallot
- ½ teaspoon kosher salt
- ¼ teaspoon ground black pepper
- ¼ cup mint leaves, coarsely chopped

1. Prepare the fish by seasoning it with salt and pepper, then set it aside for 30 minutes to allow the flavors to develop. 2. Preheat the oven to 225°F (107°C). 3. In a large, high-sided ovenproof skillet or roasting pan, heat 1 to 1½ inches of oil over medium heat, adding the lemon slices as well. Use a candy thermometer to monitor the oil temperature, bringing it to 120°F (49°C). Carefully place the fish fillets in the oil, ensuring they don't overlap and are completely submerged. 4. Transfer the skillet or pan to the preheated oven, leaving it uncovered. Bake for 25 minutes until the fish is cooked through. Once done, move the fish to a rack to drain for 5 minutes. 5. For the salad, heat the vinegar in a small saucepan until it almost reaches a boil. Remove from heat, add the tea bag, and let it steep for 10 minutes. 6. While the vinegar is steeping, prepare the citrus by cutting off the top and bottom of one orange or tangerine to reveal the flesh. Use a paring knife to slice along the inside of the peel, removing as much pith as possible. Hold the orange over a large bowl and cut between the membranes of each section to release the fruit into the bowl. Once done, squeeze the remaining membranes over a small bowl to collect the juice. Repeat this process with the second orange and the grapefruit or pomelo. 7. Add the segmented fruit, kumquats or clementines, arugula, and pomegranate seeds to the large bowl, gently tossing to mix everything together. 8. Remove the tea bag from the vinegar, squeezing out any remaining liquid. Discard the tea bag and add the vinegar to the small bowl with the citrus juice. Slowly whisk in the oil, finely chopped shallot, salt, and pepper until the vinaigrette is well blended. Drizzle 3 to 4 tablespoons of the vinaigrette over the salad and gently toss to coat. Store any leftover vinaigrette in the refrigerator for up to one week. 9. Garnish the salad with fresh mint and serve alongside the drained fish for a refreshing, balanced meal.

Per Serving:
calories: 280 | fat: 7g | protein: 29g | carbs: 25g | fiber: 6g | sodium: 249mg

Crispy Air-Fried Stuffed Shrimp with Crab Filling

Prep time: 20 minutes | Cook time: 12 minutes per batch | Serves 4

- 16 tail-on shrimp, peeled and deveined (last tail section intact)
- ¾ cup crushed panko bread

Stuffing:
- 2 (6-ounce / 170-g) cans lump crab meat
- 2 tablespoons chopped shallots
- 2 tablespoons chopped green onions
- 2 tablespoons chopped celery
- 2 tablespoons chopped green bell pepper
- ½ cup crushed saltine crackers

- crumbs
- Oil for misting or cooking spray

- 1 teaspoon Old Bay Seasoning
- 1 teaspoon garlic powder
- ¼ teaspoon ground thyme
- 2 teaspoons dried parsley flakes
- 2 teaspoons fresh lemon juice
- 2 teaspoons Worcestershire sauce
- 1 egg, beaten

1. Rinse shrimp. Remove tail section (shell) from 4 shrimp, discard, and chop the meat finely. 2. To prepare the remaining 12 shrimp, cut a deep slit down the back side so that the meat lies open flat. Do not cut all the way through. 3. Preheat the air fryer to 360ºF (182ºC). 4. Place chopped shrimp in a large bowl with all of the stuffing ingredients and stir to combine. 5. Divide stuffing into 12 portions, about 2 tablespoons each. 6. Place one stuffing portion onto the back of each shrimp and form into a ball or oblong shape. Press firmly so that stuffing sticks together and adheres to shrimp. 7. Gently roll each stuffed shrimp in panko crumbs and mist with oil or cooking spray. 8. Place 6 shrimp in air fryer basket and air fry at 360ºF (182ºC) for 10 minutes. Mist with oil or spray and cook 2 minutes longer or until stuffing cooks through inside and is crispy outside. 9. Repeat step 8 to cook remaining shrimp.

Per Serving:
calories: 223 | fat: 4g | protein: 24g | carbs: 24g | fiber: 2g | sodium: 758mg

Blackened Red Snapper

Prep time: 13 minutes | Cook time: 8 to 10 minutes | Serves 4

- 1½ teaspoons black pepper
- ¼ teaspoon thyme
- ¼ teaspoon garlic powder
- ⅛ teaspoon cayenne pepper
- 1 teaspoon olive oil
- 4 (4 ounces / 113 g) red snapper fillet portions, skin on
- 4 thin slices lemon
- Cooking spray

1. Combine the spices and oil in a small bowl, stirring until a thick paste forms. Rub this paste evenly onto both sides of the snapper steaks, making sure they are well coated. 2. Lightly spray the air fryer basket with nonstick cooking spray, then place the snapper steaks in the basket with the skin-side facing down. 3. Top each piece of fish with a slice of fresh lemon to add brightness during cooking. 4. Roast the snapper in the air fryer at 390°F (199°C) for 8 to 10 minutes. The fish should not flake apart when done, but it should be opaque and white all the way through the center. Serve immediately.

Per Serving:

calories: 128 | fat: 3g | protein: 23g | carbs: 1g | fiber: 1g | sodium: 73mg

Slow-Cooked Spicy Tomato Basil Mussels

Prep time: 20 minutes | Cook time: 5½ hours | Serves 4

- 3 tablespoons olive oil
- 4 cloves garlic, minced
- 3 shallot cloves, minced
- 8 ounces (227 g) mushrooms, diced
- 1 (28-ounce / 794-g) can diced tomatoes, with the juice
- ¾ cup white wine
- 2 tablespoons dried oregano
- ½ tablespoon dried basil
- ½ teaspoon black pepper
- 1 teaspoon paprika
- ¼ teaspoon red pepper flakes
- 3 pounds (1.4 kg) mussels

1. In a large sauté pan, heat the olive oil over medium-high heat. Cook the garlic, shallots, and mushrooms for 2 to 3 minutes, until the garlic is just a bit brown and fragrant. Scrape the entire contents of the pan into the slow cooker. 2. Add the tomatoes and white wine to the slow cooker. Sprinkle with the oregano, basil, black pepper, paprika, and red pepper flakes. 3. Cover and cook on low for 4 to 5 hours, or on high for 2 to 3 hours. The mixture is done cooking when mushrooms are fork tender. 4. Clean and debeard the mussels. Discard any open mussels. 5. Increase the heat on the slow cooker to high once the mushroom mixture is done. Add the cleaned mussels to the slow cooker and secure the lid tightly. Cook for 30 more minutes. 6. To serve, ladle the mussels into bowls with plenty of broth. Discard any mussels that didn't open up during cooking. Serve hot, with crusty bread for sopping up the sauce.

Per Serving:

calories: 470 | fat: 19g | protein: 44g | carbs: 24g | fiber: 5g | sodium: 897mg

Balsamic-Glazed Air-Fried Tilapia

Prep time: 5 minutes | Cook time: 15 minutes | Serves 4

- 4 tilapia fillets, boneless
- 2 tablespoons balsamic vinegar
- 1 teaspoon avocado oil
- 1 teaspoon dried basil

1. Sprinkle the tilapia fillets with balsamic vinegar, avocado oil, and dried basil. 2. Then put the fillets in the air fryer basket and cook at 365°F (185°C) for 15 minutes.

Per Serving:

calories: 129 | fat: 3g | protein: 23g | carbs: 1g | fiber: 0g | sodium: 92mg

Chapter 10

Snacks and Appetizers

Chapter 10 Snacks and Appetizers

Shrimp and Chickpea Fritters

Prep time: 5 minutes | Cook time: 10 minutes | Serves 6

- 2 tablespoons olive oil, plus ¼ cup, divided
- ½ small yellow onion, finely chopped
- 12 ounces (340 g) raw medium shrimp, peeled, deveined, and finely chopped
- ¼ cup chickpea flour
- 2 tablespoon all-purpose

- flour
- 2 tablespoons roughly chopped parsley
- 1 teaspoon baking powder
- ½ teaspoon hot or sweet paprika
- ¾ teaspoon salt, plus additional to sprinkle over finished dish
- ½ lemon

1. In a large skillet, heat 2 tablespoons of olive oil over medium-high heat. Add the chopped onion and cook, stirring regularly, until softened, about 5 minutes. Once softened, use a slotted spoon to transfer the onions to a medium bowl. Add the shrimp, chickpea flour, all-purpose flour, parsley, baking powder, paprika, and salt to the bowl, and stir everything together until well mixed. Let the mixture rest for 10 minutes to allow the flavors to meld. 2. In the same skillet, heat the remaining ¼ cup of olive oil over medium-high heat. Once the oil is hot, drop the batter into the pan using about 2 tablespoons for each portion. Cook for around 2 minutes, until the bottom is golden and the edges become crispy. Flip each piece and cook for another minute or two until the second side is also golden and crisp. Remove from the skillet and drain on paper towels. Serve the shrimp fritters hot, with a squeeze of fresh lemon juice over the top, and sprinkle with a pinch of salt just before serving for extra flavor.

Per Serving:
calories: 148 | fat: 6g | protein: 15g | carbs: 9g | fiber: 3g | sodium: 435mg

Mediterranean Pesto & Olive Fat Bombs

Prep time: 15 minutes | Cook time: 0 minutes | Makes 6 fat bombs

- 1 cup crumbled goat cheese
- 4 tablespoons jarred pesto
- 12 pitted Kalamata olives, finely chopped

- ½ cup finely chopped walnuts
- 1 tablespoon chopped fresh rosemary

1. In a medium bowl, combine the goat cheese, pesto, and olives and mix well using a fork. Place in the refrigerator for at least 4 hours to harden. 2. Using your hands, form the mixture into 6 balls, about ¾-inch diameter. The mixture will be sticky. 3. In a small bowl, place the walnuts and rosemary and roll the goat cheese balls in the nut mixture to coat. 4. Store the fat bombs in the refrigerator for up to 1 week or in the freezer for up to 1 month.

Per Serving:
1 fat bomb: calories: 235 | fat: 22g | protein: 10g | carbs: 2g | fiber: 1g | sodium: 365mg

Sumac-Spiced Maple Nut Mix

Prep time: 5 minutes | Cook time:10 minutes | Makes about 2 cups

- 2 cups raw walnuts or pecans (or a mix of nuts)
- 1 teaspoon extra-virgin olive oil
- 1 teaspoon ground sumac

- ½ teaspoon pure maple syrup
- ¼ teaspoon kosher salt
- ¼ teaspoon ground ginger
- 2 to 4 rosemary sprigs

1. Preheat the oven to 350ºF (180ºC). Line a baking sheet with parchment paper or foil. 2. In a large bowl, combine the nuts, olive oil, sumac, maple syrup, salt, and ginger; mix together. Spread in a single layer on the prepared baking sheet. Add the rosemary. Roast for 8 to 10 minutes, or until golden and fragrant. 3. Remove the rosemary leaves from the stems and place in a serving bowl. Add the nuts and toss to combine before serving.

Per Serving:
¼ cup: calories: 175 | fat: 18g | protein: 3g | carbs: 4g | fiber: 2g | sodium: 35mg

Citrus-Infused Melon Salad

Prep time: 5 minutes | Cook time: 0 minutes | Serves 4

- 2 cups cubed melon, such as Crenshaw, Sharlyn, or honeydew
- 2 cups cubed cantaloupe
- ½ cup freshly squeezed

- orange juice
- ¼ cup freshly squeezed lime juice
- 1 tablespoon orange zest

1. In a large bowl, combine the melon cubes. In a small bowl, whisk together the orange juice, lime juice, and orange zest and pour over the fruit. 2. Cover and refrigerate for at least 4 hours, stirring occasionally. Serve chilled.

Per Serving:
calories: 80 | fat: 0g | protein: 2g | carbs: 20g | fiber: 2g | sodium: 30mg

Sweet-and-Spicy Nuts

Prep time: 5 minutes | Cook time: 20 minutes | Serves 10 to 12

- Nonstick cooking spray
- Zest and juice of 1 lemon
- 2 tablespoons honey
- 2 teaspoons Berbere or

- baharat spice blend
- 1 teaspoon Aleppo pepper
- 1½ cups cashews
- 1½ cups dry-roasted peanuts

1. Preheat your oven to 375°F (190°C). Line a baking sheet with parchment paper and lightly coat the parchment with cooking spray. 2. Spread the nuts in an even layer on the prepared baking sheet. Bake for 8 to 10 minutes, or until the nuts are fragrant and lightly toasted. Remove from the oven and allow them to cool slightly, but keep the oven on for the next step. 3. In a small bowl, combine the lemon zest, lemon juice, honey, Berbere spice, and Aleppo pepper, stirring until well mixed. 4. Transfer the toasted nuts to a large bowl, then pour the honey-spice mixture over them. Toss the nuts thoroughly to ensure they are evenly coated. Spread the nuts back onto the baking sheet in an even layer. Bake for another 8 to 10 minutes, or until the nuts are caramelized and golden. Remove from the oven and let them cool completely before serving. 5. Store the nuts in an airtight container in the refrigerator for up to 2 weeks.

Per Serving:
calories: 336 | fat: 27g | protein: 11g | carbs: 17g | fiber: 3g | sodium: 7mg

Creamy Shrimp-Stuffed Cucumber Pirogues

Prep time: 15 minutes | Cook time: 4 to 5 minutes | Serves 8

- 12 ounces (340 g) small, peeled, and deveined raw shrimp
- 3 ounces (85 g) cream cheese, room temperature
- 2 tablespoons plain yogurt
- 1 teaspoon lemon juice

- 1 teaspoon dried dill weed, crushed
- Salt, to taste
- 4 small hothouse cucumbers, each approximately 6 inches long

1. Pour 4 tablespoons water in bottom of air fryer drawer. 2. Place shrimp in air fryer basket in single layer and air fry at 390°F (199°C) for 4 to 5 minutes, just until done. Watch carefully because shrimp cooks quickly, and overcooking makes it tough. 3. Chop shrimp into small pieces, no larger than ½ inch. Refrigerate while mixing the remaining ingredients. 4. With a fork, mash and whip the cream cheese until smooth. 5. Stir in the yogurt and beat until smooth. Stir in lemon juice, dill weed, and chopped shrimp. 6. Taste for seasoning. If needed, add ¼ to ½ teaspoon salt to suit your taste. 7. Store in refrigerator until serving time. 8. When ready to serve, wash and dry cucumbers and split them lengthwise. Scoop out the seeds and turn cucumbers upside down on paper towels to drain for 10 minutes. 9. Just before filling, wipe centers of cucumbers dry. Spoon the shrimp mixture into the pirogues and cut in half crosswise. Serve immediately.

Per Serving:
calories: 85 | fat: 4g | protein: 10g | carbs: 2g | fiber: 1g | sodium: 93mg

Nutty Apple Salad

Prep time: 25 minutes | Cook time: 0 minutes | Serves 4

- 6 firm apples, such as Gala or Golden Delicious, peeled, cored, and sliced
- 1 tablespoon freshly squeezed lemon juice
- 2 kiwis, peeled and diced
- ½ cup sliced strawberries
- ½ cup packaged shredded coleslaw mix, without dressing

- ½ cup walnut halves
- ¼ cup slivered almonds
- ¼ cup balsamic vinegar
- ¼ cup extra-virgin olive oil
- 2 tablespoons sesame seeds, plus more for garnish (optional)
- ¼ teaspoon salt
- ¼ teaspoon freshly ground black pepper

1. In a medium bowl, toss the apple slices with the lemon juice to keep them from browning. Add the kiwis, strawberries, coleslaw mix, walnuts, and almonds, and mix everything together thoroughly to combine. 2. In a small bowl, whisk the balsamic vinegar, olive oil, and sesame seeds together, seasoning with salt and pepper to taste. 3. Drizzle the dressing over the salad and toss well to evenly coat all the ingredients. 4. To serve, spoon the salad into individual bowls and sprinkle with extra sesame seeds if desired for added crunch and flavor.

Per Serving:
calories: 371 | fat: 21g | protein: 3g | carbs: 49g | fiber: 9g | sodium: 155mg

Lebanese Muhammara

Prep time: 15 minutes | Cook time: 15 minutes | Serves 6

- 2 large red bell peppers
- ¼ cup plus 2 tablespoons extra-virgin olive oil
- 1 cup walnut halves
- 1 tablespoon agave nectar or honey
- 1 teaspoon fresh lemon juice

- 1 teaspoon ground cumin
- 1 teaspoon kosher salt
- 1 teaspoon red pepper flakes
- Raw vegetables (such as cucumber, carrots, zucchini slices, or cauliflower) or toasted pita chips, for serving

1. Drizzle the bell peppers with 2 tablespoons of olive oil and place them in the air fryer basket. Set the air fryer to 400°F (204°C) and cook for 10 minutes. 2. After 10 minutes, add the walnuts to the air fryer basket, arranging them around the peppers. Continue air frying at 400°F (204°C) for an additional 5 minutes. 3. Once done, remove the peppers and place them in a resealable plastic bag to steam, letting them rest for 5 to 10 minutes. Transfer the walnuts to a plate and allow them to cool. 4. Once the peppers have softened, place them along with the cooled walnuts, agave, lemon juice, cumin, salt, and ½ teaspoon of red pepper flakes into a food processor. Purée the mixture until smooth and well combined. 5. Spoon the dip into a serving bowl, making a small indentation in the center. Pour the remaining ¼ cup of olive oil into the indentation and garnish the dip with the remaining ½ teaspoon of red pepper flakes. 6. Serve the dip with fresh vegetables or toasted pita chips for dipping.

Per Serving:
calories: 219 | fat: 20g | protein: 3g | carbs: 9g | fiber: 2g | sodium: 391mg

Mediterranean Mixed-Vegetable Caponata

Prep time: 15 minutes | Cook time: 40 minutes | Serves 8

- 1 eggplant, chopped
- 1 zucchini, chopped
- 1 red bell pepper, seeded and chopped
- 1 small red onion, chopped
- 2 tablespoons extra-virgin olive oil, divided
- 1 cup canned tomato sauce
- 3 tablespoons red wine vinegar
- 1 tablespoon honey
- ¼ teaspoon red-pepper flakes
- ¼ teaspoon kosher salt
- ½ cup pitted, chopped green olives
- 2 tablespoons drained capers
- 2 tablespoons raisins
- 2 tablespoons chopped fresh flat-leaf parsley

1. Preheat the oven to 400°F(205ºC). 2. On a large rimmed baking sheet, toss the eggplant, zucchini, bell pepper, and onion with 1 tablespoon of the oil. Roast until the vegetables are tender, about 30 minutes. 3. In a medium saucepan over medium heat, warm the remaining 1 tablespoon oil. Add the tomato sauce, vinegar, honey, pepper flakes, and salt and stir to combine. Add the roasted vegetables, olives, capers, raisins, and parsley and cook until bubbly and thickened, 10 minutes. 4. Remove from the heat and cool to room temperature. Serve immediately or store in an airtight container in the refrigerator for up to 1 week.

Per Serving:
calories: 100 | fat: 5g | protein: 2g | carbs: 13g | fiber: 4g | sodium: 464mg

Vegetable Pot Stickers

Prep time: 12 minutes | Cook time: 11 to 18 minutes | Makes 12 pot stickers

- 1 cup shredded red cabbage
- ¼ cup chopped button mushrooms
- ¼ cup grated carrot
- 2 tablespoons minced onion
- 2 garlic cloves, minced
- 2 teaspoons grated fresh ginger
- 12 gyoza/pot sticker wrappers
- 2½ teaspoons olive oil, divided

1. In a baking pan, combine the red cabbage, mushrooms, carrot, onion, garlic, and ginger. Add 1 tablespoon of water to help steam the vegetables. Place the pan in the air fryer and cook at 370ºF (188ºC) for 3 to 6 minutes, until the vegetables are crisp-tender. Once done, drain any excess liquid and set the vegetables aside to cool slightly. 2. On a clean work surface, lay out the pot sticker wrappers one at a time. Spoon about 1 tablespoon of the vegetable filling onto the center of each wrapper. Fold the wrapper in half to form a semi-circle, then lightly moisten the edges with water and press them together to seal tightly. 3. In another baking pan, heat 1¼ teaspoons of olive oil. Arrange half of the pot stickers in the pan, seam-side up, ensuring they don't overlap. Air fry for about 5 minutes, or until the bottoms turn light golden brown. Add 1 tablespoon of water to the pan, then return it to the air fryer. 4. Continue air frying for an additional 4 to 6 minutes, or until the pot stickers are heated through and the wrappers are fully cooked. Repeat the process with the remaining pot stickers, using the remaining 1¼ teaspoons of oil and another tablespoon of water.

Serve the pot stickers immediately for best results.

Per Serving:
1 pot stickers: calories: 36 | fat: 1g | protein: 1g | carbs: 6g | fiber: 0g | sodium: 49mg

Quick Garlic Mushrooms

Prep time: 10 minutes | Cook time: 10 minutes | Serves 4 to 6

- 2 pounds (907 g) cremini mushrooms, cleaned
- 3 tablespoons unsalted butter
- 2 tablespoons garlic, minced
- ½ teaspoon salt
- ½ teaspoon freshly ground black pepper

1. Slice each mushroom in half from stem to cap and place them in a bowl, ready for cooking. 2. Preheat a large sauté pan or skillet over medium heat, allowing it to warm up evenly. 3. Melt the butter in the pan and add the minced garlic, cooking for about 2 minutes while stirring occasionally to prevent burning. 4. Add the halved mushrooms and a pinch of salt to the pan, tossing them in the garlic butter to coat them thoroughly. Cook for 7 to 8 minutes, stirring every 2 minutes to ensure even cooking and browning. 5. Once done, transfer the sautéed mushrooms to a serving dish and finish by sprinkling them with freshly ground black pepper for extra flavor. Serve hot.

Per Serving:
calories: 183 | fat: 9g | protein: 9g | carbs: 10g | fiber: 3g | sodium: 334mg

White Bean Harissa Dip

Prep time: 10 minutes | Cook time: 1 hour | Makes 1½ cups

- 1 whole head of garlic
- ½ cup olive oil, divided
- 1 (15-ounce / 425-g) can cannellini beans, drained
- and rinsed
- 1 teaspoon salt
- 1 teaspoon harissa paste (or more to taste)

1. Preheat your oven to 350°F (180°C). 2. Slice about ½ inch off the top of a whole head of garlic, then lightly wrap it in aluminum foil. Drizzle 1 to 2 teaspoons of olive oil over the exposed cloves on the cut side. Place the garlic in an oven-safe dish and roast in the oven for about 1 hour, or until the cloves become soft and tender. 3. Once roasted, remove the garlic from the oven and allow it to cool. You can roast the garlic up to 2 days in advance if needed. 4. After cooling, squeeze the garlic cloves out of their skins and place them into the bowl of a food processor. Add the beans, salt, and harissa to the processor, and begin to purée the mixture, gradually drizzling in olive oil until the beans become smooth and creamy. If the dip feels too thick, add more olive oil to reach your desired consistency. 5. Taste the dip and adjust with additional salt, harissa, or olive oil, depending on your preference. 6. Store the dip in an airtight container in the refrigerator for up to one week. 7. When ready to serve, portion out ¼ cup of the dip and pair it with an assortment of fresh raw vegetables and mini pita breads for dipping.

Per Serving:
¼ cup: calories: 209 | fat: 17g | protein: 4g | carbs: 12g | fiber: 3g | sodium: 389mg

Crispy Greek Hummus Tacos

Prep time: 10 minutes | Cook time: 3 minutes | Makes 8 small tacos

- 8 small flour tortillas (4-inch diameter)
- 8 tablespoons hummus
- 4 tablespoons crumbled feta cheese
- 4 tablespoons chopped kalamata or other olives (optional)
- Olive oil for misting

1. Place 1 tablespoon of hummus or tapenade in the center of each tortilla. Top with 1 teaspoon of feta crumbles and 1 teaspoon of chopped olives, if using. 2. Using your finger or a small spoon, moisten the edges of the tortilla all around with water. 3. Fold tortilla over to make a half-moon shape. Press center gently. Then press the edges firmly to seal in the filling. 4. Mist both sides with olive oil. 5. Place in air fryer basket very close but try not to overlap. 6. Air fry at 390ºF (199ºC) for 3 minutes, just until lightly browned and crispy.

Per Serving:
1 taco: calories: 127 | fat: 4g | protein: 4g | carbs: 19g | fiber: 1g | sodium: 292mg

Crispy Tuna Almond Croquettes

Prep time: 40 minutes | Cook time: 25 minutes | Makes 36 croquettes

- 6 tablespoons extra-virgin olive oil, plus 1 to 2 cups
- 5 tablespoons almond flour, plus 1 cup, divided
- 1¼ cups heavy cream
- 1 (4 ounces / 113 g) can olive oil-packed yellowfin tuna
- 1 tablespoon chopped red onion
- 2 teaspoons minced capers
- ½ teaspoon dried dill
- ¼ teaspoon freshly ground black pepper
- 2 large eggs
- 1 cup panko breadcrumbs (or a gluten-free version)

1. In a large skillet, heat 6 tablespoons olive oil over medium-low heat. Add 5 tablespoons almond flour and cook, stirring constantly, until a smooth paste forms and the flour browns slightly, 2 to 3 minutes. 2. Increase the heat to medium-high and gradually add the heavy cream, whisking constantly until completely smooth and thickened, another 4 to 5 minutes. 3. Remove from the heat and stir in the tuna, red onion, capers, dill, and pepper. 4. Transfer the mixture to an 8-inch square baking dish that is well coated with olive oil and allow to cool to room temperature. Cover and refrigerate until chilled, at least 4 hours or up to overnight. 5. To form the croquettes, set out three bowls. In one, beat together the eggs. In another, add the remaining almond flour. In the third, add the panko. Line a baking sheet with parchment paper. 6. Using a spoon, place about a tablespoon of cold prepared dough into the flour mixture and roll to coat. Shake off excess and, using your hands, roll into an oval. 7. Dip the croquette into the beaten egg, then lightly coat in panko. Set on lined baking sheet and repeat with the remaining dough. 8. In a small saucepan, heat the remaining 1 to 2 cups of olive oil, so that the oil is about 1 inch deep, over medium-high heat. The smaller the pan, the less oil you will need, but you will need more for each batch. 9. Test if the oil is ready by throwing a pinch of panko into pot. If it sizzles, the oil is ready

for frying. If it sinks, it's not quite ready. Once the oil is heated, fry the croquettes 3 or 4 at a time, depending on the size of your pan, removing with a slotted spoon when golden brown. You will need to adjust the temperature of the oil occasionally to prevent burning. If the croquettes get dark brown very quickly, lower the temperature.

Per Serving:
2 croquettes: calories: 271 | fat: 26g | protein: 5g | carbs: 6g | fiber: 1g | sodium: 89mg

Zesty Black-Eyed Pea Salsa

Prep time: 10 minutes | Cook time: 30 minutes | Makes 5 cups

- 1 cup dried black-eyed peas
- 4 cups water
- 1 pound (454 g) cooked corn kernels
- ½ medium red onion, peeled and diced
- ½ medium green bell pepper, seeded and diced
- 2 tablespoons minced pickled jalapeño pepper
- 1 medium tomato, diced
- 2 tablespoons chopped fresh cilantro
- ¼ cup red wine vinegar
- 2 tablespoons extra-virgin olive oil
- 1 teaspoon salt
- ½ teaspoon ground black pepper
- ½ teaspoon ground cumin

1. Add black-eyed peas and water to the Instant Pot®. Close lid, set steam release to Sealing, press the Manual button, and set time to 30 minutes. 2. When the timer beeps, let pressure release naturally, about 25 minutes, and open lid. Drain peas and transfer to a large mixing bowl. Add all remaining ingredients and stir until thoroughly combined. Cover and refrigerate for 2 hours before serving.

Per Serving:
½ cup: calories: 28 | fat: 1g | protein: 1g | carbs: 4 | fiber: 1g | sodium: 51mg

Marinated Feta and Artichokes

Prep time: 10 minutes | Cook time: 0 minutes | Makes 1½ cups

- 4 ounces (113 g) traditional Greek feta, cut into ½-inch cubes
- 4 ounces (113 g) drained artichoke hearts, quartered lengthwise
- ⅓ cup extra-virgin olive oil
- Zest and juice of 1 lemon
- 2 tablespoons roughly chopped fresh rosemary
- 2 tablespoons roughly chopped fresh parsley
- ½ teaspoon black peppercorns

1. In a glass bowl or large jar, gently combine the feta and artichoke hearts. Drizzle with olive oil, lemon zest, and lemon juice, then add the rosemary, parsley, and peppercorns. Toss carefully to ensure everything is evenly coated, taking care not to break apart the feta. 2. Cover the bowl or jar and refrigerate for at least 4 hours to allow the flavors to meld, or store for up to 4 days. Remove from the refrigerator 30 minutes prior to serving for optimal flavor.

Per Serving:
calories: 108 | fat: 9g | protein: 3g | carbs: 4g | fiber: 1g | sodium: 294mg

Grilled Halloumi with Watermelon, Cherry Tomatoes, Olives, and Herb Oil

Prep time: 5 minutes | Cook time: 5 minutes | Serves 4

- ½ cup coarsely chopped fresh basil
- 3 tablespoons coarsely chopped fresh mint leaves, plus thinly sliced mint for garnish
- 1 clove garlic, coarsely chopped
- ½ cup olive oil, plus more for brushing
- ½ teaspoon salt, plus a pinch
- ½ teaspoon freshly ground black pepper, plus a pinch
- ¾ pound (340 g) cherry tomatoes
- 8 ounces (227 g) Halloumi cheese, cut crosswise into 8 slices
- 2 cups thinly sliced watermelon, rind removed
- ¼ cup sliced, pitted Kalamata olives

1. Preheat a grill or grill pan to high heat. 2. In a food processor or blender, combine the basil, chopped mint, and garlic, pulsing until finely chopped. With the machine running, slowly drizzle in the olive oil to form an herb-infused oil. Strain the oil through a fine mesh sieve, discarding the solids. Stir in ½ teaspoon of salt and ½ teaspoon of pepper to season the oil. 3. Lightly brush the grill rack with olive oil. Drizzle 2 tablespoons of the prepared herb oil over the tomatoes and cheese, and season them with a pinch of salt and pepper. Place the tomatoes on the grill, cooking for about 4 minutes, turning occasionally, until their skins blister and begin to burst. Grill the cheese for about 1 minute per side, just until grill marks appear and the cheese starts to melt slightly. 4. On a serving platter, lay out the watermelon slices, then top with the grilled cheese and tomatoes. Drizzle the remaining herb oil over everything, and garnish with olives and fresh sliced mint. Serve immediately for the best flavor and texture.

Per Serving:
calories: 535 | fat: 50g | protein: 14g | carbs: 12g | fiber: 2g | sodium: 663mg

Nutty Fig Energy Bites

Prep time: 20 minutes |Cook time: 0 minutes| Serves: 6

- ¾ cup diced dried figs (6 to 8)
- ½ cup chopped pecans
- ¼ cup rolled oats (old-fashioned or quick oats)
- 2 tablespoons ground
- flaxseed or wheat germ (flaxseed for gluten-free)
- 2 tablespoons powdered or regular peanut butter
- 2 tablespoons honey

1. In a medium bowl, mix together the figs, pecans, oats, flaxseed, and peanut butter. Drizzle with the honey, and mix everything together. A wooden spoon works well to press the figs and nuts into the honey and powdery ingredients. (If you're using regular peanut butter instead of powdered, the dough will be stickier to handle, so freeze the dough for 5 minutes before making the bites.) 2. Divide the dough evenly into four sections in the bowl. Dampen your hands with water—but don't get them too wet or the dough will stick to them. Using your hands, roll three bites out of each of the four sections of dough, making 12 total energy bites. 3. Enjoy immediately or chill in the freezer for 5 minutes to firm up the bites before serving. The bites can be stored in a sealed container in the refrigerator for up to 1 week.

Per Serving:
calories: 196 | fat: 10g | protein: 4g | carbs: 26g | fiber: 4g | sodium: 13mg

Flatbread with Ricotta and Orange-Raisin Relish

Prep time: 5 minutes | Cook time: 8 minutes | Serves 4 to 6

- ¾ cup golden raisins, roughly chopped
- 1 shallot, finely diced
- 1 tablespoon olive oil
- 1 tablespoon red wine vinegar
- 1 tablespoon honey
- 1 tablespoon chopped flat-leaf parsley
- 1 tablespoon fresh orange zest strips
- Pinch of salt
- 1 oval prebaked whole-wheat flatbread, such as naan or pocketless pita
- 8 ounces (227 g) whole-milk ricotta cheese
- ½ cup baby arugula

1. Preheat your oven to 450°F (235ºC). 2. In a small bowl, mix together the raisins, finely chopped shallot, olive oil, vinegar, honey, parsley, orange zest, and a pinch of salt. Stir well to combine and set aside. 3. Place the flatbread on a large baking sheet and toast it in the oven for about 8 minutes, or until the edges become lightly browned and crispy. 4. Spread the ricotta cheese evenly over the toasted flatbread using the back of a spoon, then scatter fresh arugula on top of the ricotta. Cut the flatbread into triangles, and add a spoonful of the raisin-shallot relish to each piece. Serve immediately for the best flavor and texture.

Per Serving:
calories: 195 | fat: 9g | protein: 6g | carbs: 25g | fiber: 1g | sodium: 135mg

Tirokafteri (Spicy Feta and Yogurt Dip)

Prep time: 10 minutes | Cook time: 0 minutes | Serves 8

- 1 teaspoon red wine vinegar
- 1 small green chili, seeded and sliced
- 2 teaspoons extra virgin
- olive oil
- 9 ounces (255 g) full-fat feta
- ¾ cup full-fat Greek yogurt

1. In a food processor, combine the vinegar, chili, and olive oil. Blend the ingredients until smooth and well combined. 2. In a small bowl, mash the feta and Greek yogurt together with a fork until a creamy paste forms. Add the blended pepper mixture to the feta-yogurt paste and stir until everything is fully incorporated. 3. Cover the mixture and transfer it to the refrigerator to chill for at least 1 hour before serving. For storage, keep it covered in the refrigerator for up to 3 days.

Per Serving:
calories: 109 | fat: 8g | protein: 6g | carbs: 4g | fiber: 0g | sodium: 311mg

Turmeric Crunch Chickpeas

Prep time: 15 minutes | Cook time: 30 minutes | Serves 4

- 2 (15-ounce / 425-g) cans organic chickpeas, drained and rinsed
- 3 tablespoons extra-virgin olive oil
- 2 teaspoons Turkish or smoked paprika
- 2 teaspoons turmeric
- ½ teaspoon dried oregano
- ½ teaspoon salt
- ¼ teaspoon ground ginger
- ⅛ teaspoon ground white pepper (optional)

1. Preheat the oven to 400°F(205°C). Line a baking sheet with parchment paper and set aside. 2. Completely dry the chickpeas. Lay the chickpeas out on a baking sheet, roll them around with paper towels, and allow them to air-dry. I usually let them dry for at least 2½ hours, but can also be left to dry overnight. 3. In a medium bowl, combine the olive oil, paprika, turmeric, oregano, salt, ginger, and white pepper (if using). 4. Add the dry chickpeas to the bowl and toss to combine. 5. Put the chickpeas on the prepared baking sheet and cook for 30 minutes, or until the chickpeas turn golden brown. At 15 minutes, move the chickpeas around on the baking sheet to avoid burning. Check every 10 minutes in case the chickpeas begin to crisp up before the full cooking time has elapsed. 6. Remove from the oven and set them aside to cool.

Per Serving:

½ cup: calories: 308 | fat: 13g | protein: 11g | carbs: 40g | fiber: 11g | sodium: 292mg

Smoky Grilled Baba Ghanoush

Prep time: 50 minutes | Cook time: 40 minutes | Serves 6

- 2 large eggplants, washed
- ¼ cup lemon juice
- 1 teaspoon garlic, minced
- 1 teaspoon salt
- ½ cup tahini paste
- 3 tablespoons extra-virgin olive oil

1. Grill the whole eggplants over a low flame using a gas stovetop or grill. Rotate the eggplant every 5 minutes to make sure that all sides are cooked evenly. Continue to do this for 40 minutes. 2. Remove the eggplants from the stove or grill and put them onto a plate or into a bowl; cover with plastic wrap. Let sit for 5 to 10 minutes. 3. Using your fingers, peel away and discard the charred skin of the eggplants. Cut off the stem. 4. Put the eggplants into a food processor fitted with a chopping blade. Add the lemon juice, garlic, salt, and tahini paste, and pulse the mixture 5 to 7 times. 5. Pour the eggplant mixture onto a serving plate. Drizzle with the olive oil. Serve chilled or at room temperature.

Per Serving:

calories: 230 | fat: 18g | protein: 5g | carbs: 16g | fiber: 7g | sodium: 416mg

Pizzas, Wraps, and Sandwiches

Chapter 11 Pizzas, Wraps, and Sandwiches

Jerk Chicken Wraps

Prep time: 30 minutes | Cook time: 15 minutes | Serves 4

- 1 pound (454 g) boneless, skinless chicken tenderloins
- 1 cup jerk marinade
- Olive oil
- 4 large low-carb tortillas
- 1 cup julienned carrots
- 1 cup peeled cucumber ribbons
- 1 cup shredded lettuce
- 1 cup mango or pineapple chunks

1. In a medium bowl, coat the chicken thoroughly with the jerk marinade, cover, and refrigerate for 1 hour to let the flavors develop. 2. Lightly spray the air fryer basket with olive oil to prevent sticking. 3. Place the marinated chicken in a single layer in the air fryer basket, ensuring the pieces do not overlap. Lightly spray the chicken with olive oil. If necessary, cook the chicken in batches. Reserve any leftover marinade for later use. 4. Air fry the chicken at 375ºF (191ºC) for 8 minutes. Flip the chicken, brush it with the reserved marinade, and continue cooking until the chicken reaches an internal temperature of at least 165ºF (74ºC), about 5 to 7 more minutes. 5. To assemble the wraps, place ¼ cup each of carrots, cucumber, lettuce, and mango onto each tortilla. Top with one-quarter of the chicken tenderloins and roll up the tortilla tightly. These wraps are delicious served warm or cold.

Per Serving:
calories: 241 | fat: 4g | protein: 28g | carbs: 23g | fiber: 4g | sodium: 85mg

Tomato Basil Melts

Prep time: 10 minutes |Cook time: 5 minutes| Serves: 4

- 2 (6- to 7-inch) whole-wheat submarine or hoagie rolls, sliced open horizontally
- 1 tablespoon extra-virgin olive oil
- 1 garlic clove, halved
- 1 large ripe tomato, cut into 8 slices
- ¼ teaspoon dried oregano
- 1 cup fresh mozzarella (about 4 ounces / 113 g), patted dry and sliced
- ¼ cup lightly packed fresh basil leaves, torn into small pieces
- ¼ teaspoon freshly ground black pepper

1. Preheat the broiler to high with the rack 4 inches under the heating element. 2. Place the sliced bread on a large, rimmed baking sheet. Place under the broiler for 1 minute, until the bread is just lightly toasted. Remove from the oven. 3. Brush each piece of the toasted bread with the oil, and rub a garlic half over each piece. 4. Place the toasted bread back on the baking sheet. Evenly distribute the tomato slices on each piece, sprinkle with the oregano, and layer the cheese on top. 5. Place the baking sheet under the broiler. Set the timer for 1½ minutes, but check after 1 minute. When the cheese is melted and the edges are just starting to get dark brown, remove the sandwiches from the oven (this can take anywhere from 1½ to 2 minutes). 6. Top each sandwich with the fresh basil and pepper.

Per Serving:
calories: 176 | fat: 9g | protein: 10g | carbs: 14g | fiber: 2g | sodium: 119mg

Moroccan Lamb Wrap with Harissa

Prep time: 10 minutes | Cook time: 10 minutes | Serves 4

- 1 clove garlic, minced
- 2 teaspoons ground cumin
- 2 teaspoons chopped fresh thyme
- ¼ cup olive oil, divided
- 1 lamb leg steak, about 12 ounces (340 g)
- 4 (8-inch) pocketless pita rounds or naan, preferably whole-wheat
- 1 medium eggplant, sliced
- ½-inch thick
- 1 medium zucchini, sliced lengthwise into 4 slices
- 1 bell pepper (any color), roasted and skinned
- 6 to 8 Kalamata olives, sliced
- Juice of 1 lemon
- 2 to 4 tablespoons harissa
- 2 cups arugula

1. In a large bowl, mix together the garlic, cumin, thyme, and 1 tablespoon of olive oil. Add the lamb to the bowl, making sure it's fully coated with the marinade. Cover the bowl and refrigerate for at least 1 hour to let the flavors develop. 2. Preheat your oven to 400°F (205ºC). 3. Heat a grill or grill pan over high heat. Take the lamb out of the marinade and grill for about 4 minutes on each side, or until it reaches medium-rare doneness. Transfer the lamb to a plate and let it rest for about 10 minutes before slicing thinly against the grain. 4. While the lamb rests, wrap the flatbread rounds in aluminum foil and heat them in the oven for about 10 minutes. 5. Meanwhile, brush the eggplant and zucchini slices with the remaining olive oil and grill them until tender, about 3 minutes per side. Dice the grilled vegetables along with the bell pepper, then toss them in a large bowl with the olives and lemon juice. 6. Spread a generous amount of harissa onto each warm flatbread. Top the flatbreads evenly with the roasted vegetables, a few slices of lamb, and a handful of fresh arugula. 7. Roll up each flatbread to form wraps, slice them in half crosswise, and serve immediately while warm.

Per Serving:
calories: 553 | fat: 24g | protein: 33g | carbs: 53g | fiber: 11g | sodium: 531mg

Greek Pita Salad Wraps

Prep time: 15 minutes | Cook time: 0 minutes | Serves 4

- 1 cup chopped romaine lettuce
- 1 tomato, chopped and seeded
- ½ cup baby spinach leaves
- ½ small red onion, thinly sliced
- ½ small cucumber, chopped and deseeded

- 2 tablespoons olive oil
- 1 tablespoon crumbled feta cheese
- ½ tablespoon red wine vinegar
- 1 teaspoon Dijon mustard
- Sea salt and freshly ground pepper, to taste
- 1 whole-wheat pita

1. Combine everything except the sea salt, freshly ground pepper, and pita bread in a medium bowl. 2. Toss until the salad is well combined. 3. Season with sea salt and freshly ground pepper to taste. Fill the pita with the salad mixture, serve, and enjoy!

Per Serving:
calories: 123 | fat: 8g | protein: 3g | carbs: 12g | fiber: 2g | sodium: 125mg

Pesto Chicken Mini Pizzas

Prep time: 5 minutes | Cook time: 10 minutes | Serves 4

- 2 cups shredded cooked chicken
- ¾ cup pesto

- 4 English muffins, split
- 2 cups shredded Mozzarella cheese

1. In a medium bowl, thoroughly coat the chicken with the pesto, ensuring all the pieces are well covered. Take each English muffin half and place one-eighth of the pesto-coated chicken on top, spreading it evenly. Follow by sprinkling ¼ cup of Mozzarella cheese over each chicken-topped muffin. 2. Arrange four of the mini pizzas in the air fryer at a time and cook at 350ºF (177ºC) for 5 minutes, or until the cheese is melted and bubbly. Repeat the process with the remaining four pizzas for a perfectly crisp and cheesy finish. Serve hot and enjoy immediately.

Per Serving:
calories: 617 | fat: 36g | protein: 45g | carbs: 29g | fiber: 3g | sodium: 544mg

Mediterranean Tuna Delight Sandwiches

Prep time: 10 minutes | Cook time: 5 minutes | Serves 2

- 1 can white tuna, packed in water or olive oil, drained
- 1 roasted red pepper, diced
- ½ small red onion, diced
- 10 low-salt olives, pitted and finely chopped
- ¼ cup plain Greek yogurt

- 1 tablespoon flat-leaf parsley, chopped
- Juice of 1 lemon
- Sea salt and freshly ground pepper, to taste
- 4 whole-grain pieces of bread

1. In a small bowl, combine all of the ingredients except the bread, and mix well. 2. Season with sea salt and freshly ground pepper to taste. Toast the bread or warm in a pan. 3. Make the sandwich and serve immediately.

Per Serving:
calories: 307 | fat: 7g | protein: 30g | carbs: 31g | fiber: 5g | sodium: 564mg

Avocado & Asparagus Rice Wraps

Prep time: 10 minutes | Cook time: 10 minutes | Serves 6

- 12 spears asparagus
- 1 ripe avocado, mashed slightly
- Juice of 1 lime
- 2 cloves garlic, minced
- 2 cups brown rice, cooked and chilled
- 3 tablespoons Greek yogurt

- Sea salt and freshly ground pepper, to taste
- 3 (8-inch) whole-grain tortillas
- ½ cup cilantro, diced
- 2 tablespoons red onion, diced

1. Steam asparagus in microwave or stove top steamer until tender. Mash the avocado, lime juice, and garlic in a medium mixing bowl. In a separate bowl, mix the rice and yogurt. 2. Season both mixtures with sea salt and freshly ground pepper to taste. Heat the tortillas in a dry nonstick skillet. 3. Spread each tortilla with the avocado mixture, and top with the rice, cilantro, and onion, followed by the asparagus. 4. Fold up both sides of the tortilla, and roll tightly to close. Cut in half diagonally before serving.

Per Serving:
calories: 361 | fat: 9g | protein: 9g | carbs: 63g | fiber: 7g | sodium: 117mg

Authentic Margherita Pizza

Prep time: 10 minutes | Cook time: 10 minutes | Serves 4

- All-purpose flour, for dusting
- 1 pound (454 g) premade pizza dough
- 1 (15-ounce / 425-g) can crushed San Marzano tomatoes, with their juices
- 2 garlic cloves

- 1 teaspoon Italian seasoning
- Pinch sea salt, plus more as needed
- 1½ teaspoons olive oil, for drizzling
- 10 slices mozzarella cheese
- 12 to 15 fresh basil leaves

1. Preheat the oven to 475ºF (245ºC). 2. On a floured surface, roll out the dough to a 12-inch round and place it on a lightly floured pizza pan or baking sheet. 3. In a food processor, combine the tomatoes with their juices, garlic, Italian seasoning, and salt and process until smooth. Taste and adjust the seasoning. 4. Drizzle the olive oil over the pizza dough, then spoon the pizza sauce over the dough and spread it out evenly with the back of the spoon, leaving a 1-inch border. Evenly distribute the mozzarella over the pizza. 5. Bake until the crust is cooked through and golden, 8 to 10 minutes. Remove from the oven and let sit for 1 to 2 minutes. Top with the basil right before serving.

Per Serving:
calories: 570 | fat: 21g | protein: 28g | carbs: 66g | fiber: 4g | sodium: 570mg

Grilled Eggplant and Feta Sandwiches

Prep time: 10 minutes | Cook time: 8 minutes | Serves 2

- 1 medium eggplant, sliced into ½-inch-thick slices
- 2 tablespoons olive oil
- Sea salt and freshly ground pepper, to taste
- 5 to 6 tablespoons hummus
- 4 slices whole-wheat bread, toasted
- 1 cup baby spinach leaves
- 2 ounces (57 g) feta cheese, softened

1. Start by preheating your gas or charcoal grill to medium-high heat, ensuring it's hot enough for grilling. 2. Generously salt both sides of the sliced eggplant and allow it to rest for 20 minutes. This helps draw out any bitterness from the eggplant. 3. After 20 minutes, rinse the eggplant slices under cold water and pat them dry with a paper towel to remove excess moisture. 4. Brush each slice with olive oil and season both sides with a pinch of sea salt and freshly ground black pepper for added flavor. 5. Place the eggplant on the grill, cooking until it's lightly charred and has grill marks on both sides while remaining slightly firm in the center. Grill for about 3–4 minutes per side. 6. To assemble the sandwich, spread a layer of hummus onto one slice of bread, then top with fresh spinach leaves, crumbled feta, and the grilled eggplant slices. Place the other slice of bread on top and serve the sandwich warm for the best taste.

Per Serving:
calories: 516 | fat: 27g | protein: 14g | carbs: 59g | fiber: 14g | sodium: 597mg

Moroccan Lamb Flatbread with Pine Nuts, Mint, and Ras Al Hanout

Prep time: 10 minutes | Cook time: 20 minutes | Serves 4

- 1⅓ cups plain Greek yogurt
- Juice of 1½ lemons, divided
- 1¼ teaspoons salt, divided
- 1 pound (454 g) ground lamb
- 1 medium red onion, diced
- 1 clove garlic, minced
- 1 tablespoon ras al hanout
- ¼ cup chopped fresh mint
- leaves
- Freshly ground black pepper
- 4 Middle Eastern-style flatbread rounds
- 2 tablespoons toasted pine nuts
- 16 cherry tomatoes, halved
- 2 tablespoons chopped cilantro

1. Preheat your oven to 450°F (235°C). 2. In a small bowl, combine the yogurt, juice of ½ lemon, and ¼ teaspoon of salt. Stir well and set aside. 3. Heat a large skillet over medium-high heat. Add the lamb and cook, stirring frequently, until it browns, about 5 minutes. Drain off any excess fat, then add the onion and garlic to the pan, cooking and stirring until softened, about 3 minutes more. Mix in the ras al hanout, mint, the remaining teaspoon of salt, and a pinch of pepper, stirring to combine. 4. Place the flatbread rounds on a baking sheet (use two if necessary) and evenly spread the lamb mixture over each one. Top with pine nuts and tomatoes, distributing them equally. Bake in the preheated oven for about 10 minutes, or until the flatbread is golden brown and the tomatoes have softened. 5. Once out of the oven, scatter fresh cilantro over

the flatbreads and squeeze the remaining lemon juice on top. Cut into wedges and serve with a dollop of the prepared yogurt sauce.

Per Serving:
calories: 463 | fat: 22g | protein: 34g | carbs: 34g | fiber: 3g | sodium: 859mg

Herbed Focaccia Panini with Burrata and Anchovies

Prep time: 5 minutes | Cook time: 8 minutes | Serves 4

- 8 ounces (227 g) burrata cheese, chilled and sliced
- 1 pound (454 g) whole-wheat herbed focaccia, cut crosswise into 4 rectangles and split horizontally
- 1 can anchovy fillets packed in oil, drained
- 8 slices tomato, sliced
- 2 cups arugula
- 1 tablespoon olive oil

1. Divide the cheese evenly among the bottom halves of the focaccia rectangles. Top each with 3 or 4 anchovy fillets, 2 slices of tomato, and ½ cup arugula. Place the top halves of the focaccia on top of the sandwiches. 2. To make the panini, heat a skillet or grill pan over high heat and brush with the olive oil. 3. Place the sandwiches in the hot pan and place another heavy pan, such as a cast-iron skillet, on top to weigh them down. Cook for about 3 to 4 minutes, until crisp and golden on the bottom, and then flip over and repeat on the second side, cooking for an additional 3 to 4 minutes until golden and crisp. Slice each sandwich in half and serve hot.

Per Serving:
calories: 596 | fat: 30g | protein: 27g | carbs: 58g | fiber: 5g | sodium: 626mg

Wholesome Greens & Beans Pizza

Prep time: 11 minutes | Cook time: 14 to 19 minutes | Serves 4

- ¾ cup whole-wheat pastry flour
- ½ teaspoon low-sodium baking powder
- 1 tablespoon olive oil, divided
- 1 cup chopped kale
- 2 cups chopped fresh baby
- spinach
- 1 cup canned no-salt-added cannellini beans, rinsed and drained
- ½ teaspoon dried thyme
- 1 piece low-sodium string cheese, torn into pieces

1. In a small bowl, mix the pastry flour and baking powder until well combined. 2. Add ¼ cup of water and 2 teaspoons of olive oil. Mix until a dough forms. 3. On a floured surface, press or roll the dough into a 7-inch round. Set aside while you cook the greens. 4. In a baking pan, mix the kale, spinach, and remaining teaspoon of the olive oil. Air fry at 350°F (177°C) for 3 to 5 minutes, until the greens are wilted. Drain well. 5. Put the pizza dough into the air fryer basket. Top with the greens, cannellini beans, thyme, and string cheese. Air fry for 11 to 14 minutes, or until the crust is golden brown and the cheese is melted. Cut into quarters to serve.

Per Serving:
calories: 181 | fat: 6g | protein: 8g | carbs: 27g | fiber: 6g | sodium: 103mg

Turkey and Provolone Panini with Roasted Peppers and Onions

Prep time: 15 minutes | Cook time: 1 hour 5 minutes | Serves 4

For the peppers and onions
- 2 red bell pepper, seeded and quartered
- 2 red onions, peeled and quartered
- 2 tablespoons olive oil

For the panini
2 tablespoons olive oil
- 8 slices whole-wheat bread
- 8 ounces (227 g) thinly sliced provolone cheese

- ½ teaspoon salt
- ½ teaspoon freshly ground black pepper

- 8 ounces (227 g) sliced roasted turkey or chicken breast

1. Preheat your oven to 375°F (190°C). 2. To prepare the roasted peppers and onions, toss them together with olive oil, salt, and pepper on a large, rimmed baking sheet. Spread the mixture out in a single layer and roast in the oven for 45 to 60 minutes, stirring occasionally, until the vegetables are tender and beginning to brown. Once done, remove from the oven and let them cool slightly until manageable. Peel the skins off the peppers and slice them thinly, then thinly slice the onions as well. 3. Preheat a skillet or grill pan over medium-high heat. 4. To assemble the panini, brush one side of each of the 8 bread slices with olive oil. Place 4 of the bread slices, oiled side down, on your work surface. Layer each with ¼ of the cheese, ¼ of the turkey, and a portion of the roasted peppers and onions. Place the remaining 4 bread slices on top, with the oiled side facing up. 5. Transfer the sandwiches to the preheated skillet or grill pan (you may need to work in batches). Cover the pan and cook until the bottoms are golden brown and grill marks appear, about 2 minutes. Flip the sandwiches and cook, covered, for another 2 minutes or until the second side is golden and the cheese has melted. Cut each sandwich in half and serve immediately while still warm and crispy.

Per Serving:
calories: 603 | fat: 32g | protein: 41g | carbs: 37g | fiber: 6g | sodium: 792mg

Vegetable Pita Sandwiches

Prep time: 15 minutes | Cook time: 9 to 12 minutes | Serves 4

- 1 baby eggplant, peeled and chopped
- 1 red bell pepper, sliced
- ½ cup diced red onion
- ½ cup shredded carrot

- 1 teaspoon olive oil
- ⅓ cup low-fat Greek yogurt
- ½ teaspoon dried tarragon
- 2 low-sodium whole-wheat pita breads, halved crosswise

1. In a baking pan, toss together the eggplant, red bell pepper, red onion, carrot, and olive oil until the vegetables are evenly coated. Transfer the mixture to the air fryer basket and roast at 390ºF (199ºC) for 7 to 9 minutes, stirring halfway through to ensure even cooking, until the veggies are tender and slightly caramelized. If needed, drain any excess liquid. 2. In a separate small bowl, whisk together the yogurt and chopped tarragon until smooth and well blended. 3. Once the vegetables are done, gently stir in the yogurt-tarragon mixture, ensuring everything is well coated. Stuff one-fourth of this vegetable and yogurt mix into each pita pocket. 4. Place the filled pita sandwiches back into the air fryer and cook for an additional 2 to 3 minutes, just until the pita is golden and crispy. Serve immediately while warm for the best taste and texture.

Per Serving:
calories: 115 | fat: 2g | protein: 4g | carbs: 22g | fiber: 6g | sodium: 90mg

Chapter 12

Pasta

Chapter 12 Pasta

Mediterranean Chicken Pasta Bake

Prep time: 15 minutes | Cook time: 4 to 6 hours | Serves 4

- 2 pounds (907 g) boneless, skinless chicken thighs or breasts, cut into 1-inch pieces
- 8 ounces (227 g) dried rotini pasta
- 7 cups low-sodium chicken broth
- ½ red onion, diced
- 3 garlic cloves, minced
- ¼ cup whole Kalamata
- olives, pitted
- 3 Roma tomatoes, diced
- 2 tablespoons red wine vinegar
- 1 teaspoon extra-virgin olive oil
- 2 teaspoons dried oregano
- 1 teaspoon sea salt
- ½ teaspoon freshly ground black pepper
- ¼ cup crumbled feta cheese

1. In a slow cooker, combine the chicken, pasta, chicken broth, onion, garlic, olives, tomatoes, vinegar, olive oil, oregano, salt, and pepper. Stir to mix well. 2. Cover the cooker and cook for 4 to 6 hours on Low heat. 3. Garnish with the feta cheese for serving.

Per Serving:
calories: 608 | fat: 17g | protein: 59g | carbs: 55g | fiber: 8g | sodium: 775mg

Rotini with Spinach, Cherry Tomatoes, and Feta

Prep time: 5 minutes | Cook time: 30 minutes | Serves 2

- 6 ounces (170 g) uncooked rotini pasta (penne pasta will also work)
- 1 garlic clove, minced
- 3 tablespoons extra virgin olive oil, divided
- 1½ cups cherry tomatoes, halved and divided
- 9 ounces (255 g) baby leaf spinach, washed and chopped
- 1½ ounces (43 g) crumbled feta, divided
- Kosher salt, to taste
- Freshly ground black pepper, to taste

1. Cook the pasta according to the package directions, making sure to reserve ½ cup of the cooking water before draining. Once drained, set the pasta aside. 2. While the pasta is cooking, combine the minced garlic with 2 tablespoons of olive oil in a small bowl and set it aside to infuse the flavors. 3. Heat the remaining tablespoon of olive oil in a medium pan over medium heat. Add 1 cup of cherry tomatoes and cook for 2–3 minutes, gently mashing them with a fork to release their juices. 4. Add the spinach to the pan and cook, stirring occasionally, until the spinach wilts and the liquid is mostly absorbed, about 4–5 minutes. 5. Transfer the drained pasta to the pan with the spinach and tomatoes. Pour in 3 tablespoons of the reserved pasta water, then add the garlic and olive oil mixture, along with 1 ounce (28 g) of crumbled

feta. Increase the heat to high and cook everything together for 1 minute, stirring to combine. 6. Finish by topping the dish with the remaining cherry tomatoes and feta. Season with kosher salt and freshly ground black pepper to taste. The dish can be stored in the refrigerator, covered, for up to 2 days.

Per Serving:
calories: 602 | fat: 27g | protein: 19g | carbs: 74g | fiber: 7g | sodium: 307mg

Pasta Pugliese with Broccoli and Anchovy Sauce

Prep time: 15 minutes | Cook time: 25 minutes | Serves 3

- 1 pound (454 g) fresh broccoli, washed and cut into small florets
- 7 ounces (198 g) uncooked rigatoni pasta
- 2 tablespoons extra virgin olive oil, plus 1½ tablespoons for serving
- 3 garlic cloves, thinly sliced
- 2 tablespoons pine nuts
- 4 canned packed-in-oil anchovies
- ½ teaspoon kosher salt
- 3 teaspoons fresh lemon juice
- 3 ounces (85 g) grated or shaved Parmesan cheese, divided
- ½ teaspoon freshly ground black pepper

1. Place the broccoli in a large pot filled with enough water to cover the broccoli. Bring the pot to a boil and cook for 12 minutes or until the stems can be easily pierced with a fork. Use a slotted spoon to transfer the broccoli to a plate, but do not discard the cooking water. Set the broccoli aside. 2. Add the pasta to the pot with the broccoli water and cook according to package instructions. 3. About 3 minutes before the pasta is ready, place a large, deep pan over medium heat and add 2 tablespoons of the olive oil. When the olive oil is shimmering, add the garlic and sauté for 1 minute, stirring continuously, until the garlic is golden, then add the pine nuts and continue sautéing for 1 more minute. 4. Stir in the anchovies, using a wooden spoon to break them into smaller pieces, then add the broccoli. Continue cooking for 1 additional minute, stirring continuously and using the spoon to break the broccoli into smaller pieces. 5. When the pasta is ready, remove the pot from the heat and drain, reserving ¼ cup of the cooking water. 6. Add the pasta and 2 tablespoons of the cooking water to the pan, stirring until all the ingredients are well combined. Cook for 1 minute, then remove the pan from the heat. 7. Promptly divide the pasta among three plates. Top each serving with a pinch of kosher salt, 1 teaspoon of the lemon juice, 1 ounce (28 g) of the Parmesan, 1½ teaspoons of the remaining olive oil, and a pinch of fresh ground pepper. Store covered in the refrigerator for up to 3 days.

Per Serving:
calories: 610 | fat: 31g | protein: 24g | carbs: 66g | fiber: 12g | sodium: 654mg

Chilled Citrus Pearl Couscous Salad

Prep time: 15 minutes | Cook time: 10 minutes | Serves 6

- 3 tablespoons olive oil, divided
- 1 cup pearl couscous
- 1 cup water
- 1 cup orange juice
- 1 small cucumber, seeded and diced
- 1 small yellow bell pepper, seeded and diced
- 2 small Roma tomatoes, seeded and diced
- ¼ cup slivered almonds
- ¼ cup chopped fresh mint leaves
- 2 tablespoons lemon juice
- 1 teaspoon grated lemon zest
- ¼ cup crumbled feta cheese
- ¼ teaspoon fine sea salt
- 1 teaspoon smoked paprika
- 1 teaspoon garlic powder

1. Press the Sauté button and heat 1 tablespoon oil. Add couscous and cook for 2–4 minutes until couscous is slightly browned. Add water and orange juice. Press the Cancel button. 2. Close lid, set steam release to Sealing, press the Manual button, and set time to 5 minutes. When the timer beeps, let pressure release naturally for 5 minutes. Quick-release any remaining pressure until the float valve drops and open lid. Drain any liquid and set aside to cool for 20 minutes. 3. Combine remaining 2 tablespoons oil, cucumber, bell pepper, tomatoes, almonds, mint, lemon juice, lemon zest, cheese, salt, paprika, and garlic powder in a medium bowl. Add couscous and toss ingredients together. Cover and refrigerate overnight before serving.

Per Serving:

calories: 177 | fat: 11g | protein: 5g | carbs: 12g | fiber: 1g | sodium: 319mg

Tahini Soup

Prep time: 5 minutes | Cook time: 4 minutes | Serves 6

- 2 cups orzo
- 8 cups water
- 1 tablespoon olive oil
- 1 teaspoon salt
- ½ teaspoon ground black pepper
- ½ cup tahini
- ¼ cup lemon juice

1. Place the pasta, water, oil, salt, and pepper into the Instant Pot®. Secure the lid, set the steam release to Sealing, press the Manual button, and set the cooking time for 4 minutes. Once the timer beeps, perform a quick pressure release until the float valve drops, then carefully open the lid. Set the pasta aside. 2. In a small mixing bowl, whisk the tahini while gradually adding the lemon juice, ensuring it's well incorporated. Slowly whisk in about ½ cup of hot broth from the Instant Pot until the mixture becomes creamy and smooth. 3. Pour the tahini mixture into the pot, stirring it thoroughly into the pasta or soup. Serve immediately for a warm, flavorful dish.

Per Serving:

calories: 338 | fat: 13g | protein: 12g | carbs: 49g | fiber: 5g | sodium: 389mg

Slow Cooker Creamy Chicken and Tomato Pasta

Prep time: 10 minutes | Cook time: 4 to 6 hours | Serves 4

- ¼ cup water
- 2 tablespoons arrowroot flour
- 2 pounds (907 g) boneless, skinless chicken breasts or thighs
- 1 (28-ounce / 794-g) can no-salt-added diced tomatoes, plus more as needed
- 1 green or red bell pepper, seeded and diced
- 1 small red onion, diced
- 2 garlic cloves, minced
- 1 teaspoon dried oregano
- 1 teaspoon dried parsley
- 1 teaspoon sea salt
- ½ teaspoon freshly ground black pepper
- 8 ounces (227 g) dried pasta
- 1 cup low-sodium chicken broth (optional)

1. In a small bowl, whisk together the water and arrowroot flour until the flour dissolves. 2. In a slow cooker, combine the chicken, tomatoes, bell pepper, onion, garlic, oregano, parsley, salt, black pepper, and arrowroot mixture. Stir to mix well. 3. Cover the cooker and cook for 4 to 6 hours on Low heat. 4. Stir in the pasta, making sure it is completely submerged. If it is not, add an additional 1 cup of diced tomatoes or 1 cup of chicken broth. Replace the cover on the cooker and cook for 15 to 30 minutes on Low heat, or until the pasta is tender.

Per Serving:

calories: 555 | fat: 12g | protein: 52g | carbs: 61g | fiber: 11g | sodium: 623mg

Walnut Spaghetti

Prep time: 10 minutes | Cook time: 20 minutes | Serves 6

- 1 pound (454 g) whole-wheat spaghetti
- ½ cup olive oil
- 4 cloves garlic, minced
- ¾ cup walnuts, toasted and finely chopped
- 2 tablespoons low-fat ricotta
- cheese
- ½ cup freshly grated, lowfat Parmesan cheese
- ¼ cup flat-leaf parsley, chopped
- Sea salt and freshly ground pepper, to taste

1. Cook the spaghetti in boiling water according to the package instructions until al dente. Before draining, reserve 1 cup of the pasta water. Drain the pasta and set it aside. 2. In a large skillet, heat the olive oil over medium-low heat. Add the minced garlic and sauté for 1–2 minutes until fragrant, being careful not to let it burn. 3. Ladle ½ cup of the reserved pasta water into the skillet with the garlic, allowing it to simmer for 5–10 minutes to develop flavor. 4. Stir in the chopped walnuts and ricotta cheese, mixing well to create a creamy walnut sauce. 5. In a large serving bowl, toss the cooked spaghetti with the walnut-ricotta sauce until the pasta is well coated. Top the dish with grated Parmesan cheese and chopped parsley for garnish. Season with salt and pepper to taste, and serve immediately.

Per Serving:

calories: 551 | fat: 31g | protein: 16g | carbs: 60g | fiber: 7g | sodium: 141mg

Rotini with Red Wine Marinara

Prep time: 10 minutes | Cook time: 25 minutes | Serves 6

- 1 pound (454 g) rotini
- 4 cups water
- 1 tablespoon olive oil
- ½ medium yellow onion, peeled and diced
- 3 cloves garlic, peeled and minced
- 1 (15-ounce / 425-g) can

- crushed tomatoes
- ½ cup red wine
- 1 teaspoon sugar
- 2 tablespoons chopped fresh basil
- ½ teaspoon salt
- ¼ teaspoon ground black pepper

1. Place the pasta and water in the Instant Pot®. Secure the lid, set the steam release to Sealing, press the Manual button, and cook for 4 minutes. Once the timer beeps, perform a quick-release of the pressure until the float valve drops, then open the lid. Press the Cancel button, drain the pasta, and set it aside. 2. Clean the Instant Pot insert and return it to the machine. Press the Sauté button and heat the oil. Add the onion and cook for about 10 minutes, stirring occasionally, until it begins to caramelize. Stir in the garlic and cook for an additional 30 seconds until fragrant. Add the tomatoes, red wine, and sugar, and let the mixture simmer for 10 minutes to develop the flavors. Stir in the basil, season with salt and pepper, and return the cooked pasta to the pot, mixing everything together. Serve immediately for a rich, flavorful meal.

Per Serving:
calories: 320 | fat: 4g | protein: 10g | carbs: 59g | fiber: 4g | sodium: 215mg

Mediterranean Orzo Salad with Feta and Marinated Peppers

Prep time:1 hour 25 minutes | Cook time: 37 minutes | Serves 2

- 2 medium red bell peppers
- ¼ cup extra virgin olive oil
- 1 tablespoon balsamic vinegar plus 1 teaspoon for serving
- ¼ teaspoon ground cumin
- Pinch of ground cinnamon
- Pinch of ground cloves
- ¼ teaspoon fine sea salt plus

- a pinch for the orzo
- 1 cup uncooked orzo
- 3 ounces (85 g) crumbled feta
- 1 tablespoon chopped fresh basil
- ¼ teaspoon freshly ground black pepper

1. Preheat the oven at 350°F (180°C). Place the peppers on a baking pan and roast in the oven for 25 minutes or until they're soft and can be pierced with a fork. Set aside to cool for 10 minutes. 2. While the peppers are roasting, combine the olive oil, 1 tablespoon of the balsamic vinegar, cumin, cinnamon, cloves, and ¼ teaspoon of the sea salt. Stir to combine, then set aside. 3. Peel the cooled peppers, remove the seeds, and then chop into large pieces. Place the peppers in the olive oil and vinegar mixture and then toss to coat, ensuring the peppers are covered in the marinade. Cover and place in the refrigerator to marinate for 20 minutes. 4. While the peppers are marinating, prepare the orzo by bringing 3 cups of water and a pinch of salt to a boil in a large pot over high heat. When the water is boiling, add the orzo, reduce the heat to medium, and cook, stirring occasionally, for 10–12 minutes or until soft, then drain and transfer to a serving bowl. 5. Add the peppers and marinade to the orzo, mixing well, then place in the refrigerator and to cool for at least 1 hour. 6. To serve, top with the feta, basil, black pepper, and 1 teaspoon of the balsamic vinegar. Mix well, and serve promptly. Store covered in the refrigerator for up to 3 days.

Per Serving:
calories: 600 | fat: 37g | protein: 15g | carbs: 51g | fiber: 4g | sodium: 690mg

Baked Ziti

Prep time: 10 minutes | Cook time: 55 minutes | Serves 8

For the Marinara Sauce:
- 2 tablespoons olive oil
- ¼ medium onion, diced (about 3 tablespoons)
- 3 cloves garlic, chopped
- 1 (28-ounce / 794-g) can whole, peeled tomatoes,

- roughly chopped
- Sprig of fresh thyme
- ½ bunch fresh basil
- Sea salt and freshly ground pepper, to taste

For the Ziti:
- 1 pound (454 g) whole-wheat ziti
- 3½ cups marinara sauce
- 1 cup low-fat cottage cheese
- 1 cup grated, low-fat

- mozzarella cheese, divided
- ¾ cup freshly grated, low-fat Parmesan cheese, divided

Make the marinara sauce: 1. Heat the olive oil in a medium saucepan over medium-high heat until shimmering. 2. Add the onion and garlic, sautéing for about 3 minutes, stirring frequently, until they turn lightly golden. 3. Stir in the tomatoes and add the herb sprigs, bringing the mixture to a boil. Once boiling, lower the heat and let it simmer, covered, for 10 minutes to develop the flavors. After simmering, remove and discard the herb sprigs. 4. Season the sauce with sea salt and freshly ground black pepper to taste.

Make the ziti: 1. Preheat your oven to 375°F (190°C). 2. Cook the ziti according to the package instructions. Once cooked, drain the pasta and place it in a large bowl. Combine the drained pasta with 2 cups of the marinara sauce, cottage cheese, and half of the mozzarella and Parmesan cheeses, stirring to mix evenly. 3. Transfer the pasta mixture to a baking dish, spreading it out evenly. Top with the remaining marinara sauce and sprinkle the remaining mozzarella and Parmesan cheeses over the top. 4. Bake for 30–40 minutes, or until the cheese is bubbly and golden brown on top. Serve warm.

Per Serving:
calories: 389 | fat: 12g | protein: 18g | carbs: 56g | fiber: 9g | sodium: 369mg

Chapter 13

Desserts

Chapter 13 Desserts

Spiced Baked Pears with Mascarpone

Prep time: 10 minutes | Cook time: 20 minutes | Serves 2

- 2 ripe pears, peeled
- 1 tablespoon plus 2 teaspoons honey, divided
- 1 teaspoon vanilla, divided
- ¼ teaspoon ginger
- ¼ teaspoon ground coriander
- ¼ cup minced walnuts
- ¼ cup mascarpone cheese
- Pinch salt

1. Preheat your oven to 350°F (180°C) and position the rack in the center. Lightly grease a small baking dish to prevent sticking. 2. Slice the pears in half lengthwise and use a spoon to remove the core from each half. Arrange the pear halves in the baking dish with the cut side facing up. 3. In a small bowl, mix together 1 tablespoon of honey, ½ teaspoon of vanilla extract, ginger, and coriander. Drizzle this mixture evenly over the pear halves to coat them. 4. Sprinkle the walnuts generously over the pears, adding a nice crunch. 5. Bake the pears for 20 minutes, or until they are golden and tender enough to be pierced easily with a knife. 6. While the pears are baking, stir together the mascarpone cheese, the remaining 2 teaspoons of honey, ½ teaspoon of vanilla extract, and a pinch of salt in a small bowl until well combined. 7. Once the pears are done, divide the mascarpone mixture among the warm pear halves and serve immediately for a sweet, creamy treat.

Per Serving:
calories: 307 | fat: 16g | protein: 4g | carbs: 43g | fiber: 6g | sodium: 89mg

Pomegranate-Wine Poached Pears with Pomegranate Seeds

Prep time: 5 minutes | Cook time: 60 minutes | Serves 4

- 4 ripe, firm Bosc pears, peeled, left whole, and stems left intact
- 1½ cups pomegranate juice
- 1 cup sweet, white dessert
- wine, such as vin santo
- ½ cup pomegranate seeds (seeds from about ½ whole fruit)

1. Slice off a bit of the bottom of each pear to create a flat surface so that the pears can stand upright. If desired, use an apple corer to remove the cores of the fruit, working from the bottom. 2. Lay the pears in a large saucepan on their sides and pour the juice and wine over the top. Set over medium-high heat and bring to a simmer. Cover the pan, reduce the heat, and let the pears simmer, turning twice, for about 40 minutes, until the pears are tender. Transfer the pears to a shallow bowl, leaving the cooking liquid in the saucepan. 3. Turn the heat under the saucepan to high and bring the poaching liquid to a boil. Cook, stirring frequently, for about 15 to 20 minutes, until the liquid becomes thick and syrupy and is reduced to about ½ cup. 4. Spoon a bit of the syrup onto each of 4 serving plates and top each with a pear, sitting it upright. Drizzle a bit more of the sauce over the pears and garnish with the pomegranate seeds. Serve immediately.

Per Serving:
calories: 208 | fat: 0g | protein: 1g | carbs: 46g | fiber: 7g | sodium: 7mg

Slow-Cooked Fruit Medley

Prep time: 10 minutes | Cook time: 3 to 5 hours | Serves 4 to 6

- Nonstick cooking spray
- 1 pound (454 g) fresh or frozen fruit of your choice, stemmed and chopped as needed
- ⅓ cup almond milk or low-sugar fruit juice of your choice
- ½ cup honey

1. Generously coat the inside of your slow cooker with cooking spray, or alternatively, line the bottom and sides with parchment paper or aluminum foil to prevent sticking. 2. Add the fruit and milk to the slow cooker, gently stirring to ensure the fruit is evenly distributed. 3. Drizzle honey over the top of the fruit mixture to add sweetness. 4. Cover the slow cooker and cook on Low heat for 3 to 5 hours, allowing the flavors to blend and the fruit to soften.

Per Serving:
calories: 192 | fat: 0g | protein: 1g | carbs: 50g | fiber: 3g | sodium: 27mg

Decadent Greek Yogurt Chocolate Mousse with Fresh Berries

Prep time: 15 minutes | Cook time: 0 minutes | Serves 4

- 2 cups plain Greek yogurt
- ¼ cup heavy cream
- ¼ cup pure maple syrup
- 3 tablespoons unsweetened cocoa powder
- 2 teaspoons vanilla extract
- ¼ teaspoon kosher salt
- 1 cup fresh mixed berries
- ¼ cup chocolate chips

1. Place the yogurt, cream, maple syrup, cocoa powder, vanilla, and salt in the bowl of a stand mixer or use a large bowl with an electric hand mixer. Mix at medium-high speed until fluffy, about 5 minutes. 2. Spoon evenly among 4 bowls and put in the refrigerator to set for at least 15 minutes. 3. Serve each bowl with ¼ cup mixed berries and 1 tablespoon chocolate chips.

Per Serving:
calories: 300 | fat: 11g | protein: 16g | carbs: 35g | fiber: 3g | sodium: 60mg

Maple Cornmeal Steamed Bread

Prep time: 5 minutes | Cook time: 1 hour | Serves 8

- ½ cup all-purpose flour
- ½ cup stone-ground cornmeal
- ½ cup whole-wheat flour
- ½ teaspoon baking powder
- ¼ teaspoon salt
- ¼ teaspoon baking soda
- ½ cup maple syrup
- ½ cup buttermilk
- 1 large egg
- 1 cup water

1. Grease the inside of a 6-cup heatproof pudding mold or baking pan. 2. Add flour, cornmeal, whole-wheat flour, baking powder, salt, and baking soda to a medium mixing bowl. Stir to combine. Add maple syrup, buttermilk, and egg to another mixing bowl or measuring cup. Whisk to mix and then pour into the flour mixture. Mix until a thick batter is formed. 3. Pour enough batter into prepared baking pan to fill it three-quarters full. 4. Butter one side of a piece of heavy-duty aluminum foil large enough to cover the top of the baking dish. Place the foil butter side down over the pan and crimp the edges to seal. 5. Add water to the Instant Pot® and place the rack inside. Fold a long piece of aluminum foil in half lengthwise. Lay foil over rack to form a sling. Place pan on rack so it rests on the sling. 6. Close lid, set steam release to Sealing, press the Manual button, set time to 1 hour, and press the Adjust button and set pressure to Low. When the timer beeps, let pressure release naturally, about 25 minutes. 7. Open lid, lift pan from Instant Pot® using the sling, and place on a cooling rack. Remove foil. Test bread with a toothpick. If the toothpick comes out wet, place the foil over the pan and return it to the Instant Pot® to cook for 10 additional minutes. If the bread is done, use a knife to loosen it and invert it onto the cooling rack. Serve warm.

Per Serving:
calories: 175 | fat: 1g | protein: 4g | carbs: 37g | fiber: 2g | sodium: 102mg

Lightened-Up Baklava Rolls

Prep time: 2 minutes | Cook time: 1 hour 15 minutes | Serves 12

- 4 ounces (113 g) shelled walnuts
- 1¼ teaspoons ground cinnamon
- 1½ teaspoons granulated sugar

Syrup:
- ¼ cup water
- ½ cup granulated sugar
- 5 teaspoons unseasoned breadcrumbs
- 1 teaspoon extra virgin olive oil plus 2 tablespoons for brushing
- 6 phyllo sheets, defrosted
- 1½ tablespoons fresh lemon juice

1. Preheat your oven to 350°F (180°C). 2. To make the syrup, combine the water and sugar in a small pan over medium heat. Bring the mixture to a boil and cook for 2 minutes, then remove from heat. Stir in the lemon juice and set the syrup aside to cool completely. 3. In a food processor, blend together the walnuts, cinnamon, sugar, breadcrumbs, and 1 teaspoon of olive oil. Pulse until the mixture has a fine, grainy texture but is not completely smooth. 4. Lay one sheet of phyllo dough on a clean work surface and brush it with olive oil. Layer a second sheet on top, brush it with olive oil, and repeat with a third sheet. Once the three sheets are stacked and oiled, cut them in half crosswise, then cut each half into 3 equal pieces, making 6 pieces total. 5. Sprinkle 1 tablespoon of the walnut mixture onto each phyllo piece. Roll each piece into a log, folding in the sides as you go to fully enclose the filling (like rolling a burrito). The rolls should be about 3½ inches long. Arrange the rolls snugly in a large baking pan. Repeat the process with the remaining phyllo sheets to create a total of 12 rolls. 6. Lightly brush the tops of the rolls with the remaining olive oil and bake in the oven for 30 minutes, or until they turn golden brown. Remove from the oven and immediately drizzle the cooled syrup over the hot rolls. 7. Let the rolls rest for 20 minutes, then flip them over and let sit for another 20 minutes to absorb the syrup evenly. Flip them back over one final time, and sprinkle any remaining walnut mixture over the top before serving. For storage, leave the rolls uncovered at room temperature for up to 2 days to maintain crispiness, then cover with plastic wrap and store at room temperature for up to 10 days.

Per Serving:
calories: 148 | fat: 9g | protein: 2g | carbs: 16g | fiber: 1g | sodium: 53mg

Honey Ricotta with Espresso and Chocolate Chips

Prep time: 5 minutes | Cook time: 0 minutes | Serves 2

- 8 ounces (227 g) ricotta cheese
- 2 tablespoons honey
- 2 tablespoons espresso,
- chilled or room temperature
- 1 teaspoon dark chocolate chips or chocolate shavings

1. In a medium bowl, beat together the ricotta cheese and honey until the mixture becomes light and smooth, about 4 to 5 minutes. 2. Divide the ricotta-honey mixture evenly between two dessert bowls. Drizzle 1 tablespoon of espresso over each serving and finish by sprinkling with chocolate chips or chocolate shavings for a delicious touch. Serve immediately.

Per Serving:
calories: 235 | fat: 10g | protein: 13g | carbs: 25g | fiber: 0g | sodium: 115mg

Honeyed Greek Yogurt with Pomegranate Seeds

Prep time: 5 minutes | Cook time: 0 minutes | Serves 4

- 4 cups plain full-fat Greek yogurt
- ½ cup pomegranate seeds
- ¼ cup honey
- Sugar, for topping (optional)

1. Evenly divide the yogurt among four bowls. Evenly divide the pomegranate seeds among the bowls and drizzle each with the honey. 2. Sprinkle each bowl with a pinch of sugar, if desired, and serve.

Per Serving:
calories: 232 | fat: 8g | protein: 9g | carbs: 33g | fiber: 1g | sodium: 114mg

Golden Crunch Sesame Cookies

Prep time: 10 minutes | Cook time: 15 minutes | Yield 14 to 16

- 1 cup sesame seeds, hulled
- 1 cup sugar
- 8 tablespoons (1 stick)
- salted butter, softened
- 2 large eggs
- 1¼ cups flour

1. Preheat the oven to 350°F(180°C). Toast the sesame seeds on a baking sheet for 3 minutes. Set aside and let cool. 2. Using a mixer, cream together the sugar and butter. 3. Add the eggs one at a time until well-blended. 4. Add the flour and toasted sesame seeds and mix until well-blended. 5. Drop spoonfuls of cookie dough onto a baking sheet and form them into round balls, about 1-inch in diameter, similar to a walnut. 6. Put in the oven and bake for 5 to 7 minutes or until golden brown. 7. Let the cookies cool and enjoy.

Per Serving:
calories: 218 | fat: 12g | protein: 4g | carbs: 25g | fiber: 2g | sodium: 58mg

Minty Watermelon Salad

Prep time: 10 minutes | Cook time: 0 minutes | Serves 6 to 8

- 1 medium watermelon
- 1 cup fresh blueberries
- 2 tablespoons fresh mint
- leaves
- 2 tablespoons lemon juice
- ⅓ cup honey

1. Cut the watermelon into 1-inch cubes and place them in a large bowl. 2. Evenly scatter the blueberries over the watermelon cubes, ensuring they're well distributed. 3. Finely chop the fresh mint leaves and transfer them to a small bowl. 4. Whisk together the lemon juice and honey with the chopped mint to create a refreshing dressing. 5. Drizzle the mint dressing over the watermelon and blueberries, tossing gently to coat the fruit. Serve chilled for a refreshing treat.

Per Serving:
calories: 238 | fat: 1g | protein: 4g | carbs: 61g | fiber: 3g | sodium: 11mg

Air-Fried S' mores Delight

Prep time: 5 minutes | Cook time: 30 seconds | Makes 8 s'mores

- Oil, for spraying
- 8 graham cracker squares
- 2 (1½-ounce / 43-g)
- chocolate bars
- 4 large marshmallows

1. Line the air fryer basket with parchment and spray lightly with oil. 2. Place 4 graham cracker squares in the prepared basket. 3. Break the chocolate bars in half and place 1 piece on top of each graham cracker. Top with 1 marshmallow. 4. Air fry at 370°F (188°C) for 30 seconds, or until the marshmallows are puffed and golden brown and slightly melted. 5. Top with the remaining graham cracker squares and serve.

Per Serving:
calories: 154 | fat: 7g | protein: 2g | carbs: 22g | fiber: 2g | sodium: 75mg

Blueberry Pomegranate Granita

Prep time: 5 minutes | Cook time: 10 minutes | Serves 2

- 1 cup frozen wild blueberries
- 1 cup pomegranate or
- pomegranate blueberry juice
- ¼ cup sugar
- ¼ cup water

1. In a saucepan, combine the frozen blueberries and pomegranate juice, bringing the mixture to a boil over medium heat. Once boiling, reduce the heat and let it simmer for about 5 minutes, or until the blueberries begin to break down and release their juices. 2. While the berries are simmering, mix the sugar and water in a small microwave-safe bowl. Microwave for 60 seconds, or until the mixture reaches a rolling boil. Stir the sugar syrup to ensure all the sugar has dissolved, and set it aside. 3. Transfer the cooked blueberry mixture to a blender and add the sugar syrup. Blend on high for about 1 minute, or until the fruit is fully puréed and smooth. 4. Pour the puréed mixture into an 8-by-8-inch baking pan or a similarly sized dish. The liquid should be about ½ inch deep in the pan. Allow the mixture to cool for 30 minutes at room temperature, then place it in the freezer. 5. For the next 2 hours, every 30 minutes, use a fork to scrape the mixture, breaking up the ice crystals to prevent it from freezing solid. This will create the granita's signature flaky texture. 6. Serve the granita after 2 hours, or transfer it to a covered container and store in the freezer until ready to serve.

Per Serving:
calories: 214 | fat: 0g | protein: 1g | carbs: 54g | fiber: 2g | sodium: 15mg

Cranberry-Orange Cheesecake-Stuffed Pears

Prep time: 10 minutes | Cook time: 30 minutes | Serves 5

- 5 firm pears
- 1 cup unsweetened cranberry juice
- 1 cup freshly squeezed orange juice
- 1 tablespoon pure vanilla extract
- ½ teaspoon ground cinnamon
- ½ cup low-fat cream cheese, softened
- ¼ teaspoon ground ginger
- ¼ teaspoon almond extract
- ¼ cup dried, unsweetened cranberries
- ¼ cup sliced almonds, toasted

1. Peel the pears and slice off the bottoms so they sit upright. Remove the inside cores, and put the pears in a wide saucepan. 2. Add the cranberry and orange juice, as well as the vanilla and cinnamon extract. 3. Bring to a boil, and reduce to a simmer. 4. Cover and simmer on low heat for 25–30 minutes, until pears are soft but not falling apart. 5. Beat the cream cheese with the ginger and almond extract. 6. Stir the cranberries and almonds into the cream cheese mixture. 7. Once the pears have cooled, spoon the cream cheese into them. 8. Boil the remaining juices down to a syrup, and drizzle over the top of the filled pears.

Per Serving:
calories: 187 | fat: 6g | protein: 4g | carbs: 29g | fiber: 6g | sodium: 88mg

Creamy Blueberry Panna Cotta

Prep time: 5 minutes | Cook time: 0 minutes | Serves 6

- 1 tablespoon gelatin powder
- 2 tablespoons water
- 2 cups goat's cream, coconut cream, or heavy whipping cream
- 2 cups wild blueberries, fresh or frozen, divided
- ½ teaspoon vanilla powder or 1½ teaspoons unsweetened vanilla extract
- Optional: low-carb sweetener, to taste

1. In a bowl, sprinkle the gelatin powder over the cold water. Set aside to let it bloom. 2. Place the goat's cream, half of the blueberries, and the vanilla in a blender and process until smooth and creamy. Alternatively, use an immersion blender. 3. Pour the blueberry cream into a saucepan. Gently heat; do not boil. Scrape the gelatin into the hot cream mixture together with the sweetener, if using. Mix well until all the gelatin has dissolved. 4. Divide among 6 (4-ounce / 113-g) jars or serving glasses and fill them about two-thirds full, leaving enough space for the remaining blueberries. Place in the fridge for 3 to 4 hours, or until set. 5. When the panna cotta has set, evenly distribute the remaining blueberries among the jars. Serve immediately or store in the fridge for up to 4 days.

Per Serving:
calories: 172 | fat: 15g | protein: 2g | carbs: 8g | fiber: 2g | sodium: 19mg

Pumpkin-Ricotta Cheesecake

Prep time: 25 minutes | Cook time: 45 minutes | Serves 10 to 12

- 1 cup almond flour
- ½ cup butter, melted
- 1 (14½-ounce / 411-g) can pumpkin purée
- 8 ounces (227 g) cream cheese, at room temperature
- ½ cup whole-milk ricotta cheese
- ½ to ¾ cup sugar-free sweetener
- 4 large eggs
- 2 teaspoons vanilla extract
- 2 teaspoons pumpkin pie spice
- Whipped cream, for garnish (optional)

1. Preheat your oven to 350°F (180°C) and line the bottom of a 9-inch springform pan with parchment paper for easy removal. 2. In a small bowl, mix the almond flour and melted butter with a fork until fully combined. Press the mixture evenly into the bottom of the prepared pan using your fingers to create a firm crust. 3. In a large mixing bowl, beat together the pumpkin purée, cream cheese, ricotta, and sweetener with an electric mixer set to medium speed until smooth and well blended. 4. Add the eggs one at a time, beating well after each addition. Stir in the vanilla extract and pumpkin pie spice, mixing just until everything is combined without overbeating. 5. Pour the pumpkin mixture over the almond flour crust, smoothing the top. Bake in the preheated oven for 40 to 45 minutes, or until the filling is set and slightly firm to the touch. 6. Let the cheesecake cool to room temperature, then refrigerate for at least 6 hours, or until fully chilled and set. 7. Serve the cheesecake chilled, and if desired, top each slice with a dollop of whipped cream for extra indulgence.

Per Serving:
calories: 230 | fat: 21g | protein: 6g | carbs: 5g | fiber: 1g | sodium: 103mg

Olive Oil Greek Yogurt Brownies

Prep time: 5 minutes | Cook time: 25 minutes | Serves 9

- ¼ cup extra virgin olive oil
- ¾ cup granulated sugar
- 1 teaspoon pure vanilla extract
- 2 eggs
- ¼ cup 2% Greek yogurt
- ½ cup all-purpose flour
- ⅓ cup unsweetened cocoa powder
- ¼ teaspoon salt
- ¼ teaspoon baking powder
- ⅓ cup chopped walnuts

1. Preheat your oven to 350°F (180°C) and line a 9-inch square baking pan with wax paper for easy removal. 2. In a small bowl, mix together the olive oil and sugar until fully combined. Stir in the vanilla extract and mix until smooth. 3. In another small bowl, beat the eggs, then add them to the olive oil mixture, mixing well. Stir in the yogurt until well incorporated. 4. In a medium bowl, whisk together the flour, cocoa powder, salt, and baking powder until evenly combined. Gradually add the olive oil mixture to the dry ingredients, stirring until smooth. Fold in the walnuts for added texture. 5. Pour the brownie batter into the prepared pan, smoothing the top with a spatula to create an even layer. Transfer the pan to the oven and bake for 25 minutes, or until the brownies are set and slightly firm. 6. Once baked, allow the brownies to cool completely. Lift them out of the pan using the wax paper, remove the paper, and cut into 9 squares. Store the brownies in an airtight container at room temperature for up to 2 days.

Per Serving:
calories: 198 | fat: 10g | protein: 4g | carbs: 25g | fiber: 2g | sodium: 85mg

Chocolate Lava Cakes

Prep time: 5 minutes | Cook time: 15 minutes | Serves 2

- 2 large eggs, whisked
- ¼ cup blanched finely
- 2 ounces (57 g) low-carb chocolate chips, melted
- ground almond flour
- ½ teaspoon vanilla extract

1. In a medium bowl, whisk together the eggs, flour, and vanilla until smooth. Gently fold in the melted chocolate, ensuring everything is fully combined into a rich batter. 2. Grease two ramekins with cooking spray and pour the batter evenly into each. Place the ramekins into the air fryer basket. Set the air fryer to 320ºF (160ºC) and bake for about 15 minutes, or until the cakes are set at the edges and firm in the center. 3. Let the cakes cool for 5 minutes before serving to allow them to firm up slightly. Enjoy warm.

Per Serving:
calories: 313 | fat: 23g | protein: 11g | carbs: 16g | fiber: 5g | sodium: 77mg

Grilled Stone Fruit with Honey Whipped Ricotta

Prep time: 10 minutes |Cook time: 10 minutes| Serves: 4

- Nonstick cooking spray
- 4 peaches or nectarines (or 8 apricots or plums), halved and pitted
- 2 teaspoons extra-virgin olive oil
- ¾ cup whole-milk ricotta cheese
- 1 tablespoon honey
- ¼ teaspoon freshly grated nutmeg
- 4 sprigs mint, for garnish (optional)

1. Spray the cold grill or a grill pan with nonstick cooking spray. Heat the grill or grill pan to medium heat. 2. Place a large, empty bowl in the refrigerator to chill. 3. Brush the fruit all over with the oil. Place the fruit cut-side down on the grill or pan and cook for 3 to 5 minutes, or until grill marks appear. (If you're using a grill pan, cook in two batches.) Using tongs, turn the fruit over. Cover the grill (or the grill pan with aluminum foil) and cook for 4 to 6 minutes, until the fruit is easily pierced with a sharp knife. Set aside to cool. 4. Remove the bowl from the refrigerator and add the ricotta. Using an electric beater, beat the ricotta on high for 2 minutes. Add the honey and nutmeg and beat for 1 more minute. Divide the warm (or room temperature) fruit among 4 serving bowls, top with the ricotta mixture, and a sprig of mint (if using) and serve.

Per Serving:

calories: 180 | fat: 9g | protein: 7g | carbs: 21g | fiber: 3g | sodium: 39mg

Chocolate Almond Butter Cups

Prep time: 5 minutes | Cook time: 0 minutes | Serves 8

- ½ cup crunchy almond butter (no sugar added)
- ½ cup light fruity extra-virgin olive oil
- ¼ cup ground flaxseed
- 2 tablespoons unsweetened cocoa powder
- 1 teaspoon vanilla extract
- 1 teaspoon ground cinnamon (optional)
- 1 to 2 teaspoons sugar-free sweetener of choice (optional)

1. In a mixing bowl, combine the almond butter, olive oil, flaxseed, cocoa powder, vanilla, cinnamon (if using), and sweetener (if using) and stir well with a spatula to combine. Mixture will be a thick liquid. 2. Pour into 8 mini muffin liners and freeze until solid, at least 12 hours. Store in the freezer to maintain their shape.

Per Serving:

calories: 239 | fat: 24g | protein: 4g | carbs: 5g | fiber: 3g | sodium: 3mg

Ricotta Cheesecake

Prep time: 2 minutes | Cook time: 45 to 50 minutes | Serves 12

- 2 cups skim or fat-free ricotta cheese (one 15-ounce / 425-g container)
- 1¼ cups sugar
- 1 teaspoon vanilla extract
- 6 eggs
- Zest of 1 orange

1. Preheat your oven to 375°F (190°C) and grease an 8-inch square baking pan with butter or cooking spray to prevent sticking. 2. In a medium bowl, mix together the ricotta cheese and sugar until well combined. Add the eggs one at a time, mixing thoroughly after each addition. Stir in the vanilla extract and orange zest to enhance the flavor. 3. Pour the ricotta mixture into the prepared baking pan, smoothing the top with a spatula. Bake in the preheated oven for 45 to 50 minutes, or until the center is set and firm to the touch. 4. Once baked, allow the dish to cool in the pan for 20 minutes before serving. Enjoy it warm for a delightful treat!

Per Serving:

calories: 160 | fat: 5g | protein: 12g | carbs: 15g | fiber: 0g | sodium: 388mg

Chapter 14

Staples, Sauces, Dips, and Dressings

Chapter 14 Staples, Sauces, Dips, and Dressings

Cilantro-Garlic Herb Sauce

Prep time: 10 minutes | Cook time: 0 minutes | Makes about 1½ cups

- 2¼ cups fresh cilantro leaves
- 8 garlic cloves, minced
- 1½ teaspoons ground cumin
- 1½ teaspoons paprika
- ½ teaspoon cayenne pepper
- ½ teaspoon table salt
- 6 tablespoons lemon juice (2 lemons)
- ¾ cup extra-virgin olive oil

1. Pulse cilantro, garlic, cumin, paprika, cayenne, and salt in food processor until cilantro is coarsely chopped, about 10 pulses. Add lemon juice and pulse briefly to combine. Transfer mixture to medium bowl and slowly whisk in oil until incorporated and mixture is emulsified. Cover and let sit at room temperature for at least 30 minutes to allow flavors to meld. (Sauce can be refrigerated for up to 2 days; bring to room temperature before serving.)

Per Serving:

¼ cup: calories: 253 | fat: 27g | protein: 1g | carbs: 3g | fiber: 1g | sodium: 199mg

Maltese Sun-Dried Tomato and Mushroom Dressing

Prep time: 10 minutes | Cook time: 5 minutes | Serves 4

- ⅓ cup olive oil (use a combination of olive oil and sun-dried tomato oil, if they were packed in oil)
- 8 ounces (227 g) mushrooms, sliced
- 3 tablespoons red wine vinegar
- Freshly ground black pepper, to taste
- ½ cup sun-dried tomatoes, drained (if they are packed in oil, reserve the oil) and chopped

1. In a medium skillet, heat 2 tablespoons of olive oil (or a blend of olive oil and oil from the sun-dried tomatoes) over high heat. Once hot, add the mushrooms and sauté, stirring frequently, until they release their moisture and become tender. 2. Pour in the vinegar and season with freshly ground black pepper to taste. Remove the skillet from heat and stir in the remaining olive oil along with the sun-dried tomatoes, mixing well to combine the flavors.

Per Serving:

1 cup: calories: 190 | fat: 18g | protein: 3g | carbs: 6g | fiber: 2g | sodium: 21mg

Garlic-Rosemary Infused Olive Oil

Prep time: 5 minutes | Cook time: 45 minutes | Makes 1 cup

- 1 cup extra-virgin olive oil
- 4 large garlic cloves, smashed
- 4 (4- to 5-inch) sprigs rosemary

1. In a medium skillet, combine the olive oil, garlic, and rosemary sprigs. Heat over low heat, allowing the flavors to infuse as you cook for 30 to 45 minutes, stirring occasionally. Be careful not to let the oil get too hot, as this can cause the garlic to burn and develop a bitter taste. 2. Once fragrant and the garlic is very tender, remove the skillet from the heat and let it cool slightly. Using a slotted spoon, carefully remove the garlic and rosemary from the oil. 3. Pour the infused oil into a glass container and allow it to cool completely before sealing. Store the oil covered at room temperature for up to 3 months, using it to enhance various dishes with its rich flavor.

Per Serving:

⅛ cup: calories: 241 | fat: 27g | protein: 0g | carbs: 1g | fiber: 0g | sodium: 1mg

Simple Vinaigrette

Prep time: 5 minutes | Cook time: 0 minutes | Makes 1 cup

- ½ cup extra-virgin olive oil
- ¼ cup red wine vinegar or freshly squeezed lemon juice
- 1 tablespoon Dijon mustard
- 1 small garlic clove, finely minced (optional)
- 1 teaspoon dried herbs (oregano, rosemary, parsley, or thyme)
- ½ teaspoon salt
- ½ teaspoon freshly ground black pepper

1. In a glass Mason jar with a lid, add the olive oil, vinegar, Dijon mustard, minced garlic (if desired), herbs, salt, and pepper. Secure the lid tightly and shake the jar vigorously until all the ingredients are well combined. 2. Store the dressing in the refrigerator until you're ready to use it. Before serving, allow it to come to room temperature and give it a good shake, as the oil and vinegar will separate naturally. Enjoy this flavorful dressing on your favorite salads or dishes!

Per Serving:

¼ cup: calories: 246 | fat: 27g | protein: 0g | carbs: 1g | fiber: 0g | sodium: 336mg

Grapefruit-Tarragon Cream Dressing

Prep time: 5 minutes | Cook time: 0 minutes | Serves 4 to 6

- ½ cup avocado oil mayonnaise
- 2 tablespoons Dijon mustard
- 1 teaspoon dried tarragon or 1 tablespoon chopped fresh tarragon
- Zest and juice of ½
- grapefruit (about 2 tablespoons juice)
- ½ teaspoon salt
- ¼ teaspoon freshly ground black pepper
- 1 to 2 tablespoons water (optional)

1. In a large mason jar or glass measuring cup, combine the mayonnaise, Dijon, tarragon, grapefruit zest and juice, salt, and pepper and whisk well with a fork until smooth and creamy. If a thinner dressing is preferred, thin out with water.

Per Serving:
calories: 49 | fat: 4g | protein: 0g | carbs: 4g | fiber: 0g | sodium: 272mg

Herbed Butter

Prep time: 10 minutes | Cook time: 0 minutes | Makes ½ cup

- ½ cup (1 stick) butter, at room temperature
- 1 garlic clove, finely minced
- 2 teaspoons finely chopped
- fresh rosemary
- 1 teaspoon finely chopped fresh oregano
- ½ teaspoon salt

1. In a food processor, combine the butter, minced garlic, rosemary, oregano, and salt. Pulse until the mixture is smooth and creamy, ensuring everything is well incorporated. Be sure to scrape down the sides of the bowl as needed. If you prefer, you can also use an electric mixer to whip the ingredients together. 2. Once combined, transfer the butter mixture into a small bowl or glass container. Cover it securely and store in the refrigerator, where it will keep for up to 1 month. Enjoy this flavorful herb butter on your favorite dishes!

Per Serving:
⅛ cup: calories: 206 | fat: 23g | protein: 0g | carbs: 206g | fiber: 0g | sodium: 294mg

Warm Anchovy Garlic Dip

Prep time: 5 minutes | Cook time: 20 minutes | Serves 8 to 10

- ½ cup extra-virgin olive oil
- 4 tablespoons (½ stick) butter
- 8 anchovy fillets, very finely chopped
- 4 large garlic cloves, finely minced
- ½ teaspoon salt
- ½ teaspoon freshly ground black pepper

1. In a small saucepan, heat the olive oil and butter over medium-low heat until the butter is melted. 2. Add the anchovies and garlic and stir to combine. Add the salt and pepper and reduce the heat to low. Cook, stirring occasionally, until the anchovies are very soft and the mixture is very fragrant, about 20 minutes. 3. Serve warm, drizzled over steamed vegetables, as a dipping sauce for raw veggies or cooked artichokes, or use as a salad dressing. Store leftovers in an airtight container in the refrigerator for up to 2 weeks.

Per Serving:
calories: 145 | fat: 16g | protein: 1g | carbs: 0g | fiber: 0g | sodium: 235mg

Arugula Walnut Pesto

Prep time: 5 minutes | Cook time: 0 minutes | Serves 8 to 10

- 6 cups packed arugula
- 1 cup chopped walnuts
- ½ cup shredded Parmesan cheese
- 2 garlic cloves, peeled
- ½ teaspoon salt
- 1 cup extra-virgin olive oil

1. In a food processor, combine the arugula, walnuts, cheese, and garlic and process until very finely chopped. Add the salt. With the processor running, stream in the olive oil until well blended. 2. If the mixture seems too thick, add warm water, 1 tablespoon at a time, until smooth and creamy. Store in a sealed container in the refrigerator.

Per Serving:
calories: 292 | fat: 31g | protein: 4g | carbs: 3g | fiber: 1g | sodium: 210mg

Honey Berry Delight

Prep time: 5 minutes | Cook time: 15 minutes | Serves 2 to 3

- ½ cup honey
- ¼ cup fresh berries
- 2 tablespoons grated orange zest

1. In a small saucepan, heat the honey, berries, and orange zest over medium-low heat for 2 to 5 minutes, until the sauce thickens, or heat for 15 seconds in the microwave. Serve the compote drizzled over pancakes, muffins, or French toast.

Per Serving:
calories: 272 | fat: 0g | protein: 1g | carbs: 74g | fiber: 1g | sodium: 4mg

Apple Cider Dressing

Prep time: 5 minutes | Cook time: 0 minutes | Serves 2

- 2 tablespoons apple cider vinegar
- ⅓ lemon, juiced
- ⅓ lemon, zested
- Salt and freshly ground black pepper, to taste

1. In a jar, combine the vinegar, lemon juice, and lemon zest. Season the mixture with salt and pepper to taste. Secure the lid tightly and shake vigorously until all the ingredients are well blended. This bright and tangy dressing is now ready to use on your salads or dishes!

Per Serving:
calories: 7 | fat: 0g | protein: 0g | carbs: 1g | fiber: 0g | sodium: 1mg

Minty Cucumber Yogurt Dip

Prep time: 5 minutes | Cook time: 0 minutes | Serves 2 to 3

- 1 cup plain, unsweetened, full-fat Greek yogurt
- ½ cup cucumber, peeled, seeded, and diced
- 1 tablespoon freshly squeezed lemon juice
- 1 tablespoon chopped fresh mint
- 1 small garlic clove, minced
- Salt and freshly ground black pepper, to taste

1. In a food processor, combine the yogurt, cucumber, lemon juice, mint, and garlic. Pulse several times to combine, leaving noticeable cucumber chunks. 2. Taste and season with salt and pepper.

Per Serving:

calories: 55 | fat: 3g | protein: 3g | carbs: 5g | fiber: 0g | sodium: 38mg

Pickled Turnips

Prep time: 5 minutes | Cook time: 0 minutes | Serves 2

- 1 pound (454 g) turnips, washed well, peeled, and cut into 1-inch batons
- 1 small beet, roasted, peeled, and cut into 1-inch batons
- 2 garlic cloves, smashed
- 1 teaspoon dried Turkish oregano
- 3 cups warm water
- ½ cup red wine vinegar
- ½ cup white vinegar

1. In a jar, add the chopped turnips, beet, minced garlic, and oregano. 2. Pour the water and vinegars over the vegetables, ensuring they are fully submerged. Secure the lid on the jar and shake vigorously to mix everything together. 3. Place the jar in the refrigerator. The turnips will be pickled and ready to enjoy after just 1 hour. These quick pickles make a flavorful addition to salads or sandwiches!

Per Serving:

calories: 3 | fat: 0g | protein: 1g | carbs: 0g | fiber: 0g | sodium: 6mg

Yogurt Tahini Dressing

Prep time: 5 minutes | Cook time: 0 minutes | Makes 1 cup

- ½ cup plain Greek yogurt
- ⅓ cup tahini
- ¼ cup freshly squeezed orange juice
- ½ teaspoon kosher salt

1. In a medium bowl, combine the yogurt, tahini, orange juice, and salt, whisking until the mixture is smooth and well blended. 2. Cover the bowl and place it in the refrigerator to chill until you are ready to serve. For any leftovers, transfer the dip to an airtight container and store in the refrigerator for up to 5 days. Enjoy this creamy and zesty dip with your favorite snacks!

Per Serving:

2 tablespoons: calories: 70 | fat: 2g | protein: 4g | carbs: 4g | fiber: 1g | sodium: 80mg

Garlic Oregano Sherry Vinaigrette

Prep time: 5 minutes | Cook time: 0 minutes | Makes about ¾ cup

- ⅓ cup sherry vinegar
- 1 clove garlic
- 2 teaspoons dried oregano
- 1 teaspoon salt
- ½ teaspoon freshly ground black pepper
- ½ cup olive oil

1. In a food processor or blender, combine the vinegar, garlic, oregano, salt, and pepper and process until the garlic is minced and the ingredients are well combined. With the food processor running, add the olive oil in a thin stream until it is well incorporated. Serve immediately or store, covered, in the refrigerator for up to a week.

Per Serving:

calories: 74 | fat: 8g | protein: 0g | carbs: 0g | fiber: 0g | sodium: 194mg

Appendix 1: Measurement Conversion Chart

VOLUME EQUIVALENTS(DRY)

US STANDARD	METRIC (APPROXIMATE)
1/8 teaspoon	0.5 mL
1/4 teaspoon	1 mL
1/2 teaspoon	2 mL
3/4 teaspoon	4 mL
1 teaspoon	5 mL
1 tablespoon	15 mL
1/4 cup	59 mL
1/2 cup	118 mL
3/4 cup	177 mL
1 cup	235 mL
2 cups	475 mL
3 cups	700 mL
4 cups	1 L

VOLUME EQUIVALENTS(LIQUID)

US STANDARD	US STANDARD (OUNCES)	METRIC (APPROXIMATE)
2 tablespoons	1 fl.oz.	30 mL
1/4 cup	2 fl.oz.	60 mL
1/2 cup	4 fl.oz.	120 mL
1 cup	8 fl.oz.	240 mL
1 1/2 cup	12 fl.oz.	355 mL
2 cups or 1 pint	16 fl.oz.	475 mL
4 cups or 1 quart	32 fl.oz.	1 L
1 gallon	128 fl.oz.	4 L

TEMPERATURES EQUIVALENTS

FAHRENHEIT(F)	CELSIUS(C) (APPROXIMATE)
225 °F	107 °C
250 °F	120 °C
275 °F	135 °C
300 °F	150 °C
325 °F	160 °C
350 °F	180 °C
375 °F	190 °C
400 °F	205 °C
425 °F	220 °C
450 °F	235 °C
475 °F	245 °C
500 °F	260 °C

WEIGHT EQUIVALENTS

US STANDARD	METRIC (APPROXIMATE)
1 ounce	28 g
2 ounces	57 g
5 ounces	142 g
10 ounces	284 g
15 ounces	425 g
16 ounces (1 pound)	455 g
1.5 pounds	680 g
2 pounds	907 g

Appendix 2: The Dirty Dozen and Clean Fifteen

The Environmental Working Group (EWG) is a nonprofit, nonpartisan organization dedicated to protecting human health and the environment Its mission is to empower people to live healthier lives in a healthier environment. This organization publishes an annual list of the twelve kinds of produce, in sequence, that have the highest amount of pesticide residue-the Dirty Dozen-as well as a list of the fifteen kinds of produce that have the least amount of pesticide residue-the Clean Fifteen.

THE DIRTY DOZEN	THE CLEAN FIFTEEN
• The 2016 Dirty Dozen includes the following produce. These are considered among the year's most important produce to buy organic:	• The least critical to buy organically are the Clean Fifteen list. The following are on the 2016 list:

THE DIRTY DOZEN

Strawberries	Spinach
Apples	Tomatoes
Nectarines	Bell peppers
Peaches	Cherry tomatoes
Celery	Cucumbers
Grapes	Kale/collard greens
Cherries	Hot peppers

- The Dirty Dozen list contains two additional items kale/collard greens and hot peppers-because they tend to contain trace levels of highly hazardous pesticides.

THE CLEAN FIFTEEN

Avocados	Papayas
Corn	Kiwi
Pineapples	Eggplant
Cabbage	Honeydew
Sweet peas	Grapefruit
Onions	Cantaloupe
Asparagus	Cauliflower
Mangos	

- Some of the sweet corn sold in the United States are made from genetically engineered (GE) seedstock. Buy organic varieties of these crops to avoid GE produce.

Appendix 3: Recipes Index

Made in United States
North Haven, CT
04 January 2025